4 Week Loan

This book is due for return on or before the last date shown below

University of Cumbria
24/7 renewals Tel:0845 602 6124

Handbooks of Investigation in Children

This is a series of unique guides to the appropriate tests to be carried out in children with suspected disorders. Instructions for the performance and evaluation of tests are clearly explained. Each title is based on the authors' personal experience in the respective field and is devoted to the investigation of children only.

Careful reference to these titles in clinical practice will help both to eliminate inadequate testing and to ensure that the practitioner will obtain the maximum information from the investigations carried out. To amplify the explicit text, case histories helpfully illustrate how the authors have used and interpreted investigations. These pocket-sized books are essential tools for all those involved in the diagnosis and management of childhood disorders.

Other titles

Handbook of Endocrine Investigations in Children
   I. A. Hughes
Handbook of Haematological Investigations in Children
   R. F. Stevens
Handbook of Renal Investigations in Children
   C. M. Taylor and S. Chapman

Handbook of Neurological Investigations in Children

John B. P. Stephenson, MA, DM, FRCP, FRCPG, DCH
Consultant in Paediatric Neurology,
Fraser of Allander Unit,
Royal Hospital for Sick Children,
Yorkhill, Glasgow

Mary D. King, MB ChB, FRCPI
Consultant Paediatric Neurologist
The Children's Hospital,
Temple Street,
The Rotunda Hospital,
and Beaumont Hospital,
Dublin

Foreword by Professor Philip Dodge

Butterworth-Heinemann Ltd
Linacre House, Jordan Hill, Oxford OX2 8DP

 PART OF REED INTERNATIONAL BOOKS

OXFORD   LONDON   BOSTON
MUNICH   NEW DELHI   SINGAPORE   SYDNEY
TOKYO   TORONTO   WELLINGTON

First published 1989
Revised reprint 1992

British Library Cataloguing in Publication Data
Stephenson, John B. P.
  Handbook of neurological investigations in children
  1. ChildrenNervous system. Diagnosis
  I. Title   II.King, Mary D.   III. Series
  618.92′80475

ISBN 0 7506 0489 1

Library of Congress Cataloguing in Publication Data
Stephenson, John B. P.
  Handbook of neurological investigations in children/John B. P.
  Stephenson, Mary D. King.
  Includes bibliographies and index.
  ISBN 0 7506 0489 1
  1. Paediatric neurology — diagnosis.   I. King, Mary D.   II. Title.
  III. Series
  2. Nervous system diseases in infancy and childhood—handbooks.   89–609
  618.92′80475—dc19   CIP

Printed and bound in Great Britain by the University Press, Cambridge

To Philippa and Rory

Foreword

An enormous amount of information is packed between the covers of this little book designed to guide clinicians in selection of the diagnostic tests used in infants and children with neurologic disease. Scattered throughout the book are tantalizing clues leading the reader to want more. Although the American reader may take exception to the terse Scot style and special phraseology, most will find it refreshing, especially the occasional reference to the high cost of certain tests. However, at times the reader may desire further elaboration on the disorder under discussion. The vast knowledge of the authors is evident as this reader encountered much with which he was unfamiliar and suspects that this may be so for other readers. The text is remarkably up-to-date as reflected in the discussion of the peroxisomal disorders and the recently identified metabolic abnormality in Canavan's disease. Those who read this book will learn much and want to know more.

Philip R. Dodge
Professor of Pediatrics and Neurology,
Washington University School of Medicine,
St Louis, Missouri, U.S.A.

Acknowledgements

The authors would like to thank the following: Audrey Dixon, Diane Henderson, Gerry Hooton, Siobhan Kennedy and Christina Nulty and Cynthia Young for help with preparation of the manuscript; Jean Hyslop and Thomas Nolan for help with the illustrations; Donald Hadley, John Stack and Mark Ziervogel for providing images; Geraldine Block, Mary Broadbery and Hilary Reidpath for preparation of EEGs; Pat Boyle, Michael Farrell, Ian Hann, Jaak Jaeken, Robert McWilliam, Christopher Rittey, James Toland, John Tolmie and Margaret Wilson for helpful comments; and Sylvia Hull for patience.

Contents

Abbreviations

Investigations

α	EEG alpha rhythm (8–13 Hz)
ALT	alanine transaminase
AST	aspartate transaminase
BAEP	brain-stem auditory evoked potential(s)
BAER	brain-stem auditory evoked response
β	EEG beta activity (over 13, commonly 14–30 Hz, i.e. 'fast' activity)
cDNA	complementary deoxyribonucleic acid
CFM	cerebral function monitor
CFAM	cerebral function analysing monitor
CK	creatine kinase
CPP	cerebral perfusion pressure
c.p.s.	cycles per second (hertz; Hz)
CSF	cerebrospinal fluid
CT	computerized tomograph(y)
δ	EEG delta activity (less than 4 Hz, i.e. 'slow' activity)
DNA	deoxyribonucleic acid
DHAP-AT	dihydroxyacetone phosphate acyl transferase
DTPA	diethylene triamine pentacetic acid (as in gadolinium-DTPA)
ECG	electrocardiogram
EEG	electroencephalogram
EMG	electromyogram
ERG	electroretinogram
FAB–MS	fast atom bombardment mass spectroscopy
GABA	gamma amino butyric acid
GAG	glycosaminoglycan(s)
GC	gas chromatography
GC–MS	gas chromatography mass spectroscopy
h	hour
HMMA	4-hydroxy-3-methoxymandelic acid
HMPAO	^{99m}Tc hexamethyl propylene amine oxime
HV	hyperventilation
HVA	homovanillic acid
Hz	hertz (cycles per second)
IAP	intra-arterial pressure
ICP	intracranial pressure
IgG	immunoglobulin G

LR+	likelihood ratio of disease given a positive test
LR−	likelihood ratio of disease given a negative test
MAP	muscle (compound) action potential
MCV	motor (nerve) conduction velocity
min	minute
MR	magnetic resonance
MRI	magnetic resonance imaging
m/s	metres per second
μV	microvolt(s)
ms	millisecond(s)
MZ	megahertz
OC	ocular compression
PAS	periodic acid Schiff
PET	positron emission tomography
PS	photic stimulation
PV+	positive predictive value
PV−	negative predictive value
RNA	ribonucleic acid
RNS	repetitive nerve stimulation
ROC	receiver (or relative) operating characteristic
s	second(s)
SAP	sensory action potential
SCV	sensory (nerve) conduction velocity
SEP	somatosensory evoked potential
S/W	EEG spike and slow wave
SPECT	single photon emission computerized tomography
θ	EEG theta activity (4–7 Hz)
TLC	thin layer chromatography
TORCH(S)	toxoplasma, rubella, cytomegalovirus, herpes simplex (syphilis)
VEP	visual evoked potential
VER	same as VEP
VLCFA	very long-chain fatty acids

Disorders or Diseases

ACTH	adrenocorticotrophic hormone
ALD	adrenoleukodystrophy
BFEC	benign focal epilepsy of childhood (with Rolandic spikes)
BH$_4$	tetrahydrobiopterin
CMV	cytomegalovirus
DMD	Duchenne muscular dystrophy
DTP	diphtheria tetanus and pertussis (vaccine)
HIV	human immunodeficiency virus
HMSN	hereditary motor and sensory neuropathy
HSES	haemorrhagic shock encephalopathy syndrome
HSN	hereditary sensory neuropathy
HSV	herpes simplex virus (typed by numbers)
INAD	infantile neuroaxonal deficiency
INCL	infantile neuronal ceroid lipofuscinosis
MCAD	medium-chain acyl coenzyme A dehydrogenase (deficiency)

MELAS	mitochondrial encephalopathy with lactic acidosis and stroke-like episodes
MERRF	myoclonic epilepsy with ragged red fibres
MPS	mucopolysaccharidosis
NAD	neuroaxonal dystrophy
NCL	neuronal ceroid lipofuscinosis (INCL: infantile type)
OTC	ornithine transcarbamylase (deficiency)
PKU	phenylketonuria
PNDC	progressive neuronal degeneration of childhood (with liver disease)
PVL	periventricular leucomalacia
SIDS	sudden infant death syndrome
SMA	spinal muscular atrophy (anterior horn cell degeneration)
SSPE	subacute sclerosing panencephalitis (post-measles)
TV	television-induced (seizures)

Introduction

We hope that this book will be of some help to all those who see children with suspected neurological disorders. We give emphasis to common tests in common conditions, but also highlight unusual investigations in those rare disorders which have important therapeutic or genetic consequences.

It would have been a Herculean task to attempt coverage of all the available investigations which may be helpful in the diagnosis and management of disorders of the central, peripheral and autonomic nervous systems and their connections. We have had to be selective in content, and pay more attention to the philosophy of tests. This is neither a textbook of child neurology nor a practical manual.

The book is divided into two parts. Part 1 deals with the investigations themselves. Because the question the clinician asks is 'How do I investigate such-and-such a neurological disorder?' we have included two types of investigations. Firstly there are investigations which are more or less primarily concerned with the function and structure of the nervous system, and secondly we consider tests which may be necessary to explain what is wrong. Thus we have to give guidance not only within the disciplines of neurophysiology and neuroradiology, but also to venture into the subtleties of biochemistry and other disciplines.

In these objectives we may be accused of attempting to teach several grannies to suck eggs. In fact we wish to encourage a personal but mutually critical dialogue between the clinician and laboratory colleagues. However, the clinician is ultimately responsible for the diagnosis and to this end must be able to seek out excellence wherever it can be found.

In Part 2 we adopt a problem-orientated approach, and discuss the most appropriate choice of investigations in selected clinical situations. We hope that overlap and repetition between the two parts will illuminate rather than irritate.

At the end of most chapters in Part 1 of the book we include a number of case histories which illustrate some of the good and bad uses of investigation. These refer to real not imaginary children. The diagnoses are listed in the Appendix.

Each chapter concludes with a list of selected references. These include texts which are major sources of further reading and descriptions of investigations or disorders which are recent or not well known. Further references to a number of genetic disorders may be found through the McKusick number given in the Index (McKusick 1988).

The Appendix includes a few normative values, but it must be emphasized that norms and ranges vary between laboratories and may have to be developed using personal control groups. Furthermore there are considerable age (and sometimes sex) variations which in many instances require further clarification. The Appendix also includes definitions of the terms used with respect to the statistical significance of investigations, and some worked examples. The general principles of such methods are alluded to below.

Philosophy of the use of tests

'Clinical medicine is basically an intellectual process whereby data from all sources, whether strictly clinical (in the restricted sense) or from the laboratory and other technical tools, is integrated and shaped into a meaningful profile' (Aicardi 1987). The first essential for the best use of investigations which will allow a meaningful diagnostic profile is for a problem to be posed, a question to be asked. This may seem an obvious point, but without a knowledge of the problem, the significance of EEG spikes in the Rolandic area, for example, cannot be determined. Also it is important to try to ask a question which the investigation may be able to answer or to seek a modification of the investigation if it cannot. For example, '? Infantile Spasms' cannot necessarily be answered by a standard short EEG, although admittedly a chaotic EEG appearance may support the diagnosis. To determine the existence and type of the spasms, prolonged recording probably with a video-recording assistance would often be necessary.

One difficulty which may be experienced by clinicians who are not specialists in the field results from the inevitable artificiality of human classifications. If one's concept of ataxia does not include neuropathy, then nerve conduction studies will not be undertaken and the correct diagnosis will not be reached.

More difficulty attaches to the plan of investigation of disorders with multiple explanations such as mental handicap and, more particularly, developmental regression. One approach, which may have economic and social advantages, is to undertake a large battery of 'screening' tests simultaneously. The authors prefer a stepwise approach and would emphasize that when a metabolic 'screen' is done it is most important to know what can be detected by the screen and what cannot.

It is worth devoting some thought to the diagnostic power of positive and negative tests, of whatever kind, and what to do when either a normal or an abnormal result which one has not expected is received.

Looking at this question in simple mathematical terms helps to explain how a totally different significance can be attributed to a result obtained in general paediatric practice compared with that obtained in a specialist unit, despite the investigations having been carried out in exactly the same way. The algebra is outlined in the Appendix but the difference may be explained as follows. If the odds in favour of the disorder being tested for are low, then a normal result tends to exclude the diagnosis. An unexpected positive result is not helpful in confirming a diagnosis in this circumstance (but it is easy for such false positives to stir up a lot of painful and unnecessary further investigations). These points apply unless the test has 100% specificity, having no false positives (see Appendix). On the other hand, if the odds in favour of the disorder being present are high, then a positive result does tend to confirm the diagnosis, while an (unexpected) negative result is not helpful in ruling out that diagnosis unless the test is 100% sensitive, with no false negatives. Put another way, the predictive value of an investigation depends on the expected prevalence of the disorder, even though the sensitivity and specificity are high (provided they are not 100%).

Finally, a word is in order about the economics of neurological investigations. Provided that the costs of patient/family transport and board can be set aside, a sequential approach to investigations is economically sound. However, a very expensive test such as magnetic resonance imaging (MRI) is justifiable not only if it can be shown to improve ;eatment', but also if it can provide a better understanding of prognosis and genetics and so help family management. In a wider context, there is an economic as well as a scientific argument for the adequate investigation of children who form part of epidemiological studies.

Further reading

Aicardi, J. (1987) The future of clinical child neurology. *Journal of Child Neurology*, **2**, 152–159
McKusick, V. A. (1988) *Mendelian Inheritance in Man*, 8th edn Johns Hopkins University Press, Baltimore
Simel, D. L. (1985) Playing the odds. *Lancet*, **1**, 329–330

Part 1

Investigations

Chapter 1

Electroencephalography

Electroencephalography (EEG) is the most commonly requested neurological test. It should never be 'routinely' ordered without having some sort of question in mind. Furthermore, the question must be one which the type of EEG ordered may be able to answer.

What is the EEG?

The electrical activity of the brain is written out on paper in a number of channels (commonly 8 or 16) using one or several montages. A montage is a topographical arrangement of electrodes, making it easier to see the location on the scalp of the various electrical rhythms or discharges. Rhythms are conventionally described in terms of frequency, ranging from fast activity (beta) at 14–30 Hz through alpha at 8–13 Hz and theta at 4–7 Hz, to slow or delta 0.5–3 Hz. Activity faster than beta activity is commonly not true EEG but rather a biological 'artefact' arising from scalp muscle electromyogram (EMG). Very slow activity also results from biological artefacts related to respiration or sweating. Activity which is recurrent but not rhythmic may still be described in terms of its approximate frequency – for example irregular slow activity might be described as being predominantly 2–3 Hz. Rhythmic and non-rhythmic activity is also described in terms of amplitude. Amplitude is usually measured in microvolts (μV) ranging from less than 2 μV in electro-cerebral silence ('flat EEG') to 400 μV or more in high-voltage spikes. Spikes are transients with a pointed appearance and a duration of less than 80 milliseconds (ms). They are often associated with a longer-duration slow wave-form and the combination may be described as a spike-and-wave complex. Very short-duration transients of a spike-like appearance of less than 30 ms duration are likely to be scalp compound muscle action potentials. Sharp waves have a duration of 80–200 ms but a similar pointed shape. There is no standard term for longer-duration steeply pointed waves, but they may be referred to as sharp components. Polyspikes are multiple closely spaced spike discharges. They may be followed by a slow wave as in polyspike and wave. High-voltage beta activity may be difficult to distinguish from polyspikes.

Provocations

Many factors influence the EEG, such as age, state of consciousness, temperature, and metabolic balance. Certain stimuli are deliberately employed to provoke abnormalities which would otherwise be missed. In photic stimulation (stroboscopic activation) a pulsed light is flashed at varying rates into the child's open eyes to detect photosensitivity. Eye closure is an important provocation which is sometimes omitted because the young child may not close his eyes on command. However, the eyes can always be closed passively. Spike-and-wave or sharp components not otherwise obvious may be induced by this manoeuvre. Hyperventilation, induced in young children by having them blow tissues or mobiles, is most useful for provoking the regular high-amplitude spike-and-wave of typical absence. Sleep may be induced naturally in the EEG department with kindness, time and patience. The use of a sedative such as chloral hydrate makes induction of sleep easier but interpretation more difficult. Night-time natural sleep recording is more difficult to obtain – most easily by cassette recording (see below, Cassette EEG). Sleep deprivation is employed to elicit spikes in other epilepsies, for example when grand mal occurs in late childhood with or without early morning myoclonus.

Special provocations

Modifications of photic stimulation are helpful in certain circumstances. Monocular occlusion is used when standard photic stimulation induces spikes or spike-and-wave, the so-called photoparoxysmal response, in a child with television-induced epilepsy (this is more for management than diagnosis, in that if the photoconvulsive response is prevented by monocular occlusion the same technique may be employed by the child to avoid television seizures). Pattern stimulation using a large printed display of alternating black and white stripes may confirm and clarify a clinical diagnosis of pattern-sensitive epilepsy in a child whose eyes flicker in the presence of striped decorations. Slow stroboscopic activation using a flash frequency of 0.5 cycles per second or less induces large occipital spikes (which are in fact giant visual evoked potentials) particularly in one cause of epilepsy and neurological deterioration (late infantile neuronal ceroid lipofuscinosis). Ocular compression has an indirect effect upon the EEG when it induces cardiac asystole due to an exaggerated vagal oculocardiac reflex.

Special montages

Different electrode arrangements and placements are used to assist the localization of the origin of electrical discharges before consideration of epilepsy surgery. These may include the insertion of subdural electrodes and implantation of depth electrodes, which are neurosurgical procedures beyond the scope of this book.

Polygraphy: additional recordings

A single channel of ECG is always recorded on the same paper as the EEG in case sudden changes in heart rate lead to changes in the EEG background activity which would not otherwise be interpretable. Likewise, a simple recording of respiration such as by strain-gauge allows recognition of the usual forms of apnoea and respiratory rhythm disturbances. Additional recordings of eye movements, surface EMG and body movements may help in particular clinical situations, for example in the EEG of the newborn when it is difficult to tell the stage within the sleep–wake cycle.

Cassette EEG

Cassette EEG monitoring allows continuous EEG to be recorded on magnetic tape for 24 h or more in ambulatory older children or from infants in their cots. This type of prolonged recording enables seizures to be captured and often to determine whether such seizures are epileptic, and if so, the type. An ECG channel is included particularly to identify syncopes.

Split-screen video EEG

Split-screen video EEG recording allows the appearance of the child in a seizure to be correlated with the EEG such as in the distinction between a myoclonic seizure (in which there is a jerk) and an atonic seizure (in which there is a sag). The addition of cable telemetry allows even more prolonged and intensive monitoring, when the identification of the precise seizure type is necessary for management. In such a system the child is confined to a living area with constant video surveillance. The EEG is transmitted to the apparatus which integrates it with the video recording via a long, flexible cable.

'Cerebral function monitors'

Cerebral function monitors are designed to be simple to use, and record usually one or two channels of EEG over hours and days when moment-to-moment evaluation is required. The authors prefer the Cerebral Function Analysing Monitor (CFAM) which writes out a slow-running derivation of the EEG, plotting the amplitude and frequency distribution. It has the additional facility of writing out raw unanalysed EEG on demand or at regular predetermined intervals. The main use of these monitors is during anaesthesia, especially during cardiac bypass surgery, but they are valuable for monitoring acute encephalophathies both in the intensive care unit and in general neonatal intensive care (Chapter 13).

Requesting an EEG

Since the interpretation of the EEG depends both on the problem and the state of the child, EEG requests should contain a certain minimum of information

Age (and gestational age in young infants).
Mention of fever, biochemical upset (in particular blood glucose level) of systemic illness at the time of the recording.
A detailed history of any seizures.
Up-to-date information on sedative medications.
A statement on what is the problem, that is, the question or questions to be answered. 'Query epilepsy', 'query a normal EEG', or 'recurrent febrile convulsions' are not appropriate reasons for requesting this test.

Some examples of the type of EEG which might be requested are listed in Table 1.1.

Indications for EEG

1. Clarification of the type of epilepsy, once a clinical diagnosis of epilepsy has been made.
2. Management of epileptic encephalopathies (conditions in which there is a potentially reversible disorganization of the EEG not brought about by extracerebral factors).
3. Follow-up of non-lesional epilepsy, for example benign focal epilepsy of childhood and other primary childhood epilepsies.
4. Any undiagnosed acute neurological illness including suspect poisoning.
5. Suspect cerebral malformation and/or mental handicap.
6. Suspect neurodegenerative disorder (subacute or chronic loss of skills).

Further details of the EEG abnormalities which may be found are discussed in the next section under these six headings.

Detailed EEG indications

1. Clarification of the type of epilepsy once a clinical diagnosis of epilepsy has been made

Certain appearances have diagnostic value:

Three per second regular spike and wave with interruption of the stream of consciousness in typical absences.
Four per second spike and wave and polyspike and wave bursts in the epilepsy of Janz (tonic clonic convulsions of late childhood with

early-morning myoclonic jerks). The most characteristic EEG finding accompanies a clinical myoclonic jerk. Prolonged polyspiking in the form of 5–20 closely spaced spikes is followed by bursts of rhythmic slow waves without spikes. In the interictal bursts less than 3 polyspikes are followed by 3–4/s spike and wave. Brief bursts of polyspike and wave (commonly with not more than 3 spikes in a polyspike complex) in myoclonic epilepsies in general. Clusters of high-amplitude spike-and-wave complexes in one or both Rolandic areas without any focal slow activity in the syndrome of benign focal epilepsy of childhood with Rolandic spikes.

2. Management of epileptic encephalopathies

High voltage (often very high voltage) chaotic slow waves and spike and sharp wave activity (hypsarrhythmia) often coexist with infantile spasms and developmental arrest. Repeat EEG after 2 weeks corticosteroid therapy usually shows this generalized disturbance to have disappeared but focal spikes or slow activity may suggest pathology which can be discerned on CT scan.

Frequent bilateral spike-and-wave complexes commonly without seizures are associated with acquired apparent 'deafness', loss of language or 'elective mutism' in the Landau–Kleffner syndrome. In some cases disappearance of this abnormality is accompanied by improved language comprehension, but often no such benefit is seen.

Long runs of slow (around 2/s) spike and wave, often irregular, may be associated with fluctuating impairments of awareness and cognitive and motor skills, and with progressive decline in mental ability. In some children, repeated EEG examinations indicate that the correlation is close, and antiepileptic therapy (especially corticosteroids or ketogenic diet) improve both the EEG and the child's competence. Unfortunately in many children neither is there a close EEG clinical correlation nor a demonstrable benefit of reducing the amount of EEG spike and wave.

3. Follow-up of non-lesional ('primary') epilepsy

In benign focal epilepsy of childhood with Rolandic spikes on the EEG, there is evidence that seizures remit before the Rolandic spike complexes disappear. Thus, disappearance of the Rolandic spikes suggests that remission has occurred. However, this does not mean that one has to wait until the spikes have gone to discontinue treatment.

In simple absences with 3/s regular spike and wave, disappearance of spikes from the EEG also suggests that the epilepsy has remitted, but this relationship is probably less secure than in Rolandic epilepsy.

In most other epilepsies the evidence is inadequate to make clear inferences with respect to prognosis or discontinuation of therapy

Table 1.1 Choice of EEG: some examples

Type of EEG	Clinical situation	Findings	Interpretation
1. Routine (without provocations)	Sick neonate with hiccups	Burst-suppression	Glycine encephalopathy
	Mental handicap (± fits)	High-voltage 8–14/s activity	Pachygyria
	Nocturnal hemifacial salivatory fits	Rolandic spike–wave clusters	BFEC
	Dementia	Periodic complexes Diffuse fast	SSPE INAD
2. Serial routine	BFEC	Spikes no longer	Epilepsy has remitted
	'Autistic' state	Decline of voltage	INCL
3. Routine with HV	Blanks	3/s symptomatic S/W	Petit mal absences
	Stroke-like episodes	Huge asymmetrical slow build-up	? Moya-moya (DANGER!)
4. Routine with PS	Infantile hemiclonic seizures Infantile atypical febrile convulsions	Photoconvulsive response	Severe polymorphous epilepsy
	TV seizures	Photoconvulsive response abolished by monocular occlusion	Simple TV epilepsy
5. Pattern stimulation	Pattern sensitive	Spikes induced	Pattern-sensitive epilepsy
6. With slow strobe	Dementia, fits, ataxia	Giant occipital spikes	Late infantile NCL
7. Routine with repeated passive eye closure	Unexplained delay/mental handicap/epileptic seizures	High-voltage 3–4/s sharp components maximum posteriorly mixed with smaller spikes or sharp waves.	Angelman syndrome
8. Sleep EEG	Clinically diagnosed epilepsy with infrequent seizures; normal routine EEG with standard provocations	Various	Depends on epilepsy type (e.g. continuous spike–wave in BFEC, spike–wave bursts in infantile spasms and other epilepsies)

Methods		EEG findings	Disorders
9. Sleep deprivation EEG	Early morning myoclonus and/or grand mal	Fast spikes then rhythmic slow, polyspike and wave, 4/s spike and wave	Primary generalized epilepsy (juvenile myoclonic epilepsy of Janz)
10. With OC	Unusual seizure in response to head bumps	Identical episode reproduced after cardiac asystole	Reflex anoxic seizure
11. With saline provocation	? 'psychic' seizures (pseudoseizures)	Seizure induced without EEG change	'hysteria'
12. EEG polygraphy	'breath-holding' seizures	Apnoea, QRS complex reduction; slow burst on EEG	Compulsive Valsalva manoeuvres
13. Cassette recording	Daily 'blanks' not defined	Focal origin ictal spikes	Partial seizures
	Acquired mutism	Continuous spike wave in slow sleep	Landau–Kleffner ('acquired epileptic aphasia')
14. Split-screen video	Nodding attacks	Atonia with spike wave	Atonic seizure
15. Ditto + cable telemetry	Frequent daily 'blanks'; normal routine EEG with HV	(a) Focal discharge during behavioural alteration;	Complex partial epileptic seizure
		(b) No EEG change during bizarre stereotypy	'Psychic' pseudoepileptic seizure
16. CFAM	Unexplained unconsciousness	Beta activity prominent	Benzodiazepine poisoning
		High voltage	Status epilepticus (obtain full EEG to clarify)

Methods		Disorders	
CFAM	cerebral function analysing monitor	BFEC	benign focal epilepsy of childhood with Rolandic spikes
HV	hyperventilation	INAD	infantile neuroaxonal dystrophy
OC	ocular compression	NCL	neuronal ceroid lipofuscinosis (INCL: infantile type)
PS	photic stimulation (stroboscopic activation)	SSPE	subacute sclerosing panencephalitis post-measles
QRS	systolic complex on electrocardiographic channel	TV	television induced
SW	spike and wave		

from the EEG appearance. On the one hand, in the epilepsy of late childhood characterized by early-morning grand mal (generalized tonic–clonic seizures) and/or morning myoclonic jerks may show a normal EEG after valproate-induced remission but will probably relapse in due course without treatment; on the other hand, some epilepsies may stay in remission despite the persistence of spikes at the time of stopping therapy.

4. Acute undiagnosed neurological illness

In the neonatal period, burst-suppression (that is, high-voltage activity of irregular type interrupted by virtual flattening of the EEG) may be seen in asphyxia, and in 'early myoclonic encephalopathy'. In glycine encephalopathy, the burst-suppression is distinguished by the presence of hiccups associated with the EEG bursts (see also Chapter 13).
Periodic lateralized high-voltage complexes may be seen in herpes encephalitis (but these can also occur after asphyxia and in static encephalopathies).
Trains of spikes which vary in position and amplitude and rhythm from moment to moment are typical of the haemorrhagic shock and encephalopathy syndrome or other severe hypoxicischaemic insult.
Generalized slowing of the background despite focal neurological signs may be seen in meningitis (meningoencephalitis) especially tuberculous meningitis.
Focal slow activity is usual in cerebral abscess but is also seen with any focal pathology and commonly after prolonged focal (partial) epileptic seizures in young children.
Focal flattening (reduction in amplitude of the background activity) is usual in subdural haemorrhage or effusion.
A very low-amplitude EEG is found in impaired cerebral perfusion (as with raised intracranial pressure) but also in certain poisonings and in severe hypothermia, and transiently after generalized tonic–clonic or clonic epileptic seizures, or during severe anoxia or ischaemia.
Diffuse moderate-amplitude fast beta activity is the result of certain drug intoxications, in particular benzodiazepine poisoning.

5. Suspect cerebral malformation and/or mental handicap

High-voltage or very high-voltage activity in the alpha frequency or in the lower part of the beta range is characteristic of lissencephaly or pachygyria. This EEG abnormality may be focal in focal pachygyria.
High-voltage or very high-voltage posterior spike and wave accentuated by passive eye closure, the waves being high voltage sharp components (broader or wider than sharp waves), is a feature of Angelman's happy puppet syndrome. The finding is present before other somatic and behavioural features of the syndrome are obvious.

Trains of spikes or sharp waves, at first only in sleep, with poorly organized background activity develop in Rett syndrome. (This disorder of females is primarily a mental handicap disorder, although it may appear as if it were a dementia.)

6. Suspect neurodegenerative disorder (subacute or chronic loss of skills)

Stereotyped high-voltage polyphasic complexes repeated every several seconds and often associated with subtle transient reduction in tone is typical of post-measles subacute sclerosing panencephalitis. Progressive reduction in EEG amplitude after infancy is typical of infantile neuronal ceroid lipofuscinosis.

High-voltage posterior complexes induced by slow stroboscopic activation at less than 0.5/s is typical of late infantile neuronal ceroid lipofuscinosis.

Diffuse beta activity of moderate amplitude develops after the age of 2 years in infantile neuroaxonal dystrophy.

Multiple spikes superimposed on lateralized large slow waves suggest progressive neuronal degeneration of childhood, and predict later hepatic involvement.

Contraindications to EEG

There are no absolute contraindications to EEG. However, potential dangers arise from misinterpretation of the findings when these are conveyed from the electroencephalographer to the clinician. Most frequently this arises when EEGs are requested for three inappropriate reasons, repeated febrile convulsions, convulsive syncope (anoxic seizures), and behaviour disorders (conduct disorders) without dementia or other neurological deterioration. The difficulty arises because EEG spikes, characteristic of epilepsy occur in a small proportion (1%–2%) of individuals who do not have epilepsy. If therefore EEGs are carried out on the basis of these inappropriate indications, a small proportion will show spikes and it will be difficult to hide this fact from the parents. To make matters worse, common normal phenomena may be misinterpreted as abnormalities. For example, the shifting 'small sharp spikes' of light sleep may be reported as multifocal spikes (*see case* 1.3) and the high-voltage sharp-notched slow bursts of the young child's drowsy state as generalized spike and wave.

A potential physical danger not of the EEG recording itself but of one of the provocations, that of hyperventilation, occurs in idiopathic moya-moya disease (in which stenosis of arteries at the circle of Willis leads to hemiplegias or transient ischaemic attacks), and in sickle-cell disease (in which moya-moya may also be found). Hyperventilation may precipitate hemiplegia in these disorders, through cerebral arteriolar vasoconstriction. In the case of sickle-cell disease the neurological deficit is more likely to be permanent. An *in vitro* sickling test must therefore be done on any non-caucasian child before hyperventilation activation is allowed.

Case illustrations

1.1 Fainting fit
1.2 School problems: 'migraine', 'epilepsy'
1.3 'Epilepsy' with regression: 'Batten's disease'
1.4 'Elective mutism'
1.5 Not periventricular leucomalacia
1.6 Acute 'encephalopathy' with hemi-seizures

See Appendix for definitive diagnoses.

In addition to the following case illustrations, *see* 2.4, 3.1, 4.1, 4.4, 4.5, 5.1, 5.3, 8.1, 9.2 and 10.1

1.1 Fainting fit

An intelligent 7-year-old girl blacked out while standing eating in the kitchen. She was pale with her eyes rolling and her teeth clenched. There was no clonic movements, incontinence or tongue biting, but she was drowsy afterwards.

Investigation
The EEG showed frequent clusters of left Rolandic spike and slow-wave complexes, the amplitude of the spikes exceeding 200 μV.

Comments
The diagnosis was of vasovagal syncope, and EEG examination was not appropriate. The hazard here was that the clinician might alarm the parents by disclosing the 'result' of the EEG or even suggest to them that this was the beginning of epilepsy (*see* Appendix: Predictive value of investigation results).

1.2 School problems: 'migraine', 'epilepsy'

This 8-year-old boy's problems began within a couple of months of school entry. A school medical officer found his vision to be reduced in one eye and he was soon told to wear spectacles at all times from waking to going to bed. His 'friends' at school called him 'specky four eyes'. He began to have episodes of pallor and vomiting, sometimes with a sore head, every 2 weeks. He was given pizotifen, with a subsequent reduction in the number of vomiting episodes, but he seemed 'doped' or 'drugged'.

Investigation
EEG aged 7 was reported 'This is a mildly abnormal record with activation procedures producing an excess of sharp outline activities. There are no overt paroxysmal features, however, and in particular no evidence of petit mal. The

slightly abnormal record in combination with the clinical history would justify a trial of anticonvulsants.'

Course
The boy's mother was told he had epilepsy and that he should not climb trees or ride a bicycle, or go swimming unless an adult was in the pool close beside him. He was treated with antiepileptic medication without effect. Episodes of vomiting continued but remitted during the summer.

Comments
This boy, on closer examination, had a considerable specific learning disability, with normal intelligence and an amblyopia not justifying spectacle management. There was no evidence that he had ever had epilepsy. The EEG was ordered without a proper question having been framed which the EEG could answer and the (normal) EEG was overinterpreted. Children with specific learning disabilities who may 'switch off' when they do not immediately respond to a question are at risk of a misdiagnosis of epilepsy. Such a diagnosis should be regarded as questionable unless 'switch off' episodes are shown to be accompanied by clear-cut simultaneous EEG spiking.

1.3 'Epilepsy' with regression: 'Batten's disease'

This boy posed considerable problems to physicians in North America. He first presented with toe walking at the age of 2 years. At that stage he could reproduce a sentence spoken by his father. At around $2\frac{1}{2}$–3 years of age his development seemed to plateau and regress and he began to have seizures. At first he would pant and then appear to stop breathing and then later he would fall to the floor. He would be clumsy at these times. Often he would fall back or stagger and his speech was garbled for a few seconds. He became disruptive and hyperactive. The seizures developed so that they were characterized by one or two deep breaths, and then a staring look for 5–10s and then a straight backward fall. Over time the seizures became more pronounced and came to include both tonic and vibratory components and what appeared to be a clonic component, aside from the loss of postural control which was a feature from early on.

Investigations (1)
EEG. A number of EEGs were said to contain multi-focal spikes, especially in sleep.
CT scan normal.
MR imaging normal.
Urinary dolichols 5.9 μg/mg of lipid (control range 1.0 ± 0.7).
Skin biopsy. A single curvilinear cytoplasmic profile was seen on electron-microscopy.

Course (1)
His parents were told that his epilepsy was secondary to Batten's disease (neuronal ceroid lipofuscinosis). His seizures did not respond consistently to any type of antiepileptic medication.

Investigations (2)
EEG. Normal recordings were obtained.
Electroretinogram. Normal flash and flicker responses were obtained.

Repeat urinary dolichols were normal.
Repeat skin biopsy showed no abnormality.

Course (2)
He did not regress further, but seizures continued. He was referred to cardiorespiratory laboratories.

Investigations (3)
Polygraphy showed that he had repeated breath-holds in which his pulse disappeared, his ECG voltage was reduced by half and his EEG became diffusely slow.

Course (3)
Although it had become clear that the boy was performing repeated compulsive Valsalva manoeuvres, his seizures were still regarded as epileptic and continued attempts were made to treat them with antiepileptic drugs.

Investigations (4)
Cassette EEG/ECG. 72-h EEG was intrinsically normal. He had small sharp waves in sleep but no epileptic abnormality. Seizures were preceded by repeated Valsalva manoeuvres and were characterized by incremental tachycardia and then slowing and disappearance of EEG activity without spikes. Biochemical studies at the time of seizures showed no major changes in glucose, growth hormone, cortisol, ACTH, and beta-endorphin, and moderate increase in prolactin, but huge increases in met-enkephalin to 3000 pmol/l.

Course (4)
Seizures did not occur if he wore a belt which prevented Valsalva manoeuvres. Oral naltrexone then made the belt unnecessary.

Comments
This boy had a milder form of autism with considerable language and communication disorder. Batten's disease was diagnosed on the basis of an inadequate battery of tests. Standard EEG was misinterpreted and, although he had clear anoxic changes on EEG during Valsalva manoeuvres, the dramatic nature of his seizures convinced the physicians that these seizures were epileptic. Prolonged cassette recordings, coupled with videotape analysis, showed that they were, in fact, all anoxic seizures. The boy seemed to have a compulsive desire to induce cerebral hypoxia and the huge met-enkephalin level was probably related to this. This case illustrates the importance of watertight investigations before progressive neurodegenerative disease is diagnosed, and the necessity for ictal EEGs in supposed refractory 'epilepsy'.

1.4 'Elective mutism'

This boy was referred to a child and family psychiatric unit towards the end of his 4th year when he had stopped talking after a number of stressful events ('life events') within the family. ' . . . there is little doubt that [he] is electively mute and that his symptoms give him a lot of power within the family' wrote the psychiatrist.

When reviewed at the age of 4 years the parents said that his speech had begun to deteriorate when he was $3\frac{1}{2}$ years old. Previously he could hold long conversations with adults about past and future events, face to face and on the telephone, using normal vocabulary and grammar. Over a weekend he was noted to be talking normally at times but at other times 'mumbling' and ignoring people who spoke to him. During the following week he seemed to be 'cut-off' at times; the 'mumbling' stopped, but no other sounds were made. Hearing was checked and found to be normal. Vocalization returned, described by his parents as 'sounds like words but they weren't words; he sounded and acted like a child wanting to talk but not knowing how.' He began to use pointing, and developed his own gestures to communicate. His behaviour began to deteriorate and he became difficult to manage. Psychiatric treatment of his behavioural difficulties was effective but his speech did not return. He had no seizures of any kind.

On examination, his success with performance items from the Stanford Binet and Merrill Palmer tests of intellectual function was at his age level; he played with toys appropriately; he followed gestures and pantomime and looked at faces and was aware of speech, but gave no proper responses to verbal labels for objects, miniature toys, or pictures. Otherwise, he seemed neurologically intact.

Investigation
EEG (Figure 1.4(a)). Frequent bursts of spike and wave recurred throughout a routine recording. The frequency was 2–3 Hz, and the distribution generalized with posterior and variably left-sided accentuation.

Course
A 2-week therapeutic trial of betamethasone abolished his EEG spikes (Figure 1.4(b)) but did not improve his language comprehension. Six months later occasional absences were reported and later characterized on EEG by 2–3 Hz spike and wave with small regular twitchings of his mouth and eyes (Figure 1.4(c)). The absences were abolished by sodium valproate, once again with no improvement in auditory verbal understanding. His needs are now being met by a special school for children with severe language disorders.

Comment
The Landau–Kleffner syndrome commonly presents as if it were a psychiatric reaction. In this context the EEG with bilateral spiking has very strong diagnostic power. All-night sleep EEG would probably have shown prolonged continuous spike and wave. 'Mutism' is one of the few indications for standard EEG in apparently psychiatric disorders.

1.5 Not periventricular leucomalacia

A girl, the sixth child of healthy, unrelated parents presented at 4 months of age with episodes in which her arms and legs extended and turned in simultaneously, with her hands fisted and the eyes rolled upwards. Her mother felt that she had never been normal and noted stiffening during feeds since birth. On examination, head circumference was 42 cm (35 cm at birth). She did not fixate, follow or smile, and exhibited extreme head lag with persistence of primitive reflexes, fisting and hypertonia. There were no dysmorphic features.

Investigations (1)
EEG was reported as showing 'borderline hypsarrhythmia' (Figure 1.5(a)(b)). Cerebral ultrasound showed a mild degree of ventriculomegaly with marked

16

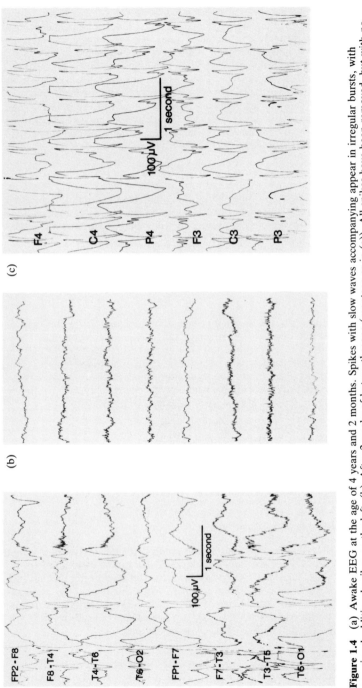

Figure 1.4 (a) Awake EEG at the age of 4 years and 2 months. Spikes with slow waves accompanying appear in irregular bursts, with occasional additional spikes on the left. (b) After 2 weeks of betamethasone (montage as in (a)). All spikes have been removed, but with no improvement in verbal auditory agnosia. (c) Six months later. Average reference EEG during a 4-s run of generalized semi-rhythmic spike and wave, associated with twitching of eyes and mouth. In these and the following EEG samples FP = fronto-polar (pre-frontal); F = frontal; C = central (Rolandic); T = temporal; P = parietal; O = occipital; Z = sagittal (mid-line); even numbers = right; odd numbers = left.

17

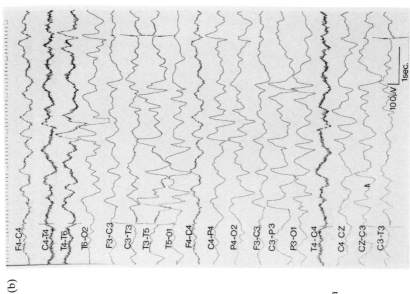

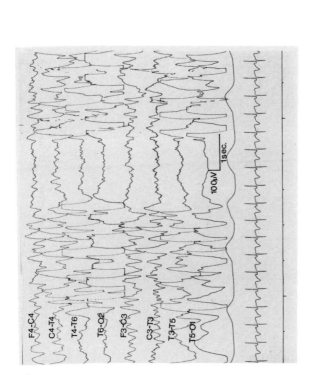

Figure 1.5 (a) EEG at age 4 months reported as 'modified hypsarrhythmia'. (b) Drowsy EEG at age 7 months without diagnostic features (very brief 'spikes' on the right are sucking artifacts).

18

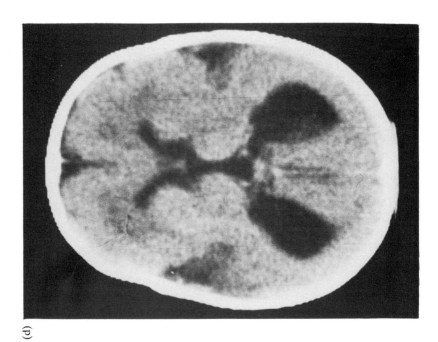

(d)

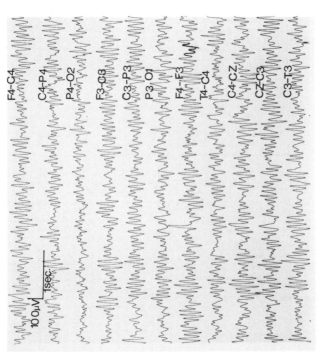

(c)

Figure 1.5 (c) EEG at 15 months now shows generalized high-voltage activity in the alpha frequency (10–11Hz). (d) CT scan showing thick cortical grey matter most obvious in frontal regions, and lack of operculation, with figure-of-eight appearance.

irregularity and cystic changes in the periventricular areas, suggesting periventricular leucomalacia.
Plasma and urinary amino acids were normal.
Plasma uric acid was normal.
CSF protein was normal.

Course
She was started on betamethasone with some response, and following the introduction of nitrazepam the tonic spasms disappeared. Over the following 9 months she made no developmental progress, and at 14 months head circumference was 44 cm and she showed signs of a spastic quadriplegia.

Investigations (2)
EEG at fifteen months showed diffuse large-amplitude activity (200 μV) at 12–15 Hz (Figure 1.5(c)).
CT brain scan (Figure 1.5(d)) showed a smooth cortex with broad Sylvian fissure and widened interhemispheric fissure anteriorly, consistent with type I lissencephaly.
Karyotype by Giemsa banding was normal.

Comment
The clinical picture suggested an underlying brain malformation rather than pre- or perinatal periventricular leucomalacia (PVL). In either of these situations, CT brain scan and/or MRI are the imaging methods of choice after the neonatal period. In type I lissencephaly, EEG will not show the characteristic high-amplitude fast activity until the end of the first year.

1.6 Acute 'encephalopathy' with hemiseizures

A 4-month-old boy with apparently normal development was transferred to intensive care shortly after admission. He had begun to have seizures that day, at first generalized, clonic and brief, and then associated with deviation of his eyes to the left, with fever developing. He had had his triple vaccine on the first occasion 6 weeks before and was due the next within a few days. On examination he localized to pain but the right side of his face and his right limbs moved less well.

Investigations (1)
EEG showed periodic lateralized complexes of high amplitude on the left.
CSF contained 0.35 g/1 protein and no cells.
White blood count was $6.4 \times 10^9/1$.
Repeated blood and CSF herpes simplex titres and other virological studies were negative.

Course
He was initially treated with acyclovir for 10 days. Continued partial epileptic seizures appeared to respond to phenytoin. He had a persistent right hemisyndrome and development was never again normal

Investigations (2)
Further EEG showed high-voltage activity in the alpha frequency over the left hemisphere and sometimes in the beta frequency, with short interludes of

relative EEG suppression. Similar activity was seen inconstantly in the right frontal region.

Ultrasound examination (echoencephalogram) showed no intracranial abnormality.

CT scan using a second and higher-generation machine showed indentation of the anterior horn of the right lateral ventricle and a thin corpus callosum with a suggestion of thick cerebral cortex over much of the left cerebral hemisphere and in the right frontal region.

MR imaging showed extensive pachygyria on the left and in the right frontal region (Figure 1.6).

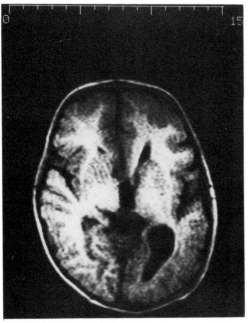

Figure 1.6   T1-weighted MR image emphasizing distinction between grey and white matter. The right side (left of this picture) is the more normal, but the grey mantle at the frontal pole may be too thick (scale is 1 cm per division). On the left (right side of this Figure) the grey matter is extensively thickened, and in the occipital region there is no clear grey/white demarcation abutting the dilated posterior horn of the left lateral ventricle.

Comments

This boy's neuronal migration disorder presented in the guise of an acute encephalopathy. Sequential EEGs were more sensitive than the CT scan, suggesting the underlying pathology, which was best seen by magnetic resonance imaging.

Further reading

Aicardi, J. (1986) *Epilepsy in Children*, Raven Press, New York

Asconape, J. and Penry, J. K. (1984) Some clinical and EEG aspects of benign juvenile myoclonic epilepsy. *Epilepsia*, **25**, 108–114

Binnie, C. D., Rowan, A. J. and Gutter, Th. (1982) *A Manual of Electroencephalographic Technology*. Cambridge University Press, Cambridge

Boyd, S. G., Harden, A., Egger, J. and Pampiglione, G. (1986) Progressive neuronal disease of childhood with liver disease (Alper's disease): characteristic neurophysiological features. *Neuropediatrics*, **17**, 75–80

Boyd, S. G., Harden, A. and Patton, M. A. (1988) The EEG in the early diagnosis of Angelman (Happy Puppet syndrome). *European Journal of Pediatrics*, **147**, 508–513

Cohen, R. J. and Suter, C. (1982) Hysterical seizures: suggestion as a provocative test. *Annals of Neurology*, **11**, 391–395

Cole, G., Harden, A. and Boyd, S. G. (1987) Serial EEG studies in haemorrhagic shock and encephalopathy. *Electroencephalography and Clinical Neurophysiology*, **67**, 73–77

Duchowny, M. S., Resnick, T. J., Deray, M. J. and Alvarez, L. A. (1988) Video EEG diagnosis of repetitive behavior in early childhood and its relationship to seizures. *Pediatric Neurology*, **4**, 162–164

Gastaut, H., Pinsard, N., Raybaud, Ch. *et al* (1987) Lissencephaly (agyria-pachygyria): clinical findings and serial EEG studies. *Developmental Medicine and Child Neurology*, **29**, 167–180

Halliday, A. M., Butler, S. R. and Paul, R. (1987) *A Textbook of Clinical Neurophysiology*. Wiley, Chichester

Stephenson, J. B. P. (1980) Reflex anoxic seizures and ocular compression. *Developmental Medicine and Child Neurology*, **22**, 380–386

Talwar, D. and Torres, F. (1988) Continuous electrophysiologic monitoring of cerebral function in the pediatric intensive care unit. *Pediatric Neurology*, **4**, 137–147

Chapter 2

Electromyography and nerve conduction

Nerve conduction studies

Many sophisticated methods of studying nerve and muscle are available. Indications and interpretation of the most commonly used methods are outlined here.

Motor nerve conduction studies

The painless magnetic stimulator is coming into use at the time of writing, but by traditional methods that part of the motor nerve which can be studied begins quite a way from its origin in the anterior horn cells.

The principle of study is that the nerve is stimulated and the evoked potential recorded in a distal muscle.

If the size of the resultant muscle action potential is smaller than expected this indicates that fewer axons are conducting, either because of degeneration of the axons themselves (axonal neuropathy) or because there has been degeneration of the anterior horn cells. If there is anterior horn cell disorder and/or proximal axonal degeneration then distal muscles will show the changes of denervation on EMG as described below.

As normally measured, the velocity depends on the myelination of the largest and fastest conducting nerve fibres. Abnormalities of myelin, either congenital hypomyelination or especially segmental demyelination, lead to slow conduction velocity throughout the measurable length of the nerve. Thus, the time taken for a proximal stimulus to reach the muscle (the proximal latency) and the time for a distal stimulus to reach the muscle (the distal latency) will be increased. The conduction velocity is calculated by subtracting the distal latency from the proximal latency and dividing this into the accurately measured distance between the two points stimulated. The conduction velocity is thus markedly reduced in hypomyelinating and demyelinating neuropathy. If, in addition to demyelination, there is axonal damage, then EMG signs of denervation in the muscle are likely as well. In pure axonal neuropathy the (fastest) conduction velocity tends to be normal.

If a nerve is trapped or compressed then 'conduction block' may be induced. In conduction block, when the nerve is stimulated proximal to the block the area under the curve of the evoked muscle potential will be less than if stimulation is carried out distal to the block. If conduction block exists at various levels, as may occur particularly in acquired demyelination (e.g. in Guillain–Barré syndrome), then muscle weakness may be considerable.

It should be remembered that if there is acute injury to a nerve in any part of its course the appearance of the expected electrophysiological signs of the damage may be delayed for weeks.

Sensory conduction

Sensory nerve conduction is normally studied by applying a supramaximal electrical stimulus to a digit via a ring electrode. The small action potential is amplified by averaging the response to a series of stimuli. The 'average' latency between the stimulus and the action potential divided into the distance gives a measure of the conduction velocity. Conduction velocity is slowed in demyelination. A reduction in the size (peak-to-peak amplitude) of the sensory action potential has several causes, including axonal neuropathy, conduction block for any reason, and demyelination (when there is also marked slowing of conduction velocity).

Repetitive nerve stimulation

Repetitive stimulation of a motor nerve as in conduction studies may be used to study the neuromuscular junction. The muscle action potential is recorded on the surface or by a subcutaneous needle electrode over a distal muscle such as abductor digitorum brevis in the case of ulnar nerve stimulation, and extensor digitorum brevis in the case of stimulation of the lateral popliteal nerve. Slow and fast rates from 2 to 50 per second assist in the diagnosis of myasthenia (in which repetitive stimulation leads to a *decremental* response) and infantile botulism (in which there is usually an *incremental* response).

EMG

The type of electromyography needed for the study of neuromuscular disorders involves recording from an intramuscular needle. Observations are made on the insertional electrical activity which accompanies the introduction of the needle, the spontaneous activity which occurs when the muscle is at rest, and the exertional activity which occurs during contraction.

The most important abnormality of insertional activity is the divebomber discharge found in myotonic dystrophy and most often determined in the mothers of floppy neonates.

Abnormal spontaneous activity is less useful diagnostically than one might suppose. The regularly recurring short-duration transients known as fibrillations are unfortunately not only found in denervation of the muscle, but may also be present in myopathies.

Abnormalities of exertional activity are more useful. In neurogenic lesions the interference pattern produced by all the available motor units is reduced and the individual motor unit potentials tend to be of long duration and often of higher amplitude. By contrast, in myopathic conditions a full interference pattern may develop before maximum effort is reached and the individual motor units tend to be of short duration.

Practical aspects of nerve conduction and EMG

Many variations of technique and the site of the study are possible in different clinical circumstances. The actual practice of EMG recording is fraught with difficulties which extensive practice reduces. In nerve conduction studies details are important. The skin temperature should be 37–38°C. Cooler extremities lead to falsely low conduction velocity results. Errors of distance measurement have a proportionally greater effect on the calculated conduction velocity the smaller the child. There is an argument for using both subcutaneous needle electrodes for stimulation and subcutaneous needle electrodes for recording when this aspect is important. Some find that the discomfort from nerve stimulation is less when subcutaneous needle electrodes are used. Intramuscular needles are always painful. Some operators seem to be able to 'hypnotize' their child patients to remain happy during needle electromyography; others use sedatives such as chloral hydrate or pethidine.

The most accessible nerves for motor conduction studies are the ulnar, median, lateral popliteal (common peroneal) and (posterior) tibial. The most accessible for sensory studies are the median and sural.

Nerve conduction and EMG abnormalities

The following Tables summarize the most useful EMG and nerve conduction abnormalities (Table 2.1) and the conditions in which these abnormalities are found (Table 2.2). The tables are arranged so that one can either go from an abnormal finding to conditions in which this may be seen, or start with a condition and work the other way. The Tables are intended for reference rather than bed-time reading.

Case illustrations

2.1 Vaccine damage
2.2 Weakness in an 11-year-old boy

Table 2.1 Abnormalities on nerve stimulation and EMG (numbers on the right refer to conditions in Table 2.2)

Motor condition

1. Slow MCV (< 60% mean)	22–31 *not* 30 early
2. Marginally slow MCV (> 60% mean)	3–20
3. Prolonged distal latency	22–31
4. Reduced MAP	3–19
5. Conduction block	30–31
6. Decremental response to RNS	33
7. Incremental response to RNS	34

Sensory conduction

8. Slow SCV	May be 15, 20–31, often *not* 30
9. Reduced SAP	14–21, less so 22–31, often *not* 30
10. Absent SAP	As above, especially 21 (lower limbs)

EMG

11. Increased insertional activity	3–13 *not* 9–10 Acute; 36, 37, 39
12. Myotonia	11, 36, 39, 40
13. Fibrillations	3–13 *not* 9–10 Acute; 31–39
14. Fasciculation potentials	9 (later), 13, 15
15. Rhythmic firing of motor units	4, 11
16. Polyphasic motor units	3–19, 34–39
17. Polyphasic motor units, long duration	3–19 (late stage) occasionally 35–36
18. Polyphasic motor units, short duration	3–19 (early stage) 34–39
19. Early recruitment of large motor units	3–19
20. Reduced interference pattern	1–19
21. Early maximum interference pattern	34–39

MCV, motor conduction velocity; MAP, muscle action potential; RNS, repetitive nerve stimulation; SCV, sensory conduction velocity; SAP, sensory action potential.

2.3 Falling from the knees down
2.4 Slowing and regression in the second year
2.5 Spinal muscular atrophy vs muscular dystrophy

See Appendix for definitive diagnoses.

In addition to the following case illustrations, *see* 4.6, 4.8, 7.2, 9.1, 10.3, 10.5 and 10.6.

2.1 Vaccine damage

A 6-month-old girl was admitted with a 4-day history of fever, lethargy, vomiting and inability to bear weight. She had received her first dose of oral polio vaccine 4 weeks previously and an intramuscular injection of diphtheria/tetanus/pertussis vaccine into her left thigh at the same time. She was irritable, dyspnoeic and hypertensive (BP 130/70). All limbs were flaccid, the left more so and the left lower limb most so, with absent tendon reflexes. She had lost neck control and made no effort to sit. Facial muscles bilaterally and the right diaphragm were paralysed. On the third day in hospital scoliosis, ocular flutter and opsoclonus were observed. The eye movements resolved within a few days but the scoliosis persisted for several months. Sensation appeared normal.

Table 2.2 Clinical settings for abnormalities of nerve conduction – EMG (numbers on the right refer to abnormalities in Table 2.1)

1.	*'Psychic' problems*	
2.	Insufficient voluntary effort, 'hysteria'	20
3.	*Anterior horn cell disorders*	
4.	SMA I (Werdnig–Hoffmann)	2, 4 (may be absent), 13, 15, 16, 18, 20
5.	SMA I diaphragmatic form (Mellins–McWilliam)	as SMA I but may be normal at first
6.	SMA II (intermediate)	4, 11, 16, 17, 19, 20
7.	SMA III (Kugelberg–Welander)	4, 11, 16, 17, 20
8.	Distal SMA	as SMA III
9.	Poliomyelitis	May be normal early; late 13, 17, 20
10.	Hopkin's syndrome (asthmatic amyotrophy)	as poliomyelitis
11.	Glycogenosis type II (Pompe's)	as SMA I, 12
12.	Hexosaminidase A + B deficiency	as SMA III
13.	Systems disorder including upper and lower motor neurone loss	as SMA III
14.	*Axonal neuropathies*	
15.	HMSN II	2, 4, 9, 13, 14, 17
16.	HMSN Ouvrier variant	as HMSN II
17.	Neuroaxonal dystrophy	as HMSN II
18.	Giant axonal neuropathy	as HMSN II
19.	Toxic and extra-CNS metabolic disorders	2–4, 9
20.	Hereditary sensory neuropathies	8–10 (details vary)
21.	Friedreich's ataxia	10 (lower limbs)
22.	*Myelin-deficient neuropathies*	
23.	Congenital hypomyelinating neuropathy	1, 3, 4, 8, 9
24.	HMSN I	.. ⎫
25.	HMSN III	.. ⎪ EMG
26.	Krabbe's disease (infantile)	.. ⎬ data commonly superfluous
27.	Metachromatic leucodystrophy (late infantile)	..
28.	Niemann–Pick disease type A	..
29.	Peroxisomal neuropathies	.. ⎭
30.	Guillain–Barré syndrome	1 (*not* early), 3, 5
31.	Chronic relapsing polyneuropathy	1, 3, 5, 9, 10, 13, 17, 20
32.	*Neuromuscular junction defects*	
33.	Myasthenia	6, (13)
34.	Infantile botulism	7, 21
35.	*Myopathies*	
36.	Polymyositis/dermatomyositis	11–13, 18, 21
37.	Duchenne and other dystrophies	11, 13, 18, 21
38.	Congenital myopathies	11, 13, 18, 21
39.	Myotonic dystrophy	11–13, 18, 21
40.	Myotonia congenita	12

SMA, spinal muscular atrophy; HMSN, hereditary motor and sensory neuropathy.

Investigations
EEG was normal.
Nerve conduction and EMG. Motor conduction velocity in right common peroneal was 44.5 metres per second with distal latency of 3.1 ms. Sensory conduction velocity in right median was 37 metres per second. EMG was

normal. The phrenic nerve was stimulated on the right and a normal latency for diaphragmatic action potential was seen. Tetanic stimulation produced a visible diaphragmatic contraction on the right.
F waves were not detected.
Repeat EMG was undertaken 2 months later in the left quadriceps and left tibialis anterior. Spontaneous activity (fibrillation and positive sharp waves) was profuse in both muscles, particularly tibialis anterior. Very few motor units could be found. Several long-duration polyphasic units were seen in the quadriceps, and one at 1.5 millivolts was of abnormally high amplitude for her age.
CSF contained 39 polymorphonuclear cells per microlitre with a protein concentration of 0.48 g/l and glucose 2.7 mmol/l, blood glucose not being measured.
Repeat CSF examination 1 week later showed 37 white cells (96 per cent lymphocytes) per microlitre, protein 0.86 g/l and glucose 2.6 mmol/l.
Immunological studies showed normal B-cell and T-cell numbers and function. IgA was persistently low at 7.3 mg/dl with an absent IgA using double diffusion immunoelectrophoresis in the saliva.
Virology. Tests for Coxsackie B and other enteroviruses were negative. Neutralizing antibody titres were raised to polio 1, polio 2 and polio 3 and these viruses were excreted in the stools, polio 2 virus up to 6 weeks after admission. The latter was identified by oligonucleotide mapping as vaccine strain, and types 1 and 3 were identified by intratypic serodifferentiation as vaccine strain.

Comments
Delayed appearance of nerve stimulation/EMG abnormalities are characteristic of both acute polyneuropathy (Guillain–Barré syndrome) and poliomyelitis. In this typical vaccine-associated case of the latter, late EMG evidence of denervation was found in muscles of the limb into which the DTP vaccine had been injected. (Gaebler, J. W., Kleiman, M. B., French, M. L. V. (1986) Neurological complications of oral polio vaccine recipients. *Journal of Pediatrics*, **108**, 878–881.)

2.2 Weakness in an 11-year-old boy

An 11-year-old boy presented with a 2-week history of difficulty climbing stairs, and tiring easily. Findings were proximal weakness, with the face and bulbar muscles spared. There was complete tendon areflexia and flexor plantar responses. After initial improvement he relapsed.

Investigations
CSF protein 1.7 g/l with IgG 10% of total protein and IgG/albumin index of 0.85.
General investigations, including aryl-sulphatase were negative apart from positive Coxsackie B IgM titre for 1 month and Coxsackie B4 neutralizing titre of 512.
Nerve conduction studies showed grossly prolonged distal latencies, conduction velocities of 19 metres per second in median nerve and 22 metres per second in peroneal. Conduction block was present proximally. Sensory potentials were normal in amplitude in the right sural, but delayed and dispersed in the median with borderline amplitude.

Needle electromyography showed occasional fibrillations and positive sharp
waves in the right deltoid. Only a single unit was recruitable in the tibialis
anterior on maximum voluntary contraction.

Repeat conduction studies 1 month later showed further slowing with velocities
around 12 metres per second and distal latencies around 17 ms.

Evidence of active denervation was demonstrated in tibialis anterior and no
units were recruitable in that muscle.

Comment

This boy had a subacute relapsing polyneuropathy associated with microbiological evidence of Coxsackie B4 infection. The neurophysiological findings
suggested segmental demyelination, with later on the possibility of axonal
neuropathy in addition. In the light of the finding of conduction block, tests for
hereditary neuropathies were superfluous.

In the event, he responded only to repeated plasmapheresis, after which he
retained full power, being able to cycle for 16 miles 3 years after onset. He
relapsed if plasmapheresis was less than once weekly.

2.3 Falling from the knees down

A 2½-year-old girl, who walked on her own at 20 months, seemed to have poor
balance and often stumbled and fell 'from the knees'. She complained that her
legs hurt if she walked any distance (100 metres). Her divorced father had been
diagnosed as having Friedreich's ataxia, but was not accessible for examination.

Investigations

Nerve conduction. Right median nerve conduction velocity was 5 metres per
second with distal latency of 16.4 ms.

CSF protein 0.49 g/l.

Sural nerve biopsy. Axons and myelination were reported as normal.

Muscle biopsy. Gastrocnemius biopsy was normal on light and electronmicroscopy.

Leucocyte aryl-sulphatase was normal.

Course

Her paternal grandmother was contacted and found to have a conduction
velocity of 15 metres per second in the right ulnar nerve with a distal latency of 9
ms, and a distal latency of 11 ms in the right median with no response obtainable
from stimulation at the elbow. Sensory potentials could not be obtained from
her. She had minimal wasting.

By examining family members an extensive dominant inheritance of hereditary motor and sensory neuropathy (HMSN type I) was determined. The girl,
who was the index case, is employed with only minor physical difficulties 17
years later.

Comments

Ataxia with Rombergism and tendon areflexia may be a presentation of hereditary motor and sensory neuropathy type I, but the diagnosis will be missed (as in
the case of her father) if nerve conduction studies are not undertaken.

2.4 Slowing and regressing in the second year

This girl was said to be normal in the first year. She reached a developmental peak at 14 months, went into a plateau until 18 months, and then regressed in motor and mental capacity. She became less able to crawl and both wrists became 'dropped'. Her output of speech diminished and her understanding dropped to the 9-month-level by the age of 2 years. On examination she had pale optic discs, general hypotonia, and absent ankle jerks and extensor plantar responses.

Investigations
EEG was normal.
24-h EEG was normal both awake and asleep (Figure 2.4(a)).
Visual evoked responses and brain-stem auditory evoked responses were normal.
Motor nerve conduction velocities were 42 metres per second in left common peroneal with distal latency 1.6 ms, and 46 metres per second in left median with 2.5 ms distal latency.
Sensory nerve action potential was absent in sural, median and ulnar nerves.
H reflex was absent.
Needle electromyography showed fibrillation, positive waves and fasciculation in abductor pollicis brevis and first dorsal interosseous.
CT scan was normal
CSF contained 2 white cells and 0.15 g/l protein.
Biochemical studies including hexosaminidase A and B in leucocytes were normal.
Skin and conjunctival biopsy showed no definite abnormalities on light or electronmicroscopy although Professor Seitelberger thought there was a 'slow axonal degeneration process', compatible with but not diagnostic of the suggested disease.
When she was 3 years of age a further EEG (Figure 2.4(b)) showed prominent high-voltage (often exceeding 100 μV) 18–20 per second fast activity diffusely.

Comments
The characteristic time course with a combination of CNS degeneration and axonal neuropathy indicated infantile neuroaxonal dystrophy, but the characteristic EEG was not well seen until the age of 3 years. The diagnosis was considered sufficiently definite without employing brain biopsy. Her younger sister developed a similar course.

2.5 Spinal muscular atrophy vs muscular dystrophy

From the age of $3\frac{1}{2}$ years this boy tended to fall easily and to walk on his toes. He had slight calf hypertrophy and selective muscle weakness, particularly of neck flexors, pectorals, serrati, spinati, deltoid, biceps, triceps, brachioradialis and lower limb muscle groups apart from plantar flexors. Tendon reflexes were not obtained apart from ankle jerks which were excessively brisk.

Investigations
Nerve conduction and EMG. Motor conduction velocities normal (for example, left ulnar 60 metres per second). On EMG he had occasional fibrillation in muscles of upper and lower limbs. Voluntary motor unit potentials were

30

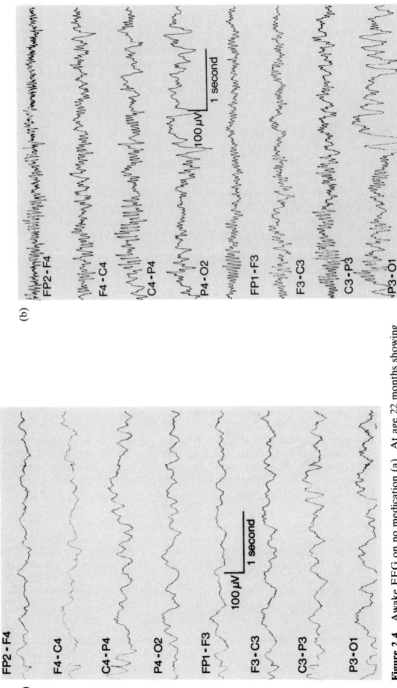

Figure 2.4 Awake EEG on no medication (a) At age 22 months showing predominant theta activity with some very low-voltage fast activity. (b) At age 3 years fast (beta) activity is of high voltage and widespread.

generally small, short and grossly polyphasic. The largest potential was 1.5 mV. Interference patterns were either normal or slightly reduced. CK varied from 1165 to 350 units per litre at the age of 10. ECG was normal. Muscle biopsy showed well-preserved architecture. There were clusters of atrophic fibres of both the main histochemical types with some tendency to fibre type grouping. Some fibres were basophilic and there was collagen proliferation.

Comments

This case illustrates a conflict of findings with important genetic implications. In favour of type III spinal muscular atrophy (Kugelberg–Welander disease) was the timing of the evolution of the symptoms and the most prominent findings on muscle biopsies, whereas in favour of a muscular dystrophy was the distribution of weakness, CK and EMG. In cases such as this in which Becker muscular dystrophy enters into the differential diagnosis, assay for the determination of dystrophin in fresh-frozen muscle biopsy will now be able to make the diagnosis exact in most cases. In the event, deterioration was slow, and the combination of elbow contractures and spinal stiffness made the diagnosis clear.

Further reading

Aminoff, M. J. (1987) *Electromyography in Clinical Practice*, Churchill Livingstone, Edinburgh

Buchtal, F. and Behse, F. (1977) Peroneal muscular atrophy (PMA) and related disorders. 1. Clinical manifestations as related to biopsy findings, nerve conduction and electromyography. *Brain*, **100**, 41–66

Goebel, H. H., Zeman, W. and De Myer, W. (1976) Peripheral motor and sensory neuropathy of early childhood simulating Werdnig–Hoffmann disease. *Neuropädiatrie*, **7**, 182–195

Harding, A. E. and Thomas, P. K. (1980a) The clinical features of hereditary motor and sensory neuropathy types I and II. *Brain*, **103**, 259–280

Harding, A. E. and Thomas P. K. (1980b) Hereditary distal spinal muscular atrophy. *Journal of the Neurological Sciences*, **45**, 337–348

McWilliam, R. C., Gardner-Medwin, D., Doyle, D. and Stephenson, J. B. P. (1985) Diaphragmatic paralysis due to spinal muscular atrophy. *Archives of Disease in Childhood*, **60**, 145–149

Miller, R. G., Gutmann, L., Lewis, R. A. and Sumner, A. J. (1985) Acquired versus familial demyelinative neuropathies in children. *Muscle and Nerve*, **8**, 205–210

Miller, R. G. and Kuntz, N. L. (1986) Nerve conduction studies in infants and children. *Journal of Child Neurology*, **1**, 19–26

Miller, R. G., Peterson, G. W., Daube, J. R. and Albers, J. W. (1988) Prognostic value of electrodiagnosis in Guillain–Barré syndrome. *Muscle and Nerve*, **11**, 769–774

Moosa, A. and Dubowitz, V. (1976) Motor nerve conduction velocity in spinal muscular atrophy of childhood. *Archives of Disease in Childhood*, **51**, 974–977

Ouvrier, R. A., McLeod, J. G., Morgan, G. J. *et al.* (1981) Hereditary motor and sensory neuropathy of neuronal type with onset in early childhood. *Journal of the Neurological Sciences*, **51**, 181–197

Packer, R. J., Brown, M. J. and Berman, P. H. (1982) The diagnostic value of electromyography in infantile hypotonia. *American Journal of Diseases of Children*, **136**, 1057–1059

Evoked potentials

Evoked potentials are generated by sensory stimuli. They may be measured from a sense organ, such as the retina or the cochlea, or from the neural pathway, or from the brain itself.

Electroretinogram

As an aid to diagnosis in paediatric neurology the electroretinogram (ERG) is commonly measured by averaging the response to repeated light flashes, either using a surface electrode at the nasion or, more sensitively, using a gold foil electrode inserted into the fornix of the lower eyelid. Contact lens electrodes are less easy to use in young children. Measurements are made of the photopic and scotopic (dark adapted) response. Sometimes the term 'mesopic' is used when the eye is considerably but not totally dark adapted.

Disorders involving the nervous system in which the ERG is low or extinguished are listed in Table 3.1. In this Table conditions with a low or extinguished ERG are divided into those in which there is congenital low vision and those in which low vision becomes manifest later, or is indeed never noticed. In the first group of conditions other handicaps may be so severe that the visual disturbance is not recognized unless the ERG is done. It is important to recognize that the ERG has substantial amplitude at birth and there should not be a difficulty in detecting these congenital retinopathies which are further discussed in Chapter 16. All these are autosomal recessive in inheritance, except that mitochondrial cytopathy may also have other inheritance patterns. In osteopetrosis (marble bones disease) the retinal defect may be limited to cone dysfunction at first, but the flash ERG becomes extinguished with time (*see* Case 4.10).

Unfortunately one of the common causes of a very low ERG associated with neurological disorder is retinopathy of prematurity (ROP), often associated with the after-effects of periventricular leuco-malacia. In this sequel of prematurity the low ERG is associated with blindness, but in several of the genetic conditions the low ERG has to be looked for, since there may be no obvious visual defect to provide a clue.

Table 3.1 Low or extinguished ERG in genetic neurological disorders

Condition	Clinical clues
1. *Congenital low vision*	
Leber's amaurosis complex	Blindness dominant (cerebral and renal malformation)
Osteopetrosis	See below: low vision is more often acquired
Joubert syndrome	Panting tachypnoea
Warburg type 2 lissencephaly	Hydrocephalus, ocular abnormalities
Peroxisomopathies (several disorders)	Hypotonia, early seizures, ± Zellweger-like
2. *Later onset low vision or vision unremarkable*	
Osteopetrosis	Hepatosplenomegaly may not be present
Bardet–Biedl syndrome	Polydactyly, obesity, hypogenitalism
Laurence–Moon syndrome	Obesity, mental handicap, ataxia
Neuronal ceroid lipofuscinosis	
Infantile	Rett-like loss of skills and hand 'knitting'
Late infantile	Seizures ataxia and regression
Juvenile	Blindness, then slowing up
Mitochondrial cytopathy	Weakness, eye movement defects
DNA repair disorder	Cockayne phenotype
Refsum's disease	Deafness, neuropathy and ichthyosis
Chronic global peroxisome deficiency	Deafness, failure to thrive
Bassen–Kornzweig syndrome (abetalipoproteinaemia)	Ataxia, previous steatorrhoea
Hunter's syndrome (MPS II)	Deaf, hepatosplenomegaly, dwarfism, face coarsening
Mucolipidosis type IV	Corneal clouding, neurodevelopmental regression
Hallervorden–Spatz disease	Rigidity, dystonia: late childhood

Visual evoked potentials

Visual evoked potentials (VEP) are recorded from surface electrodes over the visual cortex in response either to repetitive flash or pattern-reversal stimulation. In children it is often helpful to record the ERG and the VEP at the same time, and if possible the EEG also to clarify the site and the type of lesion. Pattern VEP allows more precise quantitation of the results, but although possible in young infants is usually confined to the older child who can fixate.

With diffuse retinal disorders involving the macula as well as the periphery, not only will the ERG be absent but the VEP will be absent also, as in retrolental fibroplasia.

In disorders of the peripheral retina, although the ERG may be absent the VEP may be normal, as in the early stage of retinitis pigmentosa. As the retinal damage becomes more severe, the VEP will become affected.

If the retinal ganglion cells degenerate, the ERG is normal but the VEP may be absent. This situation is found in infantile GM_2 gangliosidosis (Tay–Sachs disease).

Lesions of the anterior visual pathway, optic nerves and chiasm lead to abnormalities or complete loss of the VEP. An oversimplified interpretation of the different findings suggests that in disorders of the axons, for example with optic hypoplasia or compressive lesions, the VEP amplitude is reduced and its shape distorted, whereas in disorders of myelination such as optic neuritis, the latency is increased though the amplitude and waveform may be normal. Pathologies more posteriorly in the visual pathways are likely to show not only alterations in VEP but disturbances in the EEG, for example occipital spikes in association with periventricular leucomalacia.

Lesions of the visual cortex may be present without any appreciable change in the VEP as ordinarily detected, but with flattening of the occipital EEG.

Maturation of the VEP may be delayed so that the latency is increased for the first months of life.

Pathologies at more than one site commonly coexist and lead to more than one of these appearances being found in the same child. For example, preterm hypoxic-ischaemic damage may lead to both optic hypoplasia leading to abnormality or even loss of the VEP together with the periventricular leucomalacia associated with posterior high-voltage EEG spikes. Such a situation is one of the outcomes of the survivor when one of a pair of monozygous twins has died *in utero*.

The combination of ERG, VEP and EEG changes and their time course is very helpful in the diagnosis of certain neurodegenerative disorders, in particular the various types of neuronal ceroid lipofuscinosis. In the infantile variety, the ERG becomes progressively smaller until it is extinguished, and the VEP becomes smaller also. The EEG then also progressively diminishes until it becomes virtually isoelectric (flat). In the late infantile type, the ERG disappears early but the VEP is grossly enlarged. These giant VEPs can be seen on the ordinary EEG during photic stimulation at slow rates. In the juvenile form, the ERG also disappears early, with later reduction in amplitude of VEP and diffuse abnormality of the EEG.

Brain-stem auditory evoked potentials

Brain-stem auditory evoked potentials (BAEP) are employed both in detecting sensorineural deafness and in demonstrating abnormalities of conduction through the auditory pathway. For the test a series of monaural clicks is delivered to one or other ear. In the evaluation of hearing, the threshold in decibels at which the resulting wave forms are seen is estimated. For the analysis of the BAEP itself, the clicks are delivered to an intensity of about 70 decibels (dB) (higher if considerable sensorineural deafness is discovered). The most important and easily discriminated waves are wave I from the auditory nerve and wave V from the midbrain (inferior colliculus). The most valuable measurements are first the interwave latency between wave I and wave V, and secondly the amplitude ratio of wave V to wave I (wave V divided by wave I).

It is another oversimplification to say that increased latency will reflect a disorder of myelination and a reduction in the wave V amplitude (and therefore a reduction in the wave V : wave I ratio) will result from problems of the axon.

Somatosensory evoked potentials

The least pleasant of the evoked responses which may be undertaken in children is the somatosensory evoked potential (SEP). A peripheral nerve is stimulated by trains of electrical impulses and the SEP recorded from the scalp electrodes over the contralateral parietal cortex.

It is rather poorly tolerated in the young, but finds value during operations involving the spine and aorta, and in the intensive care unit in evaluating coma. Selective loss of lower limb reponses may sometimes assist in the diagnosis of spinal tumour.

Magnetic stimulation and central conduction time

This painless technique, whereby the motor cortex can be stimulated by brief alterations in the magnetic field in a painless manner and recordings made at various points on the pathway to a distal muscle, is likely to prove an acceptable technique for evaluating central nervous system function in childhood, but it still is in an experimental stage.

Case illustrations

3.1 Not Rett syndrome
3.2 Attention-seeking behaviour?

See Appendix for definitive diagnoses

In addition to the following case illustrations, see 1.3, 4.2, 4.3, 4.6, 4.10, 5.2, 5.3, 7.3, 8.2 and 10.3

3.1 Not Rett syndrome

An 18-month-old girl had reasonable progress in the first year and had got to the stage of saying three words and waving 'bye-bye', drinking from a cup without a lid, and trying to walk, at any rate around furniture. Then she stopped and lost skills; she had a tendency to scream and began to bring her hands together. Her head circumference declined from the 50th to the 2nd percentile.

She did not plateau, but continued to regress. Intention tremor was evident when she put her thumb to her mouth and her plantar responses were extensor. She developed myoclonic jerks at the age of 2 years, and thereafter her visual competence and head control declined, but her abilities fluctuated for a while.

Investigations

EEG at 21 months was mildly slow with maximum amplitude of about 50 μV. By 2 years the slow activity was interrupted by low-voltage fast activity and by $2\frac{1}{2}$ years it was unequivocally of low voltage, associated with non-epileptic myoclonus.

ERG at the age of 2 years was just within normal limits (Figure 3.1(a)) with a corneal electrode amplitude of 30 μV under mesopic conditions. By $2\frac{1}{2}$ years there was a marked reduction of amplitude to 8–9 μV (Figure 3.1(b)).

CSF protein was 0.05 g/1.

Conjunctival biopsy. No abnormality of nerves or abnormal storage was detected.

Rectal biopsy at age $2\frac{1}{2}$ years. Histological sections showed foamy histiocytic cells, particularly in the superficial parts of the lamina propria.

At an ultrastructural level, coarse, part membrane-bound granular material was seen in both neurones and in the smooth-muscle cells of the muscularis mucosae.

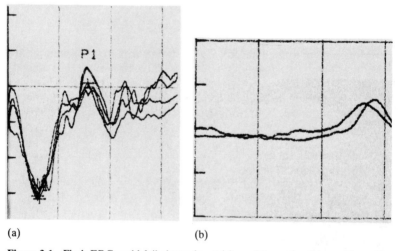

(a)   (b)

Figure 3.1 Flash ERG, gold foil electrode, at (a) age 24 months, (b) age 31 months. Note decline in amplitude (and increased latency) between these two recordings. Calibration: vertical division 10 μV, horizontal division 300 ms.

Comments

The infantile form of neuronal ceroid lipofuscinosis may have an autistic presentation with regression and a form of stereotyped hand movements, but EEG and ERG evidence of cerebroretinal degeneration soon evolves. Suction biopsy of the rectum, although to a degree invasive, remains one of the secure ways of making this devastating diagnosis.

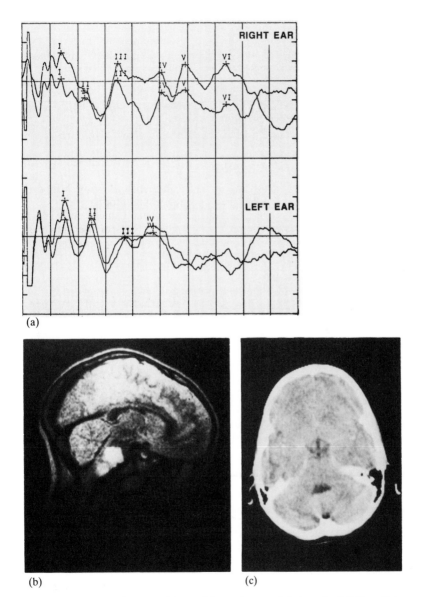

(a)

(b)   (c)

Figure 3.2 (a) BAEP from clicks to right ear is normal, but on the left there is a block before wave V. Calibration: vertical division 0.2 μV, horizontal division 10 ms. (b) Sagittal T2-weighted MR imaging shows altered signal maximum in pons. The lesion had not been recognized on contrast-enhanced CT scan (c)

3.2 Attention-seeking behaviour?

A 9-year-old girl had a history of about 3 months' alteration in voice as if she was speaking through her nose, and for a few weeks she seemed to be walking in a different way from before. She also admitted to seeing double. The family doctor saw her and thought that she was 'attention seeking' and that her condition was not medical. Actually she had a left VIth nerve weakness, disequilibrium and extensor plantar responses but mild right-sided weakness.

Investigations (1)
Second-generation CT scan showed no abnormalities of the density of the brain-stem or any contrast enhancement. However, the cisterns appeared to be obliterated about the brain-stem and there was suggestion of increased anteroposterior bulk.
Brain-stem auditory evoked potentials were normal on the right, but on the left there was an absence of wave V (Figure 3.2(a)).

Course (1)
She returned to school for a few days pending more definitive investigations.

Investigations (2)
MRI showed signal increase on T2 weighted image indicative of a brain-stem glioma involving pons and medulla (Figure 3.2(b)).

Comments
In the past the diagnosis of brain-stem glioma has often been missed on CT examination (Figure 3.2(c)). In this case the loss of wave V and subsequent waves on one side on the BAEP examination indicated an intrinsic lesion interrupting axonal transmission. The lesion was easily detected by MRI, most readily in the sagittal view.

Further reading

Aminoff, M. J. (1986) *Electrodiagnosis in Clinical Neurology*, Churchill Livingstone, Edinburgh

Fagan, E. R., Taylor, M. J. and Logan, W. J. (1987a) Sensory evoked potentials: part I. A review of neural generators and special considerations in pediatrics. *Pediatric Neurology*, **3**, 189–196

Fagan, E. R., Taylor, M. J. and Logan, W. J. (1987b) Somatosensory evoked potentials: part II. A review of the clinical applications in pediatric neurology. *Pediatric Neurology*, **3**, 249–255

Harden, A. (1982) Clinical uses of ERG/VEP/EEG in visual disorders of childhood. In *Event-Related Potentials in Children* (ed A. Rothenberger) Elsevier Biomedical Press, Amsterdam, pp. 143–160

Harden, A. (1987) Electroencephalography and evoked potentials in children with neurometabolic brain disease. *Clinical Neurology and Neurosurgery*, **89**, (Suppl. 1), 46–51

Mizrahi, E. M. and Dorfman, L. J. (1980) Sensory evoked potentials: clinical applications in pediatrics. *Journal of Pediatrics*, **97**, 1–10

Chapter 4

Diagnostic imaging

Neuroimaging

This section outlines guides for the selection and interpretation of tests with a bearing upon nervous system anatomy.

Ultrasound

High-resolution real-time sector ultrasound scanning in the initial imaging method of choice in the neonate and young infant with suspected intracranial pathology. It is also the ideal method for following over time the size of fluid-filled cavities, in particular the lateral ventricles, in early life.

The limitations of ultrasound relate to (1) less accessible anatomical sites, and (2) difficulties with respect to imaging brain parenchyma as opposed to interfaces. With the usual access via the anterior fontanelle, it is less easy to see the frontal occipital and parietal regions, and the posterior fossa is relatively poorly seen. While interfaces are very well seen within the anatomical areas that can be visualized, alterations within the brain parenchyma other than cysts may be poorly visualized, with, for example, difficulty in differentiating infarction from haemorrhage. The use of a 7.5 MHz transducer and computerized ultrasound may allow better definition of periventricular morphology, but uncertainty remains as to the optimal timing of scanning for detection of periventricular leucomalacia (PVL) which is not always recognized in the neonatal period (but may later be inferred from high-resolution CT or MR imaging). Thus cerebral ultrasound will detect intraventricular, periventricular and thalamic haemorrhage, but is less effective at demonstrating subarachnoid, subdural, and posterior fossa haemorrhage. It is less effective at recognizing PVL and differentiating ischaemic from haemorrhagic lesions than previously thought. Hydrocephalus and cystic abnormalities are easily recognized. Certain malformations may be suspected by particular features, although other imaging is commonly required for confirmation. Examples include lissencephaly (lack of sulci); agenesis of the corpus callosum (corpus callosum not visualized on parasagittal scan); holoprosencephaly (single midline cavity); absence of septum pellucidum (better seen than on CT scan); vein of Galen aneurysm (pulsating echo-free cavity behind the third ventricle); agenesis of the cerebellar vermis (dorsal extension of the fourth ventricle).

Skull X-ray

The skull X-ray gives indirect evidence about the brain and its connections. Despite the advent of newer more complex methods of imaging it has *not* become obsolete. Skull X-rays may be requested as lateral view only, lateral view and posteroanterior, or four view: lateral, posteroanterior, basal and Towne's (half-axial). Special views include those of the orbits and the pituitary fossa. As with all tests involving the interpretation of complex data, the radiologist should know precisely what is the problem to be solved.

Indications

Trauma. X-rays, with skeletal survey in addition, may be of most importance when trauma is uncertain in suspected child abuse. Computerized tomography is of more value if intracranial bleeding is suspected. When the possibility of a depressed fracture of the skull exists, then appropriately angled views are indicated.

Headache. Most cases of headache do not need any form of head imaging. A lateral skull X-ray may show splitting of the coronal sutures in increased intracranial pressure (but does not necessarily show this), and erosion of the posterior clinoids of the pituitary fossa may indicate pulsatile enlargement of the third ventricle due to obstruction of the aqueduct. Elevation of the torcula (confluence of the sinuses) above the lambda, that is, radiological evidence of enlargement of the posterior fossa, signifies gross expansion of the fourth ventricle in Dandy–Walker syndrome. Suprasellar calcification with or without erosion of the pituitary fossa may indicate craniopharyngioma. However, if the clinician thinks that increased intracranial pressure is responsible for the headache, then a CT scan is indicated irrespective of the skull X-ray findings. Splitting of the coronal suture is normally accompanied by the clinical finding of a cracked-pot percussion note over the suture, and its absence may indicate some other explanation for suture splitting such as, for example, metastatic neuroblastoma.

Epilepsy. In most children with one or other type of epilepsy, skull X-ray is not indicated. If brain imaging is needed which will help management, for example family management in tuberous sclerosis, then CT and/or MR imaging is indicated. A two-view X-ray may be helpful as an initial investigation in a child with what seems to be partial epileptic seizures of lesional type (not a benign epilepsy). These views may show asymmetry of the size of the temporal fossae or focal calcification or thinning and outward bulging of the inner table of the skull. 'Febrile convulsions' do not constitute an indication for a skull X-ray.

Abnormal head shape or size. Synostosis of one or more of the cranial sutures is best detected by a series of skull films. A small anterior fontanelle at birth or microcephaly with a pointed head (oxycephaly) later is an indication to look for extensive craniosynostosis. Skull X-ray is essential to differentiate the plagiocephaly due to fusion of a lambdoid suture (which may later lead to increased intracranial pressure) from the more common positional asymmetry found in those with a tendency to turn their heads to the right or to the left. Skull X-ray is not often of diagnostic value in a child presenting with small or a large head (*see* Chapter 5) but will detect osteopetrosis.

Ataxia. Progressive ataxia due to posterior-fossa tumours will (except in the case of the brain-stem glioma) be associated with increased intracranial pressure, and the CT and/or MR imaging will be diagnostic. Old-fashioned radiological signs such as the erosion of the jugular tubercles seen within the foramen magnum in the Towne's view are now obsolete.

Lateral skull X-ray is essential and diagnostic in platybasia (basilar impression), in which there is progressive unsteadiness with pyramidal signs, and later nystagmus and bulbar signs and possible neck pain or head tilt. The lateral skull X-ray shows the tip of the odontoid more than 5 mm above a line joining the posterior edge of the hard palate to the posterior lip of the foramen magnum. This surgically treatable disorder can be overlooked if CT scan is done and not skull X-ray.

The adenoidal pad will be missing from the lateral skull X-ray in ataxia telangiectasia but there are better ways of diagnosing this disorder (*see* Chapter 20).

Spastic diparesis. Progressive spastic diparesis may also be the presentation of basilar impression and a lateral skull X-ray is mandatory in the investigation of this.

Investigation of neurofibromatosis. When an optic glioma is suspected either because of pallor of the optic disc or a positive swinging light test then special views of the optic foramina are often necessary whatever other types of imaging are also employed.

Investigation of short stature. In this situation, in which the probability of a craniopharyngioma is low, absence of calcification or erosion of the clinoids is sufficient for reassurance.

Spine X-rays

Plain films remain of value in certain situations. Standard views are anteroposterior and lateral. Views of flexion and extension of the cervical spine are taken in special situations. Many of the indications for spine X-ray are outside the usual sphere of paediatric neurology.

Indications

Management of scoliosis in neuromuscular disorders, Friedreich's ataxia, Rett's syndrome etc. In certain situations, notably neurofibromatosis, enlargement of one of the foraminae will be looked for in addition to the degree of curve.

Down's syndrome. Cervical spine X-rays are indicated in Down's syndrome when paraparesis has become evident, but how often and at what age cervical spine X-rays should be done in such children before they have symptoms is not yet agreed.

Paraparesis is in general an indication for spine X-ray though not as the sole investigation. Evidence of extradural tumours, whether bony or neuroblastoma, may be inferred, and flattening of the pedicles indicates expansion of the spinal cord. As always, the radiologist should know that the problem is. Hemiparesis may also be the result of a cervical cord tumour (*see* Chapter 19).

Cervical spine injuries. Plain X-rays will form part but commonly not all of the imaging procedures used from the neonatal period onwards.

Acute back pain, with special attention to disorders which may need immediate neurosurgical attention, such as decompensated tumour, or abscess.

Torticollis. Atlantoaxial rotation fixation may masquerade as hysterical or neurogenic torticollis. Good cervical spine films should suggest the diagnosis, which can then be confirmed by high-resolution CT (Case 4.7).

Suspect spinal malformations. Although further imaging will probably be necessary when there are abnormalities of limb size or other evidence suggesting diastematomyelia or related malformations, spine X-ray may provide initial clues. However, normality of the plain spine X-ray does not exclude occult spinal cord abnormality.

Syndrome diagnosis. Other bony abnormalities may be helpful in syndrome diagnosis, for example the butterfly vertebrae in Aicardi's syndrome.

Spine X-ray may also give pointers towards the diagnosis of mucopolysaccharidoses, mucolipidoses, certain gangliosidoses, homocystinuria, and so forth.

Although adequate comparative studies are still insufficient, it seems likely that a combination of good plain spine films (for bone) and MR imaging (for cord) will be the preferred investigation for most suspect spinal disorders of neurological import.

CT spine

In neurological disorders the main value is when combined with metrizamide myelography (*see below*), but the method allows further analysis of bone lesions already visualized on plain spine X-rays (Case 4.7).

Myelography

The methods of imaging the spinal cord are progressively changing and improving. There has been movement from oily myelography to water-soluble myelography to CT-assisted water-soluble myelography using metrizamide. We think that MR imaging (*see below*) combined with plain spine X-rays will be the initial investigation of choice in most situations.

In general the contraindications to myelography are the same as for lumbar puncture (Chapter 5). The greatest hazard occurs when there is spinal-cord swelling. Myelography in acute spinal disease should only be undertaken when neurosurgical exploration can be arranged at short notice thereafter.

CT myelography

This is the investigation of choice for imaging spinal cord and cauda equina lesions when MR imaging is not available. It seems better than MRI at detecting cystic lesions when the cord is of normal diameter but of approximately equal resolution in most other situations below the foramen magnum.

CT (head) scan

At the time of writing, computerized tomography (CT) scanning has reached fourth-generation capability, with fine ability to detect intra-cranial detail. However, it involves ionizing radiation and is less efficient than magnetic resonance (MR) imaging in several situations and areas, particularly in the imaging of the posterior fossa and midline structures.

As with other tests, what is done depends upon the problem. The main variations of technique are in the thickness of the brain slice obtained, the plane in which the patient is scanned, and whether or not intravenous iodine-containing contrast material is administered. Contrast injection is not normally required in acute trauma or infarction, or in the follow-up of hydrocephalus, but is helpful in most other situations (e.g. suspect tumour, vascular abnormality, or cerebral malformations). The most important *contraindication* to contrast CT (aside from known sensitivity to the contrast medium) is sickle-cell disease. Sedation may be needed in those who are not expected to lie still (chloral hydrate 100 mg/kg by mouth (maximum 2 g 30 min before the procedure). Those who are expected to be very active are given trimeprazine 6 mg/kg 1 h before, in addition to the chloral hydrate. Others have used oral chlormethiazole or rectal thiopentone (25 mg/kg), which gives a shorter wake-up time.

As a general rule, as tests become more sophisticated and expensive the question tends to be posed: How will the result affect management? Improved management results not only from discovering lesions which are amenable to neurosurgical treatment, or genetic disorders which have family-planning implications, but also from parents knowing as precisely as possible what is wrong with the child, and the likely prognosis.

This being so, the range of indications for at least one good-quality CT scan is very wide and includes any situation where a structural brain lesion is thought to be likely.

Against this has to be weighed cost, hazard of ionizing radiation in the case of CT, hazard of sedation (which should be negligible with the method described) and the rare complication of anaphylaxis after contrast injection.

The relative values of different brain-imaging techniques are outlined in Table 4.1, but certain aspects relating to CT are given below.

In the neonatal period, while ultrasound is adequate for diagnosing intraventricular haemorrhage, CT is better at demonstrating intra-cerebral, subdural, subarachnoid and cerebellar haemorrhage. Which technique is most efficient in the detection of abnormalities varies with the age (developmental stage) of the child. For example, ultrasound scanning may be better than CT scanning in detecting periventricular leucomalacia (PVL) in the neonatal period, while after a few months CT is a distinctly superior method, and later still MR imaging may be even better.

The value of CT brain scan in various clinical situations is discussed in the relevant chapters. However, it may be helpful to list the correlates of certain CT findings which may have several explanations.

White-matter hypodensities

Obstructive hydrocephalus (posterior-fossa tumour, etc.)
Infection (post-ventriculitis)
Hypoxic-ischaemic encephalopathy
Leucodystrophies
Subacute sclerosing panencephalitis
Congenital muscular dystrophy
Aminoacidopathies (maple-syrup urine disease, PKU)
Peroxisomopathy (Zellweger syndrome)
Type II lissencephaly
Methotrexate encephalopathy.

Striatal hypodensities

Leigh's disease and mitochondrial disorders
Infantile striatal necrosis
Glutaric aciduria type I
Methylmalonic acidaemia
Wilson's disease
Hypoxic ischaemic encephalopathy
Carbon monoxide poisoning

Table 4.1 Comparative value of brain imaging methods

	Skull X-ray[1]	Ultrasound[2]	CT	MR
TISSUE DEFINITION				
Bone	+++	0	++	0
CSF Subarachnoid	0	0	++	+++
Ventricular	0	+++	++	++
Choroid plexus	0	+++	++	++
Gyri	+	+	++	+++
Sulci	0	++	++ (High resolution)	+++
Grey/white matter differentiation	0	–	++ (High resolution)	+++
Blood vessels	–	++ (main arteries only)	+	++ (flow voids)
ANATOMICAL SITES				
Cerebral hemisphere convexities	–	–	++	+++
Frontal pole	–	0	++	+++
Occipital pole	–	0	++	+++
Temporal pole	+	+	++	+++
Parietal	–	–	++	+++
Central white matter	0	+	++	+++
Corpus callosum	0	+++	++	+++
Basal ganglia	0	+	++	+++
Suprasellar region	+	0	++ (high resolution)	+++
Optic nerves	++	0	++ (high resolution)	++
Cerebellum	+	+	++	+++
Brain-stem	0	0	+	+++
Craniocervical junction	++	0	+	+++
PATHOLOGIES				
Bony abnormalities	+++	0	+	0
Calcification	+	+ +	+++	–
Haemorrhage				
Periventricular and intraventricular	0	+++	++	++ (not necessary)
Elsewhere	–	+	++	+++
Infarctions	0	–	++ (later)	++ (later)
Inflammation	0	–	+	+
Cysts	–	+++	++	+++
Leucomalacia				
Early	0	++	0	?
Late	0	–	++ (high resolution)	+++
Oedema	0	0	++	++
Tumour[3]	–	–	++ or +++	+++ or ++
Obstructive hydrocephalus	+	++	++	+++
Malformations[4]	–	+	++	+++

+++ Excellent; ++ Good; + Helpful; – Rarely helpful; 0 No use
[1] Not brain imaging: refers to indirect evidence
[2] When anterior fontanelle patent and trans-sonic
[3] CT with contrast is better than MRI at detecting oedema around tumours; MRI is better than CT at detecting some low-grade tumours and hamartomata (e.g. those underlying refractory focal epilepsy)
[4] Depends on structures involved

Haemolytic uraemic syndrome
Trauma.
The list of causes of *calcification* is too long to be of use on its own: *see* Diebler and Dulac (1987) for further illustrations.

Magnetic resonance imaging

If technological advances allow sufficient reduction in costs, magnetic resonance (MR) imaging will become the investigation of first choice for the nervous system in childhood. The lack of hazard, even with multiple imagings, is ideal for the developing brain. At the present time the longer duration of scanning and need for the child to be still, often coupled with the relative inaccessibility for monitoring, makes for difficulties in ill babies.

Early studies gave the impression that the superiority of MRI over CT brain scan was self-evident but more recent analyses have begun to clarify the situations in which MRI has unequivocal advantages:

Disorders of white matter. MRI is more sensitive than CT scan in defining the extent of lesions in demyelinating disorders (e.g. acute disseminated encephalomyelitis) and dysmyelinating disorders (e.g. Krabbe's disease, Canavan's disease), but is of equal sensitivity in detecting the presence of disease. It is more sensitive than CT scan in detecting developmental disorders of myelination, and grey matter heterotopias in white matter.
Brain-stem and cord malformations and tumours (*see* Case 4.8)
Descending transtentorial herniation
Some slowly growing brain tumours particularly in sites not clearly visualized on CT scan. MRI has been shown to be more sensitive at detecting the existence of lesions in patients with a propensity to intracranial tumours, for example, neurofibromatosis and tuberous sclerosis, except that CT with contrast may identify the *nature* of a tumour, for example the giant-cell tumour of tuberous sclerosis.
Mesial temporal sclerosis. MRI should form part of the work-up of patients with refractory complex partial seizures prior to surgery.
Vascular malformations, e.g. arteriovenous malformations or moya-moya disease may be demonstrated as areas of flow voids on MRI.
Recent infarction may be seen within hours on MRI rather than several days as with CT scan.
Basal ganglia lesions, for example in movement disorders and metabolic encephalopathies (Leigh's disease, glutaric aciduria type I), are often not detected on CT scan.

The main disadvantages of MRI are the lack of visualization of calcification, lack of specificity with respect to pathological diagnosis, and often the difficulty in distinguishing tumour from surrounding oedema. In these situations CT scan with contrast and variation in CT slice thickness may clarify.

SPECT

Single photon emission computerized tomography (SPECT) allows the imaging of regional cerebral blood flow at first pass after the intravenous injection of an isotope-labelled tracer such as HMPAO. It may be the investigation of first choice in stroke or suspect vascular disease (*see below* and Case 4.5). Preliminary data suggest that localized high uptake may be an early feature of herpes simplex encephalitis, focal low uptake appearing weeks subsequently. SPECT is much cheaper and more accessible than positron emission tomography (PET), but the latter is able to image metabolic functions. The use of SPECT (and PET) in the investigation of epilepsy is under study.

Angiography

Digital subtraction angiography offers considerable advantages over conventional angiography in that smaller catheters with smaller volumes of contrast are used, radiation exposure is less and contrast resolution superior, making it the investigation of choice in children with suspect cerebral vascular disease. The venous route is adequate for the visualization of thrombosis of the sagittal sinus in the neonate.

The most common indication for angiography is probably a history of stroke or transient ischaemic attack, to detect occlusive disease around the circle of Willis in 'moya-moya' disease, in which collateral vessels develop and give the disease the Japanese name. Neurosurgical options make this a disorder worth diagnosing early. At the time of writing it is uncertain whether in fact MR imaging may be a good screening test for this disorder in that moving blood leads to flow voids on the scan and hence the pattern of abnormal vessels may be detected, but it seems likely that SPECT will be a sensitive tool in this respect.

On the whole, arteriovenous malformations can be suspected by other imaging methods. Arterial aneurysms in childhood either bleed or remain silent. Thus angiography is not really indicated in the investigation of preadolescent children with ophthalmoplegic migraine (in contrast to the adult situation).

Angiography is much safer than it was, but is still hazardous in sickle-cell disease, especially in acute situations.

General imaging

A variety of imaging studies of childrens' organs may help in the diagnosis (or management) of disorders which are predominantly neurological in manifestation. Table 4.2 lists those most commonly employed.

Of the imaging methods which may be helpful in particular circumstances, two deserve mention. *Muscle imaging* by (computerized)

Table 4.2 General imaging in neurological disorders

Region	Imaging method	Clinical situation	Finding	Inference
Heart	Echocardiography	Unsteady primary school child	Thick septum	Friedreich's ataxia
Chest	Plain X-ray	Floppy neonate	Raised right hemidiaphragm	Myotonic dystrophy
	Plain X-ray	Floppy neonate	Thin horizontal ribs	Congenital myopathy or spinal muscular atrophy
Oesophagus	Plain X-ray	Ataxia and dancing eyes	Retrocardiac shadow	Neuroblastoma
	Barium swallow	Neck + upper trunk dystonia ('arching')	Hiatus hernia	Sandifer syndrome ('milk scan' and pH monitoring may be more sensitive)
Kidney	Ultrasound	Infant with suspect vision ± panting respiration	Cysts	Leber's congenital retinal blindness; Joubert's syndrome
	Ultrasound	Tuberous sclerosis probable	Mass	Angiomyolipoma
Bone	Bone age	Delay, etc.	Gross delay and dysgenesis	Hypothyroidism
		Floppy neonate	Gross delay (possible calcification)	Peroxisomopathy
	Skeletal survey	Suspect storage	Dysostosis multiplex	Mucopolysaccharidoses, mucolipidoses
			Epiphyseal calcification	Peroxisomopathy; I cell disease; β glucuronidase deficiency; multiple sulphatase deficiency
		'Optic atrophy'*/Eye wobble	Increased bone density	Osteopetrosis

* Eyes may look normal

real-time ultrasound may allow differentiation between abnormal and healthy muscles, and help in guiding needle biopsy (*see* Chapter 7). *Radionuclide 'milk scan'* is of value in detecting gastro-oesophageal reflux, which may be a manifestation of vagal impairment (*see* Chapter 6).

Case illustrations

4.1   Neontal seizures with 'subdural effusion'
4.2   Visual defect at normal school
4.3   Developmental arrest with enlarging head
4.4   Atypical familial febrile convulsions
4.5   Alternating hemiseizures
4.6   Self-injury and refusal to walk in a mentally handicapped boy
4.7   Acquired torticollis
4.8   Shakiness in a nervous 10-year-old boy
4.9   Staggering in a $1\frac{1}{2}$-year-old
4.10 Wobbly eyes diagnosed after a fall

See Appendix for definitive diagnoses.

In addition to the following case illustrations, *see* 1.5, 1.6, 3.2, 5.1, 5.3, 7.2, 8.1, 8.2, 10.1, 10.5 and 10.9.

4.1 Neonatal seizures with 'subdural effusion'

A boy was born at 35 weeks gestation by Caesarean section as his mother was having a laparotomy because of a gangrenous fallopian tube. He had respiratory distress and then began clonic epileptic seizures at the age of 9 days.

Investigations (1)
EEG showed burst suppression predominantly on the left.
Echoencephalography. Ultrasound suggested a left subdural effusion.

Course (1)
Seizures remitted for a few days on phenobarbitone but then returned.

Investigations (2)
CT scan (Figure 4.1). The left cerebral hemisphere was enlarged with an
   abnormal fissure, giving the false appearance of a subdural effusion. The
   cerebral cortex was thick and the lateral ventricle dilated.
EEG. Serial EEGs showed development from burst-suppression to high-voltage
   and very high-voltage alpha activity later speeding up to high-voltage beta
   activity in part.

Comments
Although ultrasound examination is excellent for observing fluid spaces it may not detect intrinsic brain malformation. In this case a neuronal migration disorder which took the form of predominant hemipachygyria was much better demonstrated by CT scan (and even more clearly by MRI) and was accompanied by the characteristic EEG picture of high-voltage alpha and beta activities over the affected thick cortex.

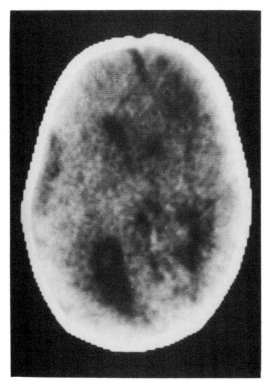

Figure 4.1 CT scan at age 1 month. It is easy to see how the CSF space below the skull table on the left (left of picture) was regarded as a subdural collection on echoencephalography. The normal relative hypodensity of the white matter, present on the right, is not seen in the enlarged left cerebral hemisphere.

4.2 Visual defect at normal school

This boy had had wobbly eyes since he was a baby. At the age of $3\frac{1}{2}$ years he had near vision equivalent to 6/9 with both eyes together using letter matching and the 7-letter Sheridan–Gardiner test. He appeared to have a right hemianopia and strong left-hand preference. His optic discs were pale and probably small.

Investigations (1)
EEG was normal.
ERG was normal.
Visual evoked potentials had prolonged latency and suboptimal amplitude.
Brain imaging was not done at this stage.

Course
At the age of 8 years the school doctor had formed the impression that his eyesight was deteriorating and had suggested that he should be taught Braille. No objective evidence of visual deterioration was obtained and he remained at normal school. At the age of 14 years a bitemporal field cut was documented by

the ophthalmologists and the question of a compressive chiasmatic lesion was raised. On examination at this stage his near vision was still equivalent to 6/9, he had visuomotor ataxia on the right, and his left hand and foot were larger than those on the right.

Investigations (2)
CT scan (Figure 4.2) showed absence of the septum pellucidum and a cleft in the left cerebral hemisphere extending from the lateral ventricle to the surface. The cleft was bordered by hyperdensities suggestive of heterotopia.

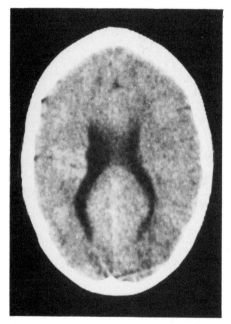

Figure 4.2   CT scan. On the left (left side of picture) there is a cleft between the lateral ventricle and the meningeal surface, abutted by a rim of increased density.

Comments
It was always presumed this boy had optic hypoplasia as part of a prenatal malformation, but over the years the question of progressive pathology was raised by the school doctor and the ophthalmologists. Eventual confirmation of his specific malformation (septal agenesis with hemispheric cleft) allowed his secondary school career to continue in a more settled manner.

4.3 Developmental arrest with enlarging head

A boy was noted to have enlarged anterior and posterior fontanelles at birth when his head circumference was 36.5 cm. Development was thought to be normal until the age of 6 weeks, but thereafter he became stiff and irritable and did not appear to see. At this stage head control was poor and head circumference was enlarging. Rigidity and irritability required increasing doses of baclofen, together with nitrazepam for intermittent spasms. On these medications he remained reasonably happy with occasional smiles until his death at 22 months.

Investigations
CT scan (Figure 4.3), showed extensive low density of all white matter.
EEG showed low-voltage fast activity.
Visual evoked potentials were of reduced amplitude and of normal latency.
ERG was normal
Haematological, chromosome and standard biochemical investigations including analysis of urinary organic acids by gas chromatography, sugar chromatography and bile acid analysis were normal.
Brain biopsy showed spongy degeneration.

Comments
The range of investigations performed was excessive in this case. The course and CT scan appearance were typical of Canavan's disease. Brain biopsy may now no longer be necessary if a specific defect of aspartocyclase is demonstrated (*see* Chapter 10).

4.4 Atypical familial febrile convulsions

An 11-month-old boy presented with prolonged unilateral febrile seizures. Development was suspect. There was a strong family history of febrile seizures in siblings and in his father. Left occipital spikes were seen on EEG. There were no dysmorphic features at the time. A series of asymmetrical febrile convulsions occurred only with fever, culminating in febrile status at the age of 3 years.

Three small, vague, hypopigmented areas were detected on Wood's light examination.

Investigations
EEG showed occasional left posterior spikes.
At the time of status epilepticus, very high-amplitude spike and poly-spike and wave was persistent on the left (Figure 4.4(a)).
CT scan at 15 months (Figure 4.4(b)) showed a small region of calcification related to the posterior aspect of the body of the left lateral ventricle. Follow-up scan at $3\frac{1}{2}$ years of age showed, in addition, several hypodense areas in the cortex.

Comment
At follow-up he developed angiofibromata of the face, and a shagreen patch typical of tuberous sclerosis. One afebrile complex partial seizure had occurred up to the age of 6 years. He had considerable cognitive difficulties, with an IQ of 65.

4.5 Alternating hemiseizures

At the age of 2 months this breast-fed girl had intermittent vomiting for a week, became irritable, and then developed a macular rash on her trunk. She was found to be febrile and had a left-sided convulsive seizure lasting 5 min. In the

53

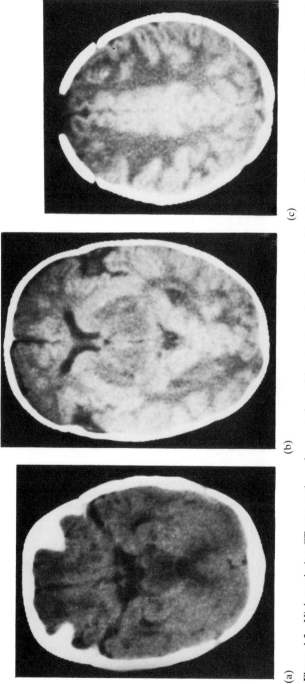

(a)

(b)

(c)

Figure 4.3 High-resolution CT scan at time of presentation, with extensive selective low densities. Note (a) appearance resembling that seen in case 10.5, but (b) white matter and thalamic hypodensities, and (c) extensive central white matter (centrum semiovale) hypodensity, with preserved cortex.

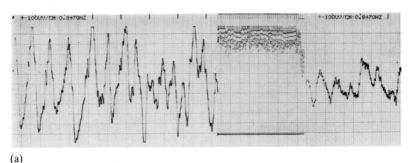

(a)

Figure 4.4 (a) Continuous CFAM trace during and after febrile status epilepticus. Time markers are at 1-s intervals during raw EEG print-out, and 1-min intervals otherwise. Note the fall in processed amplitude at the end of the status. (Note: frequency analysis is not shown).

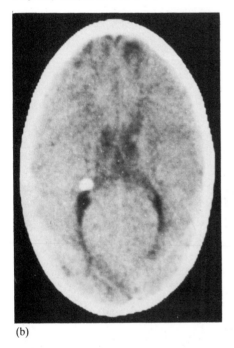

(b)

Figure 4.4 (b) CT scan showing calcified and poorly calcified subependymal nodules, and low-density tuber in right frontal pole (to right of picture).

next few hours two 'generalized' convulsions lasting 2–3 min each were reported. Investigations for viral and bacterial disorders were negative. She recovered and made normal progress. At the age of $1\frac{1}{2}$ years she had intermittent left-sided twitching for half an hour without loss of consciousness, followed by a left hemiparesis which was still obvious 48 h after the event and detectable for a further 2–3 weeks.

Investigations (1)
EEG showed excess slow activity maximum posteriorly, diminished but not abolished by photic stimulation.

CT scan. Low attenuation areas in white matter anterior to the frontal horns and extending over the roofs of the lateral ventricles. Areas of spotty high attenuation in the putamena suggested fine calcification.

Course 1
At 20 months of age she developed focal right-sided clonic seizures and a dense right hemiparesis which took a month to recover. She was thereafter able to walk, but was clumsy and unsteady, and spoke poorly. Shortly afterwards she developed left-sided twitching followed by a left hemiparesis. She became unable to smile, cough or suck, and drooled saliva.

Investigations (2)
EEG. Overall amplitude low, more so on the right which had less low-voltage fast activity.
CT scan (Figure 4.5). Punctate calcification was now not only in the basal ganglia but also in the right frontal region. Paraventricular hypodensities had around the right sylvian fissure and posteriorly to the parieto-occipital region. After contrast, there was striking enhancement of the gyri in the right frontal region and just below this there was serpiginous enhancement.
Blood lactate was 0.9 mmol/1, and pyruvate 81 μmol/1.
CSF protein was 0.19 g/1.
CSF lactate was 1.8 mmol/1, and pyruvate 105 μmol/1.
SPECT with HMPAO revealed markedly reduced cerebral blood flow in a patchy moth-eaten distribution in various areas, in particular in the neigh-

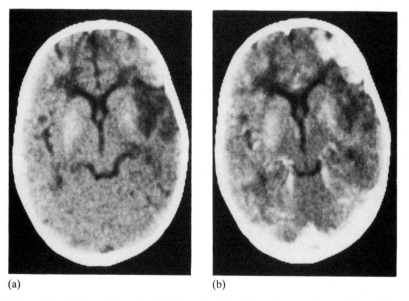

(a)   (b)

Figure 4.5   In these CT sections left is on the left of the picture. Abnormalities visible in (a) include hypodensity of white matter adjacent to the anterior horn of the left lateral ventricle, extensive hypodensity in the right central region, and increased density in the striatum, especially on the left. In (b) iodide contrast enhancement illuminates a region of the right frontal cortex.

bourhood of the hypothalamus and in the right cerebral hemisphere, but with also markedly abnormal blood flow on the left.

MRI showed multiple small cerebral infarcts and evidence of increased proliferation of small vessels.

Cerebral angiography revealed occlusion of both middle cerebral arteries with marked moya-moya collaterals in the region of the striate perforators. The posterior circulation was normal and the anterior cerebral arteries were back-filling via the collaterals.

Course (2)

The patient made a striking improvement after each general anaesthetic which was employed for the latter investigations (using ketamine and halothane, and avoiding a low $PaCO_2$). Superficial temporal arteries were dissected out and transposed onto the brain surface. She made considerable improvement but has complex deficits.

Comments

The CT appearances may be pleomorphic in moya-moya disease, but although the condition may for a time masquerade as febrile convulsions, the alternating hemipareses indicated the need for SPECT scan, and then MRI and angiography.

4.6 Self-injury and refusal to walk in a mentally handicapped boy

A dysmorphic boy with microcephaly and severe mental handicap began to walk by himself at around the age of 5 years. He did not have intelligible speech, and tended to injure himself by hitting his face if he was unhappy. At the age of 15 years he lost his happy disposition and became disinclined to walk. He started to pull out his hair, bite his fingers and rub the skin off his face. He *stopped* wetting the bed at night.

On examination he had a kyphosis, distal wasting of the lower limbs, brisk tendon reflexes and extensor plantar responses. His bladder was not at first distended.

Investigations

Nerve conduction. Motor conduction velocity was 52 metres per second in the right ulnar and 42 metres per second in the right lateral popliteal; sensory conduction was 35 metres per second in the left sural nerve.

Evoked potentials. Sensory evoked potential was normally evoked from stimulation of the upper limb but absent on stimulation of the lower limb.

Spine X-ray. This was initially reported as normal, but on review there was destruction of the left pedicle of T12.

Renal sonar. The bladder was overfilled and failed to empty on micturition, but the wall was of normal thickness and there was no upper renal tract dilatation. Normal kidneys of 8 and 6 cm long were demonstrated, with uniform cortical width.

Myelogram with CT scan. There was extradural block in the upper lumbar region. There was also severe spinal cord compression, the compression also involving the conus and cauda equina. A large bone tumour arose from the spinal process and lamina with the appearance suggestive of an osteoblastoma.

MR imaging. These appearances were confirmed.

Course
Acute urinary retention required catheterization.
His self-injurious behaviour diminished with analgesics. Unfortunately he died before it was possible to resect the benign tumour.

Comments
The radiologist had not been made aware of the question being asked by the clinician and sufficiently good plain spine X-rays were not obtained in the first instance.

4.7 Acquired torticollis

A 10-year-old girl was referred with a history of unexplained torticollis for which she had been hospitalized for the past 4 months. Her orthopaedic surgeon had sought the opinion of the child psychiatrist, the neurosurgeon and the adult neurologist. Her investigations had included X-ray of the cervical spine, and MRI which had been used down to C2, with negative results.

She said that she had previously had a wry neck which had been associated with an abscess on the neck. On the day of onset of the present condition she had been bending over to put deodorant under her left armpit when suddenly she felt an abrupt pain in her neck and could not move it normally again. When she tried to walk downstairs she felt like an astronaut with her feet floating, but when she lay down on the couch the pain went away. During the 4 months following, her neck was always twisted over to one side except on two occasions, once during a general anaesthetic.

Investigations
Plain X-rays of the cervical spine showed a wide gap between the odontoid peg and the anterior arch of the atlas.
CT of the cervical spine confirmed rotation fixation of the atlantoaxial joint.

Course
She was treated with traction, and improved.

Comments
Initial suggestions for dealing with this torticollis included psychiatric therapy, cervical rhizotomy, and thalamotomy. The diagnostic solution was indicated by the exact history and only required good plain X-rays of the cervical spine (elaborated by CT) for confirmation.

4.8 Shakiness in a nervous 12-year-old boy

This 12-year-old boy, the youngest of nine children was described by his mother and nurse sister as 'always a bit nervous, pampered and with a tendency to diarrhoea'. He hated school and at the age of 7 years his school work deteriorated and he began to be 'shaky' when walking. Two neighbouring children were affected by Friedreich's ataxia and his mother thought that the boy was imitating these children. At 8 years of age the school doctor noted that he held his head to one side. At 10 years of age he was referred to hospital. He had a broad-based gait with Rombergism and inability to stand on one leg or tandem walk. There was a mild lower dorsal and lumbar scoliosis but no head tilt. There was nystagmus on lateral gaze. Tone and tendon reflexes were normal but plantar responses were extensor. Sensory examination revealed impaired proprioception in the toes and fingers, absent vibration sensation to the iliac crests and impaired touch and pain sensation to the level T8. There was past-pointing on finger–nose testing and he was clumsy when dressing, feeding and performing fine motor tasks. There was no pain or sphincter disturbance.

Investigations (1)
Sural sensory action potential was normal.
Motor and sensory conduction velocity was normal.
EMG was normal.
Complete spine X-ray was normal.
Chest X-ray was normal.
CT scan of posterior fossa and high cervical cord was normal.
Electrocardiogram was normal.

A specific diagnosis was not made, although 'hereditary spinocerebellar ataxia' was considered possible.

Course
No deterioration occurred over the next 6 months; if anything, he was said to have improved. He was riding a bicycle, had stopped letting things fall, and was doing well at school. However, tone increased in the lower limbs, with ankle clonus and hyperreflexia.

Investigations (2)
MRI of the cervical spine and posterior fossa revealed marked widening of the spinal cord because of a large syrinx cavity extending from the level of C4 to T10. Contrast MR study using gadolinium–DTPA did not suggest an underlying tumour, as confirmed at surgery (Figure 4.8).

Comments
The clinical picture at initial presentation was consistent with a spinal-cord lesion. Nystagmus, sensory ataxia and normal tendon reflexes were misleading. MRI of spinal cord (or myelography with neurosurgical consultation) is the investigation of choice in this situation.

4.9 Staggering in a $1\frac{1}{2}$-year-old

A 20-month-old presented with a story of gradual worsening of his gait for 4 months with staggering and then inability to walk, followed by difficulty putting his spoon into his mouth. He had developed an aggressive personality. He had both ataxia and myoclonus together, with bouts of ocular flutter and opso-clonus, exacerbated by flashing a light into his eyes.

Investigations
EEG was normal.
Blood count was normal.
Viral titres were consistent with oral polio immunization.
HMMA 6.3 μmol/mmol of creatinine, HVA 12 μmol/mmol of creatinine.
Chest X-ray showed a left paraspinal lesion behind the heart.

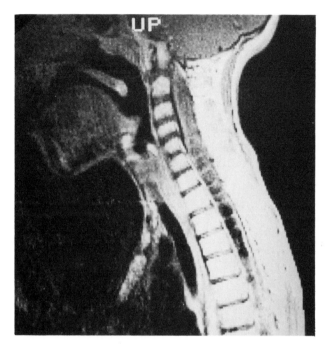

Figure 4.8 MRI of cervical spine. Sagittal T1-weighted spinecho sequence post IV gadolinium-DTPA demonstrates cystic dilatation of the cord from the level of C4. Note the synechiae segmenting the syrinx cavity.

Biopsy of the left posterior mediastinal tumour showed a partially differentiated neuroblastoma which had invaded adjacent lymph nodes.

Comment
His 'dancing eyes' syndrome markedly improved after surgical resection of the tumour and radiotherapy, but later relapsed and required prednisolone treatment. After 5 years there were no further cerebellar signs or eye movement abnormality, but his development was in the dull–normal range and he used to vomit every morning before going to school.

4.10 Wobbly eyes diagnosed after a fall

A 10-month-old girl had been referred first to the ophthalmologist because of squint and roving eye movements. She could fix and follow, and apart from nystagmus no definite ocular abnormality was detected. General development was normal. The skull shape 'resembled hydrocephalus' but the head circumference, though on the 98th percentile, was on the same trajectory as her parents.

Investigations (1)
ERG: Scotopic b wave 75 μV (regarded as normal).
VEP: Low-amplitude but normal latency.

Echoencephalography was normal
CT scan (at 18 months; Figure 4.10a) showed borderline dilatation of the lateral
    ventricles. High-resolution scan (Figure 4.10b) showed no abnormality of the
    optic nerves.

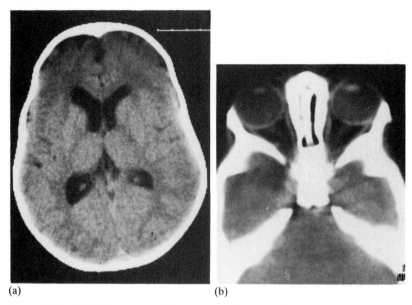

(a)   (b)

Figure 4.10   (a) High-resolution CT scan at age 18 months shows no more than
borderline dilatation of the lateral ventricles. The bony abnormality is not recognized.
(b) Magnified section of the same scan demonstrating normal optic nerves

Course (1)
From age 12 months her parents noted that she 'missed things' and felt about for
    objects. By 2 years her vision was exceedingly low. Her optic discs were
    somewhat pale and the size of her retinal arteries was questioned.

Investigations (2)
ERG at 29 months was extinguished, using gold foil electrodes and flash stimuli.

Course (2)
Shortly thereafter she fell over and injured her arm (Figure 4.10c) and the
    District General Hospital made the diagnosis.

Investigations (3)
On skeletal survey, all bones were exceedingly dense, with typical findings of
    the severe type of osteopetrosis (Figure 4.10d).
Peripheral blood count normal (haemoglobin 11.4, WBC 11.4, platelets 277).
Iliac crest bone marrow biopsy: no haemopoietic marrow seen; no osteoclasts
    detected.

Comments
In the absence of additional clinical clues (there was still no anaemia or
hepatosplenomegaly at $2\frac{1}{2}$ years) the diagnosis of osteopetrosis was not con-

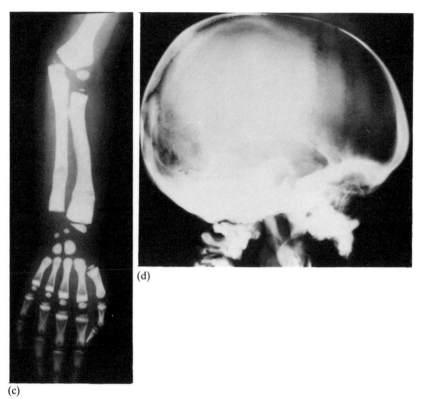

(d)

(c)

Figure 4.10 (c) Appearance of the upper limb after a minor accident, at age $2\frac{1}{2}$ years. (d) Skull X-ray at the same age, confirming universal osteopetrosis.

sidered until it was accidentally revealed 18 months after the initial presentation. The initial low VEP amplitude presumably reflected reduced cone function. Retinopathy as the explanation of the blindness in osteopetrosis is well described (e.g. Hoyt C. S., Billson F. A. Visual loss in osteopetrosis. *Am J Dis Child* 1988; 133; 955–958), but the diagnosis will be missed unless *plain* X-rays are taken. In this case a histocompatible sibling was available for bone marrow donation.

Further reading

Adams, C., Babyn, P. S. and Logan, W. J. (1988) Spinal cord birth injury: value of computed tomographic myelography. *Pediatric Neurology*, **4**, 105–109

Aicardi, J., Gordon, N. and Hagberg, B. (1985) Holes in the brain. *Developmental Medicine and Child Neurology* **27**, 249–260

Baarsma, R., Laurini, R. N., Baerts, W. and Okken, A. (1987) Reliability of sonography in non-hemorrhagic periventricular leucomalacia. *Pediatric Radiology*, **17**, 189–191

Cooper, L. S., Chalmers, T. C., McCally, M. *et al.* (1988) The poor quality of early evaluations of magnetic resonance imaging. *Journal of the American Medical Association*, **259**, 3277–3280

Crichton, J. H. (1981) Acute spinal cord disease in childhood. *Developmental Medicine and Child Neurology*, **23**, 643–646

Diebler, C. and Dulac, O. (1987) *Pediatric Neurology and Neuroradiology*, Springer-Verlag, Berlin

Dobyns, W. B. and McCluggage, C. W. (1985) Computed tomographic appearance of lissencephaly syndromes. *American Journal of Neuroradiology*, **6**, 545–550

Echenne, B., Arthuis, M., Billard, C. *et al.* (1986) Congenital muscular dystrophy and cerebral CT scan anomalies. *Journal of the Neurological Sciences*, **75**, 7–22

Feldmann, E., Gandy, S. E., Becker, R. *et al.* (1988) MRI demonstrates descending transtentorial herniation. *Neurology*, **38**, 697–701

Fischer, A. Q., Carpenter, D. W., Hartlage, P. L. *et al.* (1988) Muscle imaging in neuromuscular disease using computerised real-time sonography. *Muscle and Nerve*, **11**, 270–275

Flodmark, O., Roland, E. H., Hill A. and Whitfield, M. F. (1987) Periventricular leukomalacia: radiologic diagnosis. *Radiology*, **162**, 119–124

Goutières, F. and Aicardi, J. (1982) Acute neurological dysfunction associated with destructive lesions of the basal ganglia in children. *Annals of Neurology*, **12**, 328–332

Goutières, F., Aicardi, J. and Boulloche, J. (1987) Pelizaeus-Merzbacher disease. *Neuropediatrics*, **18**, 116

Gray, J. and Swaiman, K. F. (1987) Brain tumors in children with neurofibromatosis: computed tomography and magnetic resonance imaging. *Pediatric Neurology*, **3**, 335–341

Green, S. H. (1987) Who needs a brain scan? *Archives of Disease in Childhood*, **62**, 1094–1096

Guthkelch, A. N. (1983) Spinal tumours in children. *Developmental Medicine and Child Neurology*, **25**, 801–803

Heckmatt, J. Z. and Dubowitz, V. (1985) Diagnostic advantage of needle muscle biopsy and ultrasound imaging in the detection of focal pathology in a girl with limb girdle dystrophy. *Muscle and Nerve*, **8**, 705–709

Hope, P. L., Gould, S. J., Howard, S. *et al.* (1988) Precision of ultrasound diagnosis of pathologically verified lesions in the brains of very preterm infants. *Developmental Medicine and Child Neurology*, **30**, 457–471

Johnson, M. A. Pennock, J. M., Bydder, G. M. *et al.* (1983) Clinical NMR imaging of the brain in children: normal and neurological disease. *American Journal of Roentgenology*, **141**, 1005–1018

Konishi, Y., Kuriyama, M., Sudo, M. *et al.* (1987) Superior sagittal sinus thrombosis in neonates. *Pediatric Neurology*, **3**, 222–225

Kurokawa, T., Chen, Y. J., Tomita, S. *et al.* (1985) Cerebrovascular occlusive disease with and without the moyamoya vascular network in children. *Neuropediatrics*, **16**, 29–32

Launes, J., Nikkinen, P., Lindroth, L. *et al.* (1988) Diagnosis of acute herpes simplex encephalitis by brain perfusion single photon emission computed tomography. *Lancet*, **1**, 1188–1191

Neal Rutledge, J., Hilal, S. K., Silver, A. J. *et al.* (1987) Study of movement disorders and brain iron by MR. *American Journal of Neuroradiology*, **8**, 397–411

Nowell, M. A., Grossman, R. I., Hackney, D. B. *et al.* (1988) MR imaging of white matter disease in children. *American Journal of Roentgenology*, **151**, 359–365

Packer, R. J., Zimmermann, R. A., Sutton, L. N. *et al.* (1986) Magnetic resonance imaging of spinal cord disease of childhood. *Pediatrics*, **78**, 251–256

Quinn, N., Bydder, G., Leenders, N. and Marsden, C. D. (1985) Magnetic resonance imaging to detect deep basal ganglia lesions in hemidystonia that are missed by computerised tomography. *Lancet*, **2**, 1007–1008

Roach, E. S., Smith, T., Teury, C. V. *et al.* (1987) Magnetic resonance imaging in pediatric neurologic disorders. *Journal of Child Neurology*, **2**, 111–116

Rolak, L. A. and Rokey, R. (1986) Magnetic resonance imaging in moyamoya disease. *Journal of Child Neurology*, **1**, 67–70

Teodori, J. B. and Painter, M. J. (1984) Basilar impression in children. *Pediatrics*, **74**, 1097–1099

Chapter 5

Cerebrospinal fluid

What is cerebrospinal fluid

The cerebrospinal fluid (CSF) is formed by the choroid plexuses within the ventricles, passes into the subarachnoid space around the spinal cord and finally over the surface of the brain, to be absorbed in the arachnoid villi in the sagittal sinus. The composition of the CSF changes during its circulation from its creation to its final absorption. For example, the CSF protein is lowest in the lateral ventricles, intermediate in the lumbar subarachnoid space, and highest in the subarchnoid spaces over the surface of the cerebral hemisphere (where it is occasionally sampled in mistake for subdural fluid). Except when there is an obstruction to the flow of CSF from the ventricular system or potential downward herniation of the brain, CSF is obtained from the lumbar route.

The technique of lumbar puncture should be too well-known to require further description, except to emphasize that needles must contain stylets to avoid the possibility of inducing implantation dermoids, and leading to paraparesis some years later.

Appearance

A cloudy appearance normally indicates infection. More important is the distinction between traumatic haemorrhage and subarachnoid bleeding. In subarachnoid haemorrhage the CSF, however red, runs like CSF and does not have the viscosity of blood. Xanthochromia of the supernatant may reflect bleeding several hours previously, but a similar colour is seen when the protein content is very high from any cause. No difficulty is usually experienced in distinguishing the yellow colour of jaundice or carotinaemia.

Pressure

Ideally a transducer should be used so that no CSF escapes before the measurement of the pressure. In the absence of this technology, a manometer should be attached to the needle at the onset, otherwise pressure measurements will be meaningless.

Pressure measurements obtained by the manometric method will be in centimetres of water (cmH_2O), while those obtained with the aid of a transducer will be in millimetres of mercury (mmHg). The conversion factor is approximately 1.3, by which the pressure in mmHg must be multiplied to give the value in cmH_2O.

The normal CSF pressure in the neonate has a range of 0–5.7 mmHg with a mean of 2.8 mmHg (0–7.6 cmH_2O with a mean of 3.8 cmH_2O). The upper limit of the CSF pressure in older children is said to be similar to the adult value of 14 mmHg (19 cmH_2O). The upper limit in the infant must be lower, but information is limited.

Cells

Beyond the neonatal period the upper limit of normal for total cell number is $5/\mu l$ but the normal distribution is skewed to smaller numbers. There are several methods in use for determining the nature of the cells seen. The appearance of the cells unstained in the counting chamber should not be relied on. In many hospitals CSF is examined by bacteriologists who may use rapid commercial staining kits, adequate enough for most cases of meningitis with large numbers of cells but of limited sensitivity. Improved accuracy is obtained when the CSF is subjected to cytospin. The cells, stained by the Wright, Giemsa, or Romanowsky methods, are then examined by the haematologist or pathologist. This is of crucial importance when the CSF cell count is low, and it is the only method for diagnosing eosinophilic meningitis. Further special stains should be used after cytospin when malignant cells are being sought.

Theoretically, traumatic lumbar puncture will increase the CSF white cell count by 1 for every 700–800 red cells, but inferences based on such calculations must be made with caution.

Proteins

The protein in the CSF consists mostly of albumin, but also includes many other proteins, of which immunoglobulins are the most important. The total protein (see Appendix) starts high in the neonatal period and then falls so that from the age of 6 months there is an upper limit of 0.25 g/l (25 mg/dl) for the remainder of preadolescent childhood. Data are then sparse until the adult upper level of 0.4 g/l (40 mg/dl) is reached.

Traumatic blood contamination may be expected to increase the CSF protein by around 0.01 g/l for each 1000 red cells per microlitre, but as with similar calculations on cell counts, caution is indicated.

The proportion of immunoglobulin may be increased either because of disruption of the blood–brain barrier or because of synthesis of immunoglobulins within the nervous system (*see* end of this section). A useful ward technique for detecting increased globulin is the Pandy test, in which a drop of CSF is added to a saturated solution of phenol. Excess globulin in the CSF will lead to clouding of the solution, but the test will also be positive if the total protein is more than 0.7 g/l (70 mg/dl).

Another old-fashioned test which is of value when modern electrophoretic methods are not available is the Lange colloidal gold test, originally used in the diagnosis of neurosyphillis. This test detects positively charged immunoglobulins, and is likely to be abnormal in disorders such as subacute sclerosing panencephalitis.

By means of immunoelectrophoresis, the proportion or the absolute amount of immunoglobulin may be determined more precisely, despite the low concentration found in CSF. The total protein concentration in serum is very much higher than in CSF and the proportion of immunoglobulin is considerably higher also. Therefore, one of the reasons for an increased amount of immunoglobulin in the CSF is an impairment of the blood–brain barrier, in which case both the total protein concentration and also the proportion of immunoglobulin will be increased. Another important cause of increased immunoglobulin is abnormal synthesis within the central nervous system. This may be inferred, knowing the concentrations of albumin and immunoglobulin in the serum and CSF. Increased synthesis of immunoglobulin may occur both in infection of the nervous system such as viral encephalitis, and in immunological disorders such as encephalomyelitis. Electrophoresis can determine that these immunoglobulins are either the product of a single clone of lymphocytes in which case they are described as monoclonal, the product of a small number of clones of lymphocytes in which case they are described as oligoclonal, or formed by a large number of clones in which case they are polyclonal. Immunoglobulin which is produced within the nervous system is either monoclonal or oligoclonal. If the monoclonal or oligoclonal pattern detected is more evident in the CSF than it is in the serum, this is additional evidence of local synthesis of the immunoglobulin.

Understanding of the significance of increased concentrations of albumin and globulin is made easier if certain ratios are calculated and compared with age-related normative values.

CSF/serum albumin index

$$\frac{\text{CSF albumin}}{\text{serum albumin}}$$

An increased ratio indicates blood–CSF barrier impairment.
IgG/albumin ratio

$$\frac{\text{CSF IgG}}{\text{CSF albumin}}$$

A ratio of more than 0.27 suggests increased intrathecal IgG synthesis.

CSF IgG index

$$\frac{\text{CSF IgG} \times \text{Serum albumin}}{\text{serum IgG} \times \text{CSF albumin}}$$

An increased ratio suggests increased intrathecal IgG synthesis.

It must be emphasized, however, that such calculations of intrathecal IgG synthesis have limited validity when the blood–CSF barrier is impaired.

Glucose

The normal CSF glucose is $\frac{2}{3}$ of the blood glucose which must always be estimated simultaneously. Low CSF glucose is found when there is hypoglycaemia. Glucose levels are low in all forms of infective and malignant meningitis apart from viral meningitis, mumps also being a possible exception. Persistent low CSF glucose occurs after subarachnoid haemorrhage and occasionally it may be a feature of chronic multisystem inflammatory disorders. It has been noted in a steroid-sensitive aseptic meningitis. See also Recent Advances, page 00 Appendix II.

Microbiology

Cultural and serological tests are well established. It is worth emphasizing the necessity for repeat CSF virological studies in suspected acute encephalitis. Measurements of alpha-interferon levels are likely to prove useful as an indicator of viral infection within the nervous system: alpha-interferon is increased in this situation.

Special biochemistry

In special circumstances a number of further biochemical studies of CSF may be helpful.

Lactate and pyruvate are generally measured together, although the lactate level (upper limit of normal 2.5 mmol/l) is the most useful. Lactate levels are increased in certain mitochondrial disorders (such as Leigh's disease from, for example, cytochrome c oxidase deficiency), in progressive neuronal degeneration of childhood (otherwise known as Alper's disease or Huttenlocher's disease) and in various organic acidaemias. It is also increased in tuberculous meningitis requiring ventriculoperitoneal shunting.

CSF amino-acid estimation is of established value in confirming the diagnosis of glycine encephalopathy (non-ketotic hyperglycinaemia) in the neonate or infant. In this disorder the CSF glycine is high, whereas the blood glycine may be only mildly elevated or normal for age. The most sensitive discriminant is the CSF:plasma glycine ratio which is increased from the normal 0.025 to 0.1 or more. The measurement of gamma-aminobutyric acid (GABA) is of emerging importance in infantile encephalopathies. It is measured as free GABA and as the compound homocarnosine in CSF which has been frozen at the bedside.

Succinylpurines have been detected in the CSF of children with a recently recognized inborn error of metabolism with mental handicap and autistic presentation (*see* Chapter 18). This example illustrates the importance of freezing CSF from children with undiagnosed mental handicap disorders.

Estimation of biogenic amines and their metabolites (available in special centres only) are of value in patients with hyperphenylalaninaemia who have disorders of biopterin metabolism. Low CSF homovanillic acid (HVA) is found in dopa-sensitive dystonia ('progressive dystonia with marked diurnal variation'). (See also Recent Advances Appendix II).

Blood sampling with all diagnostic lumbar punctures

Although it has been indicated in the various sections above it cannot be over emphasized that blood must be taken at the same time as lumbar puncture to allow proper interpretation of the CSF findings. Unless the clinical situation indicates that one or more of these tests are unnecessary, blood at the time of lumbar puncture in an acute illness should be analysed for:

Glucose
Albumin
Immunoglobulins
Bacterial culture
Viral titres.

Indications for CSF Examination

Lumbar puncture is indicated in all cases of suspect meningitis or encephalitis, except when skin petechiae make meningococcal infection virtually certain, or if brain swelling, mass lesion, or obstructive hydrocephalus is thought likely (*see below*, Contraindications).

The remaining indications may be summarized thus, with findings in brackets:

Acute polyneuropathy or Guillain–Barré syndrome (increased total protein without increased cells).

Subacute polyneuropathy (increased total protein and increased immunoglobulin synthesis).
Acute disseminated encephalomyelitis (increased total protein, increased immunoglobulin synthesis, mild or moderate increase in lymphocytes).
Suspect dementia, neurodegenerative disease or neurometabolic disease (*see* Chapter 25, but NB *cells* in Aicardi–Goutières syndrome).
Suspect haemorrhage.
Benign intracranial hypertension, after CT scan (increased pressure).

In several disorders affecting the central and peripheral nervous system it is likely that the increased CSF protein is a reflection of the peripheral neuropathy. However, the diagnostic base is more secure if one has both the CSF protein estimation and the nerve conduction studies (e.g. Krabbe's disease, metachromatic leucodystrophy, etc.).

CSF examination is rarely indicated in chronic headache or chronic epilepsy, but discovery of lymphocytosis may lead to therapeutic manoeuvres (*see* Chapter 23).

Contraindications

The most important contraindication to lumbar puncture for CSF examination is the suspicion of an intracranial mass lesion, brain swelling, obstructive hydrocephalus, spinal-cord mass, or spinal-cord swelling. Clinical judgement is necessary here because no single sign or constellation of signs is consistently present in any of these situations.

In the subacute situation in which the history is of the order of 2–4 weeks, with some features such as headache, vomiting, weight loss, or fever, important differential diagnoses are Haemophilus or tuberculous meningitis, brain abscess, and posterior fossa tumour. Evidence suggesting a danger of cerebral herniation in this situation includes a larger than expected head size, a cracked-pot percussion note over the coronal sutures, papilloedema or loss of retinal venous pulsation even when the globes are gently compressed, and an abnormal head posture either tilted or held stiffly in an anxious manner.

In the acute situation where the history is measured in hours or days and the symptoms suggest pyogenic meningitis, a critical matter is to select those few children in whom immediate diagnostic lumbar puncture is not indicated. Failure to localize a painful stimulus applied to the head (using Glasgow coma scale methodology) is an absolute contraindication to lumbar puncture. Antibiotic therapy and mannitol can be given and the position reconsidered after several hours, during which time CT scan may be obtained. Tonic seizures or deterioration in the Glasgow coma scales score are strong warning signs of impending herniation and therefore indicate that the lumbar puncture may be hazardous. In these situations it is possible to obtain CSF if necessary by the ventricular route using the method of McWilliam and Stephenson (1985).

The dangers of lumbar puncture in the presence of mass lesions or swelling of the spinal cord are sometimes forgotten. This applies whether or not myelography is being performed. Medical methods of dealing with resultant spinal-cord compression are limited (possibly dexamethasone and mannitol), so advance contact and collaboration with the paediatric neurosurgeon is desirable whenever this possibility arises.

Finally, the Queckenstedt test seems no longer to have any valid indication, and is often dangerous. It should be abandoned.

Case illustrations

5.1 Cerebral 'infarction' in an infant
5.2 'Meningitis in a 4-year-old girl
5.3 'Febrile convulsions' with fatal outcome

See Appendix for definitive diagnoses.

In addition to the following case illustrations, *see* 2.1, 2.3, 7.2, 7.3, 8.1, 10.3, 10.5 and 10.7.

5.1 Cerebral 'infarction' in an infant

A 4-month-old boy was on holiday with his parents when he developed right-sided twitching and was then reluctant to move the right limbs. On admission to the district hospital he was febrile at 38°C, irritable, and had increased tone in the right limbs, no neck stiffness, bilateral upgoing plantars and no evidence of bruising or other external injury.

Investigations (1)
Investigations at that time were haemoglobin 11 g/l; white cell count 12 900 with 20% neutrophils; electrolytes were normal.
CSF. 37 white cells, 99% lymphocytes. Weak positive globulin; no organisms.
Aminoacid chromatography was normal in blood and urine.
Heaf test was negative.
Viral antibodies and virus cultures were negative from blood and CSF.
CT scan (Figure 5.1(a–c)). Patchy haemorrhage with adjacent areas of low density in right and left parietal regions. Venous sinuses showed up well. No subdural haemorrhage. No venous sinus occlusion. Conclusion was 'query venous sinus occlusion and query bilateral contusion', but very little history was provided on the request form sent to the regional neuroradiological department.
EEG showed symmetrical 2–6 Hz activity.
Subdural taps revealed sterile blood-stained fluid 2–3 ml from the left side, with dry tap on the right side.

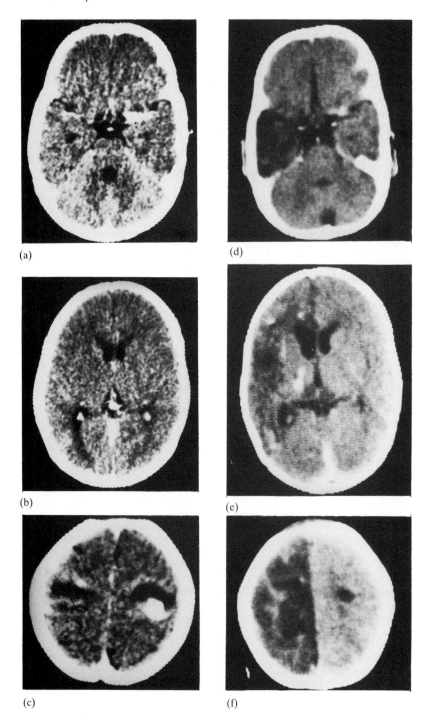

(a)

(b)

(c)

(d)

(e)

(f)

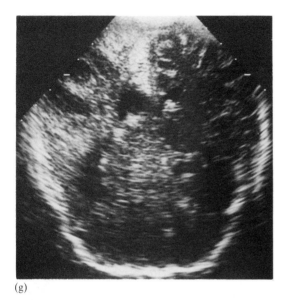

(g)

Figure 5.1 (a) (b) and (c): contrast-enhanced CT at three levels on the 4th day of illness. In all the images, left is to the left of the picture. The only abnormalities seen are low densities close to the vertex in both parietal regions, with minimal surrounding enhancement. On the right there is definite associated haemorrhage (c). (d) (e) (f): comparable levels on the enhanced CT 1 month after onset, showing extensive destruction on the left, but only a small low density in the high parietal region on the right, in (c). For comparison, a section of the ultrasound scan at the same time as the second CT (d,e,f) is shown (g). The gyral markings, easily seen on the right, are missing on the left, on which side the lateral ventricle is obviously enlarged. There are vague low densities on the left, but the parenchymal destruction is not well seen.

Course (1)

The patient's initial course was stormy with continued right-sided epileptic seizures requiring diazepam infusions. By the 8th admission day he was able to take oral fluids, but was then started on acyclovir infusions. However, 2 days later on the 10th admission day, the acyclovir was discontinued once the CT report was transmitted indicating bilateral parietal cortical infarctions probably due to venous thrombosis.

The patient made considerable improvement, moving his right limbs more, ceasing to have right-sided seizures, showing more interest in his surroundings and continuing afebrile. The paediatrician was puzzled as to why he might have venous thromboses, but was optimistic about the prognosis. He told the parents that the child should not have a second or third pertussis immunization.

Course (2)

Ten days later the patient got to the stage of holding up his head and reaching, but over 24 h developed breathing difficulty, loss of head control and attention, and increased weakness of the right limbs. He was now admitted to the children's hospital in his home area.

Investigations (2)
EEG. Occasional sharp complexes on the right.
Visual evoked potentials normal on the right, very low amplitude on the left.
CT scan. Extensive areas of low attenuation in the left involving the temporal
   lobe and parietal lobe and indeed much of the left cerebral cortex, with
   relative sparing of the lower portion of the frontal lobe and the occipital
   cortex, but extending to the midline at the vertex. A further area of low
   attenuation in the right parietal lobe close to the vertex was at the site of the
   previous haemorrhagic area.
CSF.18 cells per µl, lymphocytes. Protein 0.5 g/l. IgG was 38% of total protein
   (normal less than 10%) and the IgG:albumin ratio was 3.2 (normal
   0.26–0.66).
Alpha-interferon was 4.4 units/ml of CSF (upper limit of normal, 1.5)
Virology. Herpes-simplex-specific IgG was present at a titre of 128–256 in the
   CSF. The original CSF on day 1 of admission to the first hospital was
   obtained, and by the same test the herpes simplex titre was less than 8.
   Complement fixation test for herpes simplex was 4 on the CSF and 512 in the
   blood, IgM being positive. Maternal herpes simplex complement fixation test
   in blood was 64, IgG 256, IgM positive.

Course (3)
A full course of acyclovir was given, with further improvement. Six months later
   he was looking, smiling, and holding up his head, with a right hemiplegia.

Comments
This case well illustrates the difficulties of diagnosis of herpes encephalitis in the
young infant. The EEG is not a reliable indicator. Tests for virus isolation are of
no value. Initial virus titres are expected to be negative. Brain CT scan may be
normal or show appearances which may mimic haemorrhagic infarction or other
aetiology. Acyclovir has to be given when the diagnosis is suspected and must
never be stopped before the full course is given. Recent evidence in adults
suggests that SPECT is most likely to indicate abnormal perfusion at the time of
admission. Brain biopsy is no longer recommended as an essential aid to
diagnosis, but diagnosis can be difficult even with detailed virological studies. In
the present case the evidence rested on non-specific evidence of viral infection in
the form of intrathecal IgG synthesis and increased alpha-interferon levels in the
CSF, together with the acquisition of specific herpes simplex IgG in the CSF,
and serological evidence of acquired herpes simplex infection. His mother
appeared to have had recent herpes simplex infection, but the titres in the child
could not have been due to transmitted maternal antibodies.

5.2 'Meningitis' in a 4-year-old girl

This girl presented with a 1-week history of misery, headache and fever. She was
febrile on admission and had neck stiffness.

Investigations (1)
Peripheral white cell count 27.6 (84% neutrophils).
CSF. 21 white cells (41% lymphocytes, 59% neutrophils); protein, 0.42 g/l;
   glucose, 2.9 mmol/l; Gram stain – no organisms; culture negative.
Blood culture was negative.
Urine culture was negative.
Viral titres of blood and CSF were negative.

Course
Ampicillin and chloramphenicol were started but the patient remained pyrexial, became more irritable, and would not sit up.

Investigations: (2) 4 days after admission
Peripheral white cell count 27 000 (85% neutrophils).
CSF. 199 white cells (80% lymphocytes, 20% neutrophils); protein 0.38 g/l; glucose 2.4 mmol/l; Gram stain was negative; ZN stain was negative; Culture was negative.
CT brain scan was normal.
Mantoux 1:10 000 to 1:100 negative.

Course 2
Antituberculous therapy was added to the regimen, but the patient did not improve, and on the tenth hospital day had blurred optic disc margins, incoordination, brisk tendon reflexes, and extensor plantar responses.

Investigations (3)
EEG showed diffuse high-amplitude slow activity.
VEP showed prolonged latency at 160 ms.

Course 3
The patient was started on dexamethasone, and antibacterial and tuberculous treatment was discontinued. She was up and playing, but still ataxic within one week, when repeat CSF was normal. She was neurologically normal 6 weeks later when steroid therapy was discontinued and repeat EEG and VEP were normal.

Comments
The diagnosis of acute disseminated encephalomyelitis was delayed in this child because of the long prodrome before characteristic signs developed. This disorder should be considered in any child with unexplained CSF pleocytosis. Prolongation of the VEP is a useful diagnostic pointer.

5.3 'Febrile convulsions' with fatal outcome

A girl whose early history milestones were normal had a vague history of staggering gait from 18 months. At the age of 4 years she had a febrile convulsion lasting 30 min, said to be generalized. Within a few weeks she had episodes of twitching for 15 min or more on the left and then on the right.

Investigations (1)
EEG (Figure 5.3). At first there was slow activity on the right, but soon afterwards repeated very high-voltage slow waves with poly-spikes superimposed on the initial rise of each wave up to the crest.
ERG was normal.
Visual evoked potentials. Asymmetrical amplitude.
CSF protein 1.75 g/l.

Course
She had increasingly frequent jerks, developing into proximal high-amplitude repetitive flails resembling ballismus. Neurological decline was followed by liver failure within 2 months.

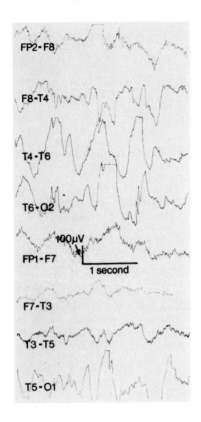

Figure 5.3 EEG at the age of $4\frac{1}{2}$ years shows high-voltage slow (delta) activity over much of the right hemisphere, admixed with polyspikes. A similar appearance is less well seen in the left occipital region.

Investigations (2)
Pre-terminal investigations included:
Rise in AST and ALT to around 200 U/l
Coagulation impairment (for example, prolonged prothrombin time).
Liver biopsy showing swollen hepatocytes, microvesicular fatty change, patchy chronic inflammatory cell infiltrate, portal fibrosis linking portal tracts and extending into lobules.
CT scan and brain biopsy were unhelpful.
All virus studies were negative.

Comment
This girl had progressive neuronal degeneration of childhood with hepatic involvement, otherwise called Alper's disease or Huttenlocher's disease. Blood and CSF lactate were not measured terminally but would probably have been markedly increased. The CSF protein and the notched EEG appearance were early clues to this disorder, the rise in transaminases preceding the terminal liver failure occurring later.

Further reading

Aicardi, J. and Goutières, F. (1984) A progressive familial encephalopathy in infancy, with calcifications of the basal ganglia, and chronic cerebrospinal fluid lymphocytosis. *Annals of Neurology*, **15**, 49–54.

Barthez, M. A., Billard, C., Santini, J. J. *et al.* (1987) Relapse of herpes encephalitis. *Neuropediatrics*, **18**, 3–7

Epstein, L. G., Sharer, L. R., Oleske, J. M. *et al.* (1986) Neurologic manifestations of human immunodeficiency virus infection in children. *Pediatrics*, **78**, 678–687

Jaeken, J. and Casaer, P. (1987) Pyridoxine non-responsive convulsions with CSF GABA and homocarnosine deficiency. *Neuropediatrics*, **18**, 126

Jaeken, J. and Van der Berge, G. (1984) An infantile autistic syndrome characterised by the pressence of succinylpurines in body fluids. *Lancet*, **2**, 1058–1061

Lefvert, A. K. and Link, H. (1985) IgG production within the central nervous system: a critical review of proposed formulae. *Annals of Neurology*, **17**, 13–20

McWilliam, R. C. and Stephenson, J. B. P. (1985) Bedside intracranial pressure monitoring. *Lancet*, **2**, 341

Ouvrier, R. A. (1978) Progressive dystonia with marked diurnal fluctuations. *Annals of Neurology*, **4**, 412–418

Schuller, E. A. C., Benabdullah, S., Sagar, H. J. *et al.* (1987) IgG synthesis within the central nervous system. Comparison of three formulas. *Archives of Neurology*, **44**, 600–604

Stephenson, J. B. P. and King, M. D. (1987) Clinical justification for cerebrospinal fluid investigation. *Lancet*, **1**, 222

Tourtellotte, N. W. Staugaitis, S. M., Walsh, M. J. *et al.* (1985) The basis of intra-blood-brain barrier IgG synthesis. *Annals of Neurology*, **17**, 21–27

Chapter 6

Cardiac tests; autonomic function

In this chapter a summary of the contribution of cardiological investigation to neurological diagnosis is followed by an outline of tests of autonomic nervous function.

Electrocardiography

Abnormalities of cardiac rhythm may lead to anoxic seizures which may be mistakenly regarded as primary epileptic seizures. The most common disturbance is probably reflex cardiac asystole. If this diagnosis seems probable it can be confirmed by an excessive response to ocular compression, but in practice it is seldom necessary except to aid management.

More serious are the QT disorders in which there is paroxysmal ventricular tachycardia or fibrillation. A QTc interval of more than 0.44 s with or without an abnormally short T wave and prominent U wave suggests one of these disorders. At the present time there is controversy regarding the genuinenness of a syndrome in which the QTc interval is normal at ordinary heart rates but does not shorten rapidly enough on induction tachycardia. Reports of anoxic seizures induced by paroxysmal ventricular fibrillation without prolonged QTc interval suggests that some such mechanism may operate.

Marked alterations in heart rate may occur during epileptic seizures with both tachycardia and bradycardia. Confusion only arises if ECG is recorded without EEG during unexplained episodes of loss of consciousness.

Marked changes in cardiac rhythm may also be seen in cassette recordings in which suffocation (as in Meadow's syndrome) or repeated Valsalva manouevres have occurred, or with intermittent brain-stem herniation in high intracranial pressure.

Intermittent reduction of the amplitude of the QRS complex (to 50% of its baseline amplitude) for many seconds may be observed in prolonged expiratory apnoea (blue breath-holding) and in the syndrome of repetitive compulsive Valsalva manouevres which has been recorded in children with mental handicap, autism, and Rett's syndrome. The intermittent ECG voltage dampening may be the first clue to the non-epileptic nature of the child's refractory seizures, and the existence of repeated Valsalvas can then be confirmed by more complex polygraphy.

Certain ECG abnormalities are common in disorders whose main manifestations are neurological or neuromuscular, but their diagnostic value is limited. These include:

Muscular dystrophy
Deep left ventricular Q waves in Duchenne
Heart block in Emery–Dreifuss (older patients)
Spinal muscular atrophy
Tremulous baseline from chest muscle fasciculation
Friedreich's ataxia
Inverted left ventricular T waves
Glycogenosis type 2
Short P–R interval, depressed S–T segments, inverted T waves
Mitochondrial cytopathy
Heart block, often complete; Wolff–Parkinson–White syndrome

Changes in cardiac rhythm during acute neurological illness rarely have specific diagnostic value, but sometimes suggest the need for tests of autonomic nervous function (*see below*).

Echocardiography

The most consistent diagnostic role of echocardiography is in the confirmation of the clinical diagnosis of *Friedreich's ataxia* in the schoolchild. A characteristic thickening of the interventricular septum is universal. Asymmetrical septal hypertrophy may also be seen in the different clinical circumstances of type 2 glycogenosis, GM_1 gangliosidosis, I-cell disease, tuberous sclerosis, and neurofibromatosis.

In many situations in the intensive care unit echocardiography helps to clarify the nature of an apparently neurological disorder. Instances include the discovery of cardiac tumours responsible for paroxysmal ventricular fibrillation, evidence of a cardiomyopathy associated with an encephalitis and therefore suggesting Coxsackie B infection, and the discovery of vegetations or abnormal heart valves in stroke or cerebral abscess.

Echocardiography is the method of choice for detecting rhabdomyomata in infancy. Such rhabdomyomata may be detected in a high proportion of infants with *tuberous sclerosis* at a time when other evidence of this disorder is lacking. Since these rhabdomyomata regress with time, early echocardiography is indicated in unexplained infantile epilepsy with suspect cerebral pathology (with seizures such as complex partial, simple partial, and infantile spasms).

Autonomic function tests

Disorders of autonomic nervous system function are probably not rare in childhood, but reliable testing is often difficult. Patient cooperation may be required, some of the tests are unpleasant, and the means for testing are not widely available.

Autonomic testing at present assumes the existence of only two components: the parasympathetic and the sympathetic nervous systems, but other testable neurotransmitter organizations will doubtless soon be discovered. Currently available autonomic tests can be used as part of a general or local evaluation of the autonomic nervous system. Tests are listed under the functions subserved.

Cardiovascular

The heart rate response to respiration and to tilt from the horizontal to the upright are tests of vagal parasympathetic activity, but methodology and norms need to be further refined. The use of a digital instantaneous heart rate monitor eases acquisition of the data.

Vagal and sympathetic tone may be investigated by plotting the effect of sequential doses of intravenous atropine and sequential doses of intravenous propranolol on heart rate.

The arterial pressure response to vertical tilt detects sympathetic malfunction, with subsequent postural hypotension.

Oesophageal function

Oesophageal motility and gastro-oesophageal sphincter competence depend on vagal parasympathetic control. The reliability of such tests as barium swallow, oesophageal pH monitoring, radionuclide 'milk scans', and oesophageal pressure measurements in infants is not completely defined, but two or even three types of test may be necessary to detect gastro-oesophageal reflux. Such reflux may reflect vagal hypofunction, which bethanechol will reverse.

Bladder function

The very complex control of bladder function is best evaluated by videourodynamic study. The degree of detrusor contractility reflects parasympathetic activity, and the degree of bladder-neck resistance sympathetic (alpha$_1$ adrenergic) activity.

Pupils

Pilocarpine 0.1% as eye drops is more readily available than freshly prepared 2.5% methacholine. This acetylcholine agonist does not alter the size of a normal pupil, nor of one that is large because of sympathetic overactivity (as may be seen in certain encephalopathies), but it leads to constriction due to denervation hypersensitivity in the localized situation of the Holmes–Adie pupil, and in the general autonomic disorder of the Riley–Day syndrome and related sensory neuropathies. No change is produced with pilocarpine if a large pupil is due to accidental (or non-accidental) instillation of mydriatic.

Homatropine (initially 1%) dilates the normal pupil and induces no change when there is complete sympathetic block, as in Horner's syndrome.

Phenylephrine 1% (easier to use than adrenaline 1:1000) induces no change in the normal pupil, but leads to dilatation in postganglionic sympathetic dernervation, as in some cases of Horner's syndrome.

Cocaine 4% (which blocks the reuptake of noradrenaline) dilates the normal pupils but has no affect on Horner's syndrome, whatever the site of the lesion.

Hydroxyamphetamine 1%, which promotes the release from the terminal axon of noradrenaline, if present, causes dilatation of the pupil unless there is postganglionic sympathetic denervation.

Tears

The Schirmer filter paper test is difficult to employ and interpret in young infants. It may show adequate tearing (parasympathetic activity) below the age (6 months) at which overflow tears are expected.

Sweat

Many methods are available for determining the degree of sweating in response to stimuli such as heating or intradermal acetylcholine. In the sweat spot test, sympathetic denervation is evaluated by estimating the degree of sweating in alcohol-painted skin after intradermal acetylcholine (0.1 ml of 1%) (Ryder et al. 1988).

Clinical situations

Widespread autonomic disorder is of course a feature of the Riley–Day syndrome. In acute demyelinating neuropathy (Guillain–Barré syndrome) autonomic neuropathy may be severe with, in particular, dramatic rapid changes in heart rate and blood pressure. Acute autonomic disturbance may also accompany traumatic spinal cord lesions. An increasing cause of general autonomic failure is HIV infection. Selective noradrenergic deficiency has been described in a short paper which well clarifies the complexities of autonomic testing (Man in't Veld et al. 1987).

Localized autonomic disturbances include Horner's syndrome, the Holmes–Adie pupil, and vagal parasympathetic deficiency secondary to a lower brain-stem glioma. The prominent gastro-oesophageal reflux in many children with cerebral palsy and other chronic central nervous system disorders suggests vagal parasympathetic impairment, a suggestion supported by the frequent beneficial response of the acetylcholine agonist bethanechol. When there is deterioration in any bodily function it is helpful to consider whether autonomic investigations might aid diagnosis.

Case illustrations

6.1 Werdnig–Hoffmann-like syndrome

See Appendix for definitive diagnoses.

In addition to the following case illustration, *see* 1.3 and 7.2.

6.1 Werdnig–Hoffmann-like syndrome with pneumonia

A 6-month-old boy of an unmarried mother had previously presented with constipation at the age of 4 weeks. The mother said that he had never kicked the covers off, couldn't hold his head straight and had had weak crying and whimpering for the previous 10 days. On examination he was an unwell baby with generalized floppiness and weakness; head control was absent. He was sweaty and his alae nasae were working. There were no murmurs but his heart seemed enlarged. The neurological findings were minor facial weakness particularly on the left, absent tendon reflexes (except crossed adduction on the left when the right knee jerk was attempted), and spontaneous clonus at the right ankle. Plantar responses were absent. A flare response to cutaneous stimulation was not elicited. His anus was lax.

Investigations
EEG was normal or showed a mild excessive slow activity.
Nerve conduction studies and EMG were not carried out for organizational reasons.
Brain imaging was not carried out.
Chest X-ray showed that the heart was displaced to the left because of collapse. Cardiothoracic ratio was 56%.
Echocardiography showed extremely thickened septum and posterior left ventricular wall.
CSF protein was 0.21 g/l (IgG 10 mg/l).
Muscle biopsy indicated glycogen storage.
Rectal biopsy contained occasional ganglion cells which had an abnormal granular or vacuolated appearance in their cytoplasm. Numerous glycogen-containing macrophages were present in the lamina propria of the mucosa.
Leucocytes and fibroblasts were grossly deficient in alpha-glucosidase (acid maltase).

Comment
An invasive course was taken to the diagnosis of Pompe's disease in this floppy baby. The most direct route would be from evidence of denervation to

echocardiography to the specific enzyme deficiency. In the event, the mother married, antenatal enzyme diagnosis was undertaken and the second child was normal.

Further reading

Axelrod, F. and Pearson, J. (1984) Congenital sensory neuropathies. Diagnostic distinction from familial dysautonomia. *American Journal of Diseases of Children*, **138**, 947–958

Bannister, R. (1988) Editor. *Autonomic Failure. A Textbook of Clinical Disorders of the Autonomic Nervous System*, Oxford University Press, Oxford

Craddock, C., Pasvol, G., Bull, R. *et al.* (1987) Cardiorespiratory arrest and autonomic neuropathy in AIDS. *Lancet*, **2**, 16–18

Man in 't Veld, A. J., Boomsma, F., Moleman, P. and Schalekamp, M. A. D. H. (1987) Congenital dopamine-beta-hydroxylase deficiency – a novel orthostatic syndrome. *Lancet*, **1**, 183–188

Mundy, A. R., Borzyskowski, M. and Saxton, H. M. (1982) Video-urodynamic evaluation of neuropathic vesico-urethral dysfunction in children. *British Journal of Urology*, **54**, 645–649

Nanayakkara, C. S. and Paton, J. Y. (1985) Sandifer syndrome: an overlooked diagnosis? *Developmental Medicine and Child Neurology*, **27**, 816–819

Ryder, R. E. J., Marshall, R., Johnson, K. *et al.* (1988) Acetylcholine sweatspot test for autonomic denervation. *Lancet*, **1**, 1303–1305

Chapter 7

Microscopic examinations: cells and biopsies

Many cells and tissues have appearances which assist in the diagnosis of neurological disorders in children. It is important to select the appropriate method and to ensure in advance that the microscopist will be happy about the specimen (*and* that you will be confident in the microscopist!) Tests are listed approximately in order of invasiveness. Some of the conditions for which these tests are helpful are emphasized.

Hair

The twisted hair (pili torti) of Menkes' disease and arginosuccinic aciduria can easily be demonstrated using a dissecting microscope. Trichorrhexis nodosa (intermittent swollen breaks) may be found in the Pollitt syndrome (trichothiodystrophy), some cases of biotinidase deficiency, Menkes' disease, and arginosuccinic aciduria.

Blood (*see also* Chapter 8)

Red cells

Acanthocytes (burr-shaped red cells) suggest abetalipoproteinaemia or Wolman's disease (acid lipase deficiency). The clinical pictures differentiate these disorders. Acanthocytes may also be found in certain anaemias and in hepatic cirrhosis, and rarely have been described in other disorders such as familial chorea and Hallervorden–Spatz disease.

Evidence of macrocytosis will suggest vitamin B_{12} deficiency, and evidence of haemolytic anaemia rare hereditary defects of red cell enzymes.

White cells

Examination of a well-stained blood film by a haematologist will be sufficient to detect vacuolation in lymphocytes, which may be very numerous and small in the mucolipidoses (but *not* in the mucopolysaccharidoses) or larger and fewer in juvenile Batten's disease (neuronal ceroid lipofuscinosis, NCL). Vacuolated lymphocytes may also be found in a number of other disorders in which a lysosomal enzyme deficiency is either known or presumed. These include GM_1 gangliosidosis of the infantile type, Niemann–Pick disease type A, mannosidosis, fucosidosis, Wolman's disease, aspartylglycosaminuria, sialidosis, sialic acid storage disease, and Salla disease. Toluidine blue staining may detect metachromatic inclusions in lymphocytes in certain of the mucopolysaccharidoses, but these disorders are much better identified in the first instance by urinary glycosaminoglycans. Metachromatic inclusions may also be seen in the white cells in GM_1 gangliosidosis. Small glycogen-containing vacuoles are seen in Pompe's disease.

If NCL is suspected, the buffy coat should be separated, fixed with glutaraldehyde, and examined by electronmicroscopy for membrane-bound granular osmophilic deposits (infantile NCL) or curvilinear bodies in many lymphocytes (late infantile NCL). In the case of infantile NCL, yellow autofluorescence under ultraviolet light should also be sought.

Urine sediment

Golden-yellow metachromatic material *within* renal epithelial cells is found in all forms of metachromatic leucodystrophy. The second urine specimen of the day may be the most useful, but as many specimens can be analysed as necessary so that renal epithelial cells can be found and stained with toluidine blue. (The same intracellular sulphatide can be found on toluidine blue staining in the urinary sediment in multiple sulphatase deficiency, but the clinical picture – coarse facies, dysostosis – is completely different.)

Renal epithelial cells may show greenish birefringence in polarized light in metachromatic leucodystrophy, and yellow autofluorescence with ultraviolet light in infantile NCL.

Conjunctiva

The ophthalmologist will help with the procedure of conjunctival biopsy, which is actually not difficult or traumatic. Fixation for electronmicroscopy is essential. It is most useful for the diagnosis of neuroaxonal dystrophy (NAD) because of the high density of nerves, but it may be negative in this condition. It is also helpful in the diagnosis of mucolipidosis IV where multilaminate bodies may be seen in epithelial and endothelial cells.

Skin

Skin biopsy may be obtained in a standard manner or with the aid of a punch. It may also be sampled when other tissues are biopsied. The specimen can be processed for fibroblast culture at the same time, if help for future pregnancies is likely to be needed.

Skin biopsies contain sweat glands and are thus helpful in the mucolipidoses and may give positive if not diagnostic information in a wide range of genetic disorders, even when the aetiology is not known (for example in Lowe's syndrome, where cytoplasmic electronlucent membrane-bound vacuoles are seen).

Like conjunctival biopsy, skin biopsy is used to look for the spheroids characteristic of neuroaxonal dystrophy.

Skin or conjunctival biopsy with electronmicroscopy is one 'metabolic' test which can justifiably be considered in any child with unexplained mental handicap, even if static, since lysosomal storage disorders exist in which the enzyme defect has not yet been discovered (e.g. sialic acid storage).

Muscle

Samples large enough for light and electronmicroscopy and histochemistry can be obtained by a needle muscle biopsy using a Bergstrom needle (4 mm in the neonate and 5 mm in the older infant and child). The authors have employed the technique of Heckmatt *et al.* (1984). It is important to select a muscle for biopsy which is involved clinically, is unlikely to be fibrotic, and has not been used for EMG. Guidance by (real-time) muscle ultrasound may help here.

Muscle biopsy will show evidence of denervation more often than will EMG, and is particularly useful in the diagnosis of spinal muscular atrophy, provided an adequate sample can be obtained. It is necessary for the distinction of (steroid-responsive) infantile myositis from congenital muscular dystrophy, albeit the interpretation may be taxing for the histopathologist (*see* Chapter 2). Although it is obvious that muscle biopsy is likely to clarify the diagnosis of disorders in which intrinsic muscle weakness is clinically obvious, biopsy may also be helpful in demonstrating certain metabolic disorders (for example the finding of ragged red fibres by Gomori stain in mitochondrial disorders), and biopsy may add to the understanding of particular malformations (for example, congenital muscular dystrophy associated with type II lissencephaly of the Warburg type).

The use of histochemistry is routine for the identification of fibre types which allows the recognition of denervation and certain myopathies. Abnormalities of the succinic dehydrogenase reaction may suggest a primary mitochondrial disorder, even when ragged red fibres are not present.

Open muscle biopsy should not be necessary for routine morphological studies although it may be needed for biochemical analysis in certain mitochondrial disorders for example. The indications for open biopsy may be summarized as:

1. For more elaborate biochemical studies, e.g. to analyse mitochondrial electron transport components.
2. For *in vitro* studies of neuromuscular transmission in (a) malignant hyperthermia and (b) congenital myasthenia.
3. In dermatomyositis/polymyositis, when closed biopsy has not yielded a blood vessel for histological examination.

In most of these situations it is likely that the much less invasive semi-open method of *conchotome* biopsy will be satisfactory. This instrument, borrowed from the ear, nose and throat surgeon, can obtain more than one substantial bite through an incision similar to that used for needle biopsy. This method might be expected to be valuable in neuroaxonal dystrophy, when seeking an intramuscular nerve in biceps for diagnostic confirmation.

Nerve

The sural nerve is accessible and no important deficit follows its biopsy. Diagnostic information not inferred by other means is not often elicited, except in rare situations such as giant axonal neuropathy. In the case of HMSN, biopsy should probably be reserved for those patients with atypical features and a negative family history. It is reasonable to discuss the matter with the pathologist before a biopsy is undertaken, and consider looking at smaller nerves in advance (e.g. in conjunctiva, skin, or biceps).

Bone marrow

Although bone marrow aspiration may reveal characteristic cells in Gaucher's disease and classical Niemann–Pick disease, it is more specifically helpful in the condition known as vertical supranuclear palsy with visceral storage, in which both foamy Niemann–Pick-like cells and sea-blue histiocytes are found together in almost all cases. Bone marrow *smears* stained by conventional Romanowski methods, not fixed sections, are essential for diagnosis.

Liver

The liver may be safely biopsied by needle, provided coagulation is normal. Of the various disorders involving the nervous system in which histological information of diagnostic value may be obtained, the peroxisomopathies are worthy of emphasis. Peroxisomes may be grossly deficient in number, or alternatively they may be normal in number but enlarged and sometimes of peculiar shape in isolated defects of single enzymes in the peroxisomal beta-oxidation pathway (*see* Chapter 10). In the progressive myoclonic epilepsy with Lafora bodies, branching filaments on electronmicroscopy have been reported within peroxisomes, in addition to the PAS-positive material in liver cell cytoplasm. In Wilson's disease, histological appearances are not specific, and biochemical tests relating to liver copper are of more importance. In progressive neuronal degeneration of childhood (Alper's disease/ Huttenlocher's disease) fatty infiltration and/or cirrhosis may be observed. In neurovisceral storage disease with supranuclear ophthalmoplegia the foamy storage cells show electron-dense pleomorphic bodies on electronmicroscopy (case 7.1).

Knowledge about the histological state of the liver in association with acute encephalopathies is in a state of flux, but the present position appears to be as follows:

In classical Reye's syndrome, not secondary to an identifiable inherited metabolic disorder, liver biopsy within the first 48 h shows (a) panlobular microvesicular fatty infiltration, (b) severely reduced succinic dehydrogenase activity, and (c) abnormal mitochondria lacking cristae. Micro- and macrovesicular fatty infiltration may accompany other metabolic encephalopathies (for example those associated with fatty acid oxidation or urea cycle defects), but succinic dehydrogenase activity is normal and mitochondria show a condensed appearance or little abnormality on electronmicroscopy.

Rectum

Biopsy of the rectum (or appendix) is necessary for the diagnosis of various forms of neuronal ceroid lipofuscinosis when other simpler biopsies (especially electronmicroscopy of lymphocytes in buffy coat pellets) have been negative or equivocal. Serial cryostat sections of fresh-frozen material are examined. The combination of autofluorescence under ultraviolet light and typical findings on electronmicroscopy, together with the histochemical findings on the snap-frozen specimen will allow a definitive diagnosis. When bone marrow smear findings are suggestive, rectal biopsy is desirable to confirm the diagnosis of neurovisceral storage disease with supranuclear ophthalmoplegia, in which water-soluble PAS-positive material (and pleomorphic lipid bodies on electronmicroscopy) is present in neurones. Rectal biopsy is justified even if bone marrow is negative should the clinical features be sufficiently suggestive (hepatosplenomegaly, vertical defect in saccadic eye movement, slow dementia, cataplexy). Rarely, biopsy will indicate a storage disorder, suggesting malfunction of an enzyme which conventional tests have shown to be present. This will lead to a search for a more subtle defect such as a lack of activator protein.

Brain

With suitably judged and interpreted alternative investigations, biopsy of the brain itself is now seldom indicated. When it is there must be advance planning so that the maximum information can be obtained in addition to standard neuropathology.

There are three types of pathology in which biopsy is sometimes indicated.

Cortical dysplasia

Type I and type II lissencephaly, widespread pachygyria, and hemimegalencephaly may all be confirmed by biopsy, but at the present time diagnostically suggestive EEG and MRI findings (and the ophthalmic and muscle biopsy features of type II lissencephaly) make this very seldom necessary.

The recognition of focal cortical dysplasia (neuronal dysgenesis) as an explanation of refractory partial epilepsy may be demonstrated by biopsy, but commonly only when this is a by-product of epilepsy surgery.

Progressive disorders of unknown origin

Alexander's disease and Canavan's disease could until very recently only be confirmed pathologically by a brain biopsy, although the diagnosis of the latter with its genetic implications, could be virtually certain on clinical and CT features. Biochemical and enzymatic diagnosis of Canavan's disease is now possible in some cases (see Chapter 10). Neuroaxonal dystrophy is diagnosed if possible by examination of nerves in skin, conjunctiva or biceps muscle, but brain biopsy with esterase histochemistry may be confirmatory. Novel disorders may sometimes be revealed by brain biopsy in children with undiagnosed chronic encephalopathies, but this is not a justification for the use of brain biopsy as a 'fishing expedition'.

Inflammatory disorders

Brain biopsy is no longer indicated in the diagnosis of acute herpes encephalitis. The position may change as antiviral agents become available for other viruses such as Coxsackie, which may induce acute encephalitis. Brain biopsy may be necessary in the management of presumed encephalitis in the immunocompromised child, whether after leukaemia therapy or related to HIV infection.

Biopsy may be undertaken either as an elective procedure or as part of an attempt at epilepsy surgery in Rasmussen's progressive focal encephalitis.

Case illustrations

7.1 A whole Charlie Chaplin film with his head on his knees
7.2 Not Friedreich's ataxia after all
7.3 Emotional lability and incontinence in a schoolboy

See Appendix for definitive diagnoses.

In addition to the following case illustrations, *see* 1.3, 2.3–2.5, 3.1, 4.9, 5.3, 6.1 and 10.3–10.7.

7.1 A whole Charlie Chaplin film with his head on his knees

A 4-year-old who had walked at 18 months was referred with a subtle but definite increase in unsteadiness such that he tended to crawl instead of walking from time to time. Also his parents had noted that if he laughed he would lose all control and go down in a heap, first his head and then his whole body falling. Previously at the age of 6 weeks he had been referred with persistent jaundice and liver biopsy had suggested paucity of intrahepatic bile ducts. Since then he had had hepatosplenomegaly, the spleen being larger.

On examination he had impaired vertical eye movements, both saccadic and pursuit, together with ataxia and disequilibrium.

Investigations (1)
EEG was normal.
Motor nerve conduction velocity and distal latency were normal. Sural sensory potential was normal. Needle EMG was normal.
Skeletal survey was normal.
Lysosomal enzyme studies were normal.
Bone marrow examination showed no evidence of 'sea-blue' histiocytes nor foamy cells.
Plasma lipids and vitamin E were normal.

Course
The negative bone marrow examination was surprising. The course was slow. Cataplexy was a prominent symptom, but was at first improved by protriptyline (Kandt *et al.* (1982) *Annals of Neurology*, **12**, 284–288). Definitive investigation was requested.

Investigations (2)
Liver biopsy was repeated at the age of 5 years. There was no intrinsic abnormality of the intrahepatic bile ducts. The important finding was of scattered, large, foamy storage cells in the sinusoids and in the portal tracts. These cells stood out clearly in the periodic acid-Schiff stained sections after diastase. Electronmicroscopy showed this stored material to consist of pleomorphic electron-dense bodies.

Comment
Neurovisceral storage disease with vertical supranuclear ophthalmoplegia, sometimes included within the umbrella of Niemann–Pick type C, can usually be confirmed by the bone marrow appearance of both 'sea-blue' histiocytes and

Niemann–Pick foamy cells, but occasionally the bone marrow may be negative and more invasive biopsies of liver, appendix or rectum are necessary. At the time of writing, the presumed lysosomal enzyme deficiency cannot be detected by a simple investigation.

7.2 Not Friedreich's ataxia after all

An 8-year-old boy was referred by the school medical officer to the consultant paediatrician because of clumsiness and abnormal gait which had not been noticed at his school entrance examination. His parents agreed that his balance had deteriorated, but they also felt that he might be less clever than he had been. The educational psychologist and the paediatrician thought that the motor disability had contributed to the apparent lowering of his IQ. He was found to have a slow dysarthria, mild ataxia with possibly a sensory component, possible Rombergism, absent tendon reflexes, extensor plantar reflexes, and pes cavus. Eye movements were entirely normal.

Investigations
ECG and spine X-ray had already been shown to be normal.
Echocardiography did not show thickening of the interventricular septum.
EEG showed no definite abnormality.
Nerve conduction velocity was 28 metres per second in right posterior tibial, with 10 ms distal latency.
CT scan showed areas of low attenuation in relation to the anterior horns and bodies of the lateral ventricles.
CSF protein was 0.53 g/l.
Smears of centrifuged deposit of the second morning urine specimen stained with acidified toluidine blue showed several aggregates of brown meta-chromatic granules, some of which appeared to be within the cytoplasm of epithelial cells of the upper urinary tract. These granules were not present in the lower urinary tract squamous cells or in polymorphs.
Leucocyte arylsulphatase A was virtually absent, arylsulphatase B and beta-galactosidase being normal.

Comment
The clinical presentation of this boy with juvenile metachromatic leucodystro-phy resembled that of Friedreich's ataxia, only the completely normal eye movements and the subtle intellectual deterioration arguing against the latter condition. The normal echocardiogram and the neurophysiological investiga-tions completely distinguished the two conditions.

7.3 Emotional lability and incontinence in a schoolboy

This 11-year-old presented in the early 1970s with a story of 2–3 years decline in school performance, with emotional lability, loss of confidence, and recent incontinence of urine. He had impaired attention in his left visual field.

Investigations
EEG showed excess slowing, more on the right than on the left.
Visual evoked potentials were mildly delayed.
Nerve conduction was normal.

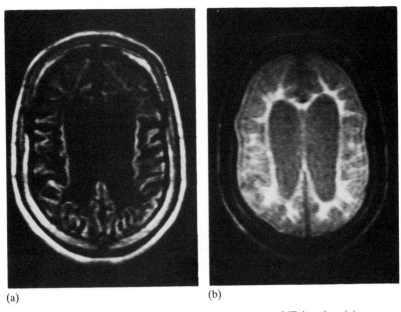

(a)   (b)

Figure 7.3 Late appearance at age 21 years of the brain on MR imaging. (a) T1-weighted image shows approximately normal grey matter cortical mantle thickness, but virtual absence of central white matter. (b) T2-weighted image confirms small volume of white matter with abnormal signal (i.e, appearing 'white').

CSF protein was 0.6 g/l, with IgG 96 mg/l.

CT scan and cerebral angiography were normal.

Right temporal biopsy showed myelin to be almost totally deficient in deeper white matter, with numerous sudanophilic lipid phagocytes and numerous large gemistocytic astrocytes. There was striking intense perivascular cuffing by lymphocytes with hypertrophied microglia and occasional plasma cells. In the subcortical white matter there was moderate myelin loss, a few sudanophilic-laden phagocytes and perivascular spaces with occasional vessels lightly cuffed with lymphocytes, and a few gemistocytic astrocytes with some loss of axons and occasional axonal swelling. In the cortex there was no abnormality.

Comment

The course and brain biopsy were in fact typical of adrenoleucodystrophy, for which biopsy is certainly no longer required. In fact this boy never developed adrenal dysfunction, still having normal cortisols and a plasma ACTH level not over 30 ng/l 7 years later. His late MRI is shown in Figure 7.3.

In due course his plasma was found to contain a marked excess of very long-chain fatty acids and the plasma of his mother and one of his sisters had the increased values characteristic of heterozygotes for adrenoleucodystrophy.

Further reading

Bowles, N. E., Dubowitz, V., Sewry, C. A. and Archard, L. C. (1987) Dermatomyositis, polymyositis and Coxsackie B virus infection. *Lancet*, **1**, 1004–1007

Di Mauro, S., Bonilla, E., Zeviani, M. *et al.* (1986) Mitochondrial myopathies. *Annals of Neurology*, **17**, 521–538

Heckmatt, J. Z., Moosa, A., Hutson, C. *et al.* (1984) Diagnostic needle muscle biopsy. *Archives of Disease in Childhood*, **59**, 528–532

Henriksson, K. G. (1979) 'Semi-open' muscle biopsy technique, a simple outpatient procedure. *Acta Neurologica Scandinavica*, **59**, 317–323

Lake, B. D. (1981) Metabolic disorders: general considerations. In *Pediatric Pathology* (ed C. L. Berry), Springer-Verlag, Berlin, pp. 617–639

Lake, B. D., Clayton, P. T., Leonard, J. V. *et al.* (1987) Ultrastructure of liver in inherited disorders of fat oxidation. *Lancet*, **1**, 382–383

Miike, T., Ohtani, Y., Nishiyama, S. and Matsuda, I. (1986) Pathology of skeletal muscle and intramuscular nerves in infantile neuroaxonal dystrophy. *Acta Neuropathologica*, **69**, 117–123

Neville, B. G. R., Lake, B. D., Stephens, R. and Sanders, M. D. (1973) A neurovisceral storage disease with vertical supra-nuclear ophthalmoplegia and its relationship to Niemann–Pick disease. A report of nine patients. *Brain*, **96**, 97–120

Ramaekers, V. T. L., Lake, B. D., Harding, B. *et al.* (1987) Diagnostic difficulties in infantile neuroaxonal dystrophy. A clinicopathologic study of eight cases. *Neuropediatrics*, **18**, 170–175

Rossi, L. N., Lutschg, J., Meier, C. and Vasella, F. (1983) Hereditary motor sensory neuropathies in childhood. *Developmental Medicine and Child Neurology*, **25**, 19–31

Thompson, C. E. (1982) Infantile myositis. *Developmental Medicine and Child Neurology* **24**, 307–313

Thompson, C. E. (1985) Pitfalls in muscle biopsy of hypotonic children. *Developmental Medicine and Child Neurology*, **27**, 675–677

Wisniewski, K. E., Kieras, F. J., French, J. H. *et al.* (1984) Ultrastructural, neurological and glycosaminoglycan abnormalities in Lowe's syndrome. *Annals of Neurology*, **16**, 40–49

Chapter 8

Microbiology; haematology; immunology

Microbiology

This section addresses some of the many important aspects of central nervous system infection. Bacterial and tuberculous meningitis and their CSF findings have been discussed in Chapter 5.

Congenital viral infections

The so-called TORCH screen is not adequate, because congenital cytomegalovirus infection will be missed unless urine and throat swabs are cultured for virus in the first 2 weeks of life. After that time, positive virus culture or serological findings may be due to postnatally acquired infections.

Human immunodeficiency virus infection (HIV)

At the time of writing it seems likely that HIV infections of the nervous system may become common and enter the differential diagnosis of early dementias and other progressive neurological disorders of childhood. In children under 15 months of age the diagnosis may be difficult to confirm, due to the presence of maternal antibodies, and special tests (polymerase chain reaction and *in vitro* antibody production) may be necessary in suspicious circumstances.

Chronic enteroviral infections

It is becoming apparent that certain viruses, in particular Coxsackie, may persist, as shown by prolonged elevation of the specific IgM in blood. Specific enteroviral RNA may be found in muscle biopsy specimens in cases of polymyositis.

Subacute sclerosing panencephalitis (SSPE)

Although measles-specific serum IgM is usually high in post-measles SSPE, CSF titres are essential to confirm the diagnosis. In leukaemia patients with measles encephalitis, titres are not necessarily elevated because of the coexisting immunosuppression. The same applies to the much rarer post-rubella subacute encephalitis.

Other viral infections

Many viral infections involve the nervous system, and persistent, obsessional attempts to determine blood and CSF serology are necessary, besides obtaining specimens for culture. CSF α-interferon assays may indicate a diagnosis of central nervous system virus infection even if a specific virus cannot yet be identified.

Sydenham's chorea

The ASO titre is known to be elevated in many but not all cases of rheumatic chorea. Use of the anti-DNAase B titre has been recommended as being more sensitive.

Borreliosis

Borrelia burgdorferi is a tick-borne spirochaete causing aseptic meningitis, facial palsy, myelitis, or progressive dementia. Antibody titres (by immunofluorescence or enzyme-linked immunosorbent assay) may be raised in blood and CSF without the florid features of Lyme disease. If the IgM only is elevated the test should be repeated, as by the time that neurological symptoms appear, IgG antibodies are usually high. False positive results may be found in autoimmune disorders and other borrelia infections.

Toxoplasmosis

Toxoplasma titres may be slow to rise over many weeks after acute *T. gondii* encephalitis.

Haematology

This section gives notes on the significance of routine and special haematological tests for the diagnosis of neurological disorders.

Haemoglobin

Anaemia may be coincidental or part of the specific process leading to the neurological dysfunction as in vitamin B_{12} deficiency or some of the rare metabolic disorders associated with haemolytic anaemia (e.g. phosphoglycerokinase deficiency).

Blood film

Inclusions in white cells, characteristic of various metabolic disorders, have been mentioned in Chapter 7. Red cell macrocytosis, confirmed by a raised MCV on automated blood counting, will be found in B_{12} deficiency. Polychromasia, reflecting reticulocytosis in haemolytic anaemia may also be seen in certain rare disorders such as triphosphate isomerase deficiency (confirmed by specific enzyme assay in red cells).

Full blood count

In addition to all the very well-known causes of neutrophil leucocytosis, important are tuberculous meningitis, acute or subacute disseminated encephalomyelitis, and brain necrosis from any cause (e.g. herpes simplex encephalitis, suffocation-induced infarctions). Pancytopenia (or leucopenia or thrombocytopenia) may be features of organic acidaemias (e.g. propionic or methylmalonic acidaemia).

Screening for sickle-cell disease

Screening (Sickledex) or more specific tests for sickle-cell disease may be indicated in the investigation of acute neurological illness, but should also be done before EEG examinations (sickle-cell disease is a contraindication to hyperventilation) or contrast injection (especially for cerebral angiography but also for CT) in a non-Caucasian child.

General tests of haemostasis and thrombosis

Coagulation 'screens' and tests for disseminated intravascular coagulation are too well known to require further description. However, it is worth mentioning that in clinical practice it may not be possible to determine whether a neurological lesion results from haemorrhage or thrombosis (e.g. in the 'ischaemic' lesions of prenatal isoimmune thrombocytopenia).

Special tests of haemostasis and thrombosis

In a way analogous to the term 'haemophilia' as in a congenital haemorrhagic disorder, the concept of *thrombophilia* has recently been formulated to cover disorders leading to premature thrombotic events. For example, in cases of unexplained cerebrovascular occlusion from the neonatal period onwards, the haematologist should advise on newer tests of specific thrombophilias, such as assays of protein C, protein S and antithrombin III, and special tests for lupus anticoagulant.

With respect to the isoimmune thrombocytopenia alluded to above, specialized testing of platelet antigens (PLA 1 status) and maternal platelet antibody levels may aid diagnosis, even years later (*see* case 8.2).

In the investigation of cerebral haemorrhage after the early neonatal period, consideration has to be given to alpha-1-antitrypsin deficiency, which will need biochemical and genetic studies to confirm.

CSF Cytospin

The haematologist is essential for interpretation of this test when the CSF study is a neurological investigation. It has been discussed in Chapter 5.

Immunology

Immunological deficiency is most commonly seen as a sequel of treatment of acute leukaemia, or HIV infection. However, progressive neurological disease may be apparent in HIV infection before immune deficiency is detectable.

Gross hypogammaglobulinaemia will be suggested by the history, but deficiency of an IgG subclass needs to be specifically sought. There is evidence of IgG subclass deficiency in some varieties of refractory epilepsy, but a critical assessment of the significance and therapeutic implications of such a finding has yet to be made.

T-Cell deficiency has been associated with

> Ataxia telangiectasia
> Purine nucleoside phosphorylase deficiency (disequilibrium–diplegia)
> Chronic progressive poliovirus encephalitis (in this case a cause rather than a consequence).

'Normal' hyperreactivity of the immune system (IgG responses etc.) is referred to in the section on microbiology and in the chapter on CSF (5). Specific search for abnormal autoantibodies is indicated in certain clinical situations:

Acetylcholine receptor antibody is increased in acquired myasthenia gravis.

Antinuclear antibody is present at high titre in systemic lupus erythematosus with cerebral involvement (chorea, dystonia etc.), even in the absence of systemic features.

Case illustrations

See Appendix for definitive diagnoses.

In addition to the following case illustrations, *see* 2.1, 2.2 and 5.1–5.3.

8.1 Episodes of blankness in a shy schoolchild

A 6-year-old boy had never progressed well at school, and also seemed to have lost control of his pencil in recent months. In the past weeks he had begun to spill his tea and look blank or slightly unsteady, sometimes at regular intervals every 8 seconds. He had had measles at 15 months, as his parents were not allowed to have him immunized earlier. He seemed to lose concentration during examination, with occasional interruption in his speech.

Investigations
EEG (Figure 8.1) showed polyphasic complexes with large, slow deflections and a fast component occurring in a stereotyped manner about every 8 s. There was excess slow activity in the frontal regions but the alpha rhythm was moderately well formed.
CT scan showed extensive white matter hypodensity around the anterior horns of the lateral ventricles. Contrast was not given.
CSF protein was 0.46 g/l with IgG 15 mg/l.
Serum measles titre was reported as 32.
Repeat testing of the serum gave measles titre of 1024.
CSF measles titre was 256.

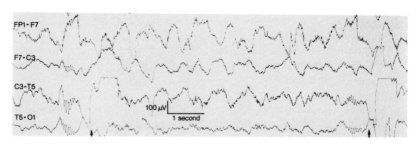

Figure 8.1 The EEG at the time of clinical presentation was symmetrical between the two sides: that from the left is shown in the Figure. Excess slow (delta) activity is maximum in frontal regions, and polyphasic complexes – consisting of 20/s beta activity followed by a large bidirectional slow wave – recur at 8-s intervals. A short spasm (marked by an arrow) begins within 150–300 ms of the onset of each slow wave. The appearance in this particular example closely resembles that seen in the different context of periodic spasms.

Comment
The diagnosis of subacute sclerosing panencephalitis was obvious, but the initial measles titre appeared to contradict this. Immunological therapy including isoprenosine had no apparent effect. He was treated symptomatically and with good effect by methylphenidate, carbamazepine and clonazepam sequentially. He has stable dystonia in flexion, with occasional smiles 4 years later.

8.2 Optic hypoplasia explained

A 10-year-old boy had always been thought to have septo-optic dysplasia, although brain imaging had not been carried out. A previous sibling had died aged 2 h with 'hydrocephalus'. The neonatal period of the present child was complicated by thrombocytopenia which had not been explained. On examination he had bilateral optic hypoplasia and mild spastic diplegia, being able to stand on one leg for only about a second.

Investigations
EEG was normal.
ERG was normal.
VEP. Reproducible visual evoked responses could not be obtained.
CT scan (Figure 8.2). Normal septum pellucidum, low density posterior to right trigone.
Hypothalamic–pituitary function was normal.
Platelet studies. The boys's platelets were PLA 1 positive, while his mother's were PLA 1 negative. She had a strong anti-PLA 1 antibody with a titre of 1/16 in her serum. The boy's platelets were incompatible with his mother's serum.

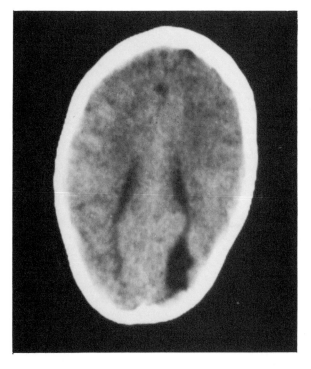

Figure 8.2 CT scan showing right occipital lucency abutting posterior horn or lateral ventricle (right side of picture).

Comment

Isoimmune thrombocytopenia was confirmed retrospectively 10 years later in this case. The combination of isoimmune thrombocytopenia (acting prenatally) with optic hypoplasia and cerebral and cerebellar destructive lesions has recently become well recognized.

Sporadic so called 'septo-optic dysplasia' should not be diagnosed without either absence of the septum pellucidum on imaging or hypothalamic–pituitary endocrine abnormalities. Absence of the septum and optic hypoplasia may also be seen in combination with hemispheric clefts ('schizencephaly'). *See* Case illustration 4.2.

Further reading

Christen, H.-J., Bartlau, N., Hanefeld, F. *et al.* (1987) Lyme borreliosis in children – a prospective study. *Neuropediatrics*, **18**, 121

De Rossi, A., Amadori, A., Chieco-Bianchi, L. *et al.* (1988) Polymerase chain reaction and in-vitro antibody production for early diagnosis of paediatric HIV infection. *Lancet*, **2**, 278

Epstein, L. G., Sharer, L. R., Oleske, J. M. *et al.* (1986) Neurologic manifestations of human immunodeficiency virus infection in children. *Pediatrics*, **78**, 678–687

Gobbi, G., Bruno, L., Pini, A. *et al.* (1987) Periodic spasms: an unclassified type of epileptic seizure in childhood. *Developmental Medicine and Child Neurology*, **29**, 766–775.

Jenkins, H. R., Leonard, J. V., Kay, J. D. S. *et al.* (1982) Alpha-1-antitrypsin deficiency, bleeding diathesis and intracranial haemorrhage. *Archives of Disease in Childhood*, **57**, 722–723

King, J., Aukett, A., Smith, M. F. *et al.* (1988) Cerebral systemic lupus erythematosus. *Archives of Disease in Childhood*, **63**, 968–970

Muhlemann, M. F. and Wright, D. J. M. (1987) Emerging pattern of lyme disease in the United Kingdom and Irish Republic. *Lancet*, **1**, 260–262

Naidu, S., Messmore, H., Caserta, V. and Fine, M. (1983) CNS lesions in neonatal isoimmune thrombocytopenia. *Archives of Neurology*, **40**, 552–554

Neves, J. F., Lopes, D., Casal, M. I. *et al.* (1988) 'Botryoid nuclei' of leucocytes in the haemorrhagic shock and encephalopathy syndrome. *Lancet*, **1**, 112

Simmonds, H. A., Fairbanks, L. D., Morris, G. S. *et al.* (1987) Central nervous system dysfunction and erythrocyte guanosine triphosphate depletion in purine nucleoside phosphorylase deficiency. *Archives of Disease in Childhood*, **62**, 385–391

Vomberg, P. P., Breederveld, C., Fleury, P. and Arts, W. F. M. (1987) Cerebral thromboembolism due to antithrombin III deficiency in two children. *Neuropediatrics*, **18**, 42–44

Wintzen, A. R., Broekmans, A. W., Bertina, R. M. *et al* (1985) Cerebral haemorrhagic infarction in young patients with hereditary protein C deficiency: evidence for 'spontaneous' cerebral venous thrombosis. *British Medical Journal*, **290**, 350–352

Chapter 9

Genetic investigations

Karyotyping

Apart from confirmation of the diagnosis of established chromosomal disorders, the highest yield will come from children with mental handicap and dysmorphic features. The yield of chromosome abnormalities with no dysmorphic features is low but not negligible, for example, sex chromosome aberrations (XXX, XXY) in some children with language delay.

Routine and prometaphase analysis

For routine karyotyping, approximately 5 ml of heparinized venous blood is required, and chromosomes derived from lymphocytes are stained by the Giemsa banding technique. Each chromosome pair has a characteristic pattern of light and dark bands. Usually 300–400 bands in total are visualized, but higher resolution banding techniques (prometaphase banding) may result in up to 1200 bands being visible. This is obviously better for the identification of very small aberrations such as those associated with specific syndromes (Table 9.1). Prometaphase banding is also indicated if a routinely banded karyotype fails to confirm a strong clinical suspicion of a recognized chromosomal disorder such as Wolf syndrome (4p–) or cri du chat syndrome (5p–). It is being increasingly undertaken in any child with a normal karyotype who nevertheless 'looks chromosomal' i.e., is mentally handicapped, growth retarded and dysmorphic. Blood samples from very young infants do not give the best technical results, so it is preferable to defer high-resolution analysis for several months.

After discovery of an unusual chromosome abnormality, further blood samples from the patient and parents are often requested by the laboratory for special staining techniques and to determine whether the observed abnormality is of clinical significance. If an unbalanced aberration in the child is derived from a balanced rearrangement in one parent it is important to study other family members so that recurrences may be avoided.

Table 9.1 Chromosomal microdeletions in some neurological disorders in childhood

Disorder	Site of microdeletion
Angleman syndrome	15 q 12
Prader–Willi syndrome	15 q 12
Duchenne muscular dystrophy ± Adrenal hypoplasia ± Glycerol kinase deficiency	} X p 21
Miller–Dieker syndrome (Some type I lissencephaly)	17 p 13

Karyotypes may be prepared from tissues other than blood. A convenient alternative is fibroblasts derived from a small (2 mm) skin biopsy. This may be especially helpful in investigating chromosome mosaicism detected in a previous blood sample, and excluding syndromes such as tetrasomy 12p, diploid/triploid mosaicism, and trisomy 8 mosaicism, where the abnormal cell line might not be found in blood lymphocytes.

In some centres, flow cytometry is available to give a flow karyotype which comprises a histogram with grouping of chromosomes according to their DNA content. It is useful for assessing variation in individual chromosomes and estimating the size of very small deletions or duplications. Family studies are usually necessary to interpret the results of flow karyotyping.

Analysis in folate-deficient medium to exclude fragile-X-associated mental retardation

This is the second commonest chromosomal cause of mental handicap after trisomy 21. As it is inherited as an X chromosome-linked trait, identification of affected males is imperative if recurrences within a family are to be avoided. Clinical features in males (which are not always present) include large ears, a long face and prominent jaw, and post-pubertal macro-orchidism. If the chromosomes from an affected male are analysed after lymphocyte culture in folate-depleted medium, the X chromosome is usually seen to have a fragile site at Xq 27.3 in 4%–60% of cells examined. This cytogenetic abnormality will not be detected if chromosomes are analysed under routine conditions after culture in folate-replete medium, so the laboratory has to be specifically informed that fragile X syndrome is suspected. Also, in view of the hereditary implications, all mentally retarded males who have had normal chromosome analysis in the past should be restudied in appropriate conditions to exclude fragile X syndrome.

Approximately one-third of carrier females are mentally impaired by the syndrome, which probably accounts for almost 10% of mild to moderate mental handicap in females. Unfortunately, many of these women remain undiagnosed because they do not have the clinical features displayed by affected males; in addition the fragile site is only present in 50% of cases, and in a still smaller percentage of cells examined.

Chromosome breakage syndromes

Normally there is a low rate of spontaneous chromosome breakage in karyotypes derived from cultured lymphocytes. Several autosomal recessive syndromes are associated with markedly increased rates of spontaneous breakage, especially if the chromosomes are subjected to specific stresses such as ultraviolet X or gamma irradiation, or exposure to DNA cross-linking agents such as mitomycin C. Under these conditions, specific defects in DNA repair may also be found. The neurological chromosome breakage syndromes are ataxia telangiectasia, Cockayne syndrome, and de Sanctis–Cacchione syndrome. All have striking clinical features and are associated with a predisposition to malignancy. The appropriate confirmatory tests should be arranged by prior consultation with the laboratory, as they are complex and may only be available at specialist centres.

Molecular genetic investigations

The use of DNA probes which reveal restriction fragment length polymorphisms (RFLPs) has resulted in mapping within the human genome of a rapidly increasing number of genes responsible for diverse neurological disorders. Some of these genes have been cloned, and the disease-causing mutations identified (*see* Case 10.4). Even if direct analysis of the mutant gene is not possible, in many families it can be 'tracked' by following RFLPs closely linked to it. The chromosomal localization of genes responsible for various neurological disorders are listed in McKusick (1988).

A pitfall for the unwary in this type of analysis is genetic heterogeneity, i.e. similar disease phenotypes may be produced by different mutant genes. Thus, although hereditary motor and sensory neuropathy type I (HMSN I) segregates with chromosome 1 RFLPs in some families, enabling predictions to be based on their pattern of inheritance, similarly based predictions in another family will be totally wrong if the disease is in fact segregating with markers on a different, unidentified chromosome.

Clearly, gene tracking requires that blood samples from many family members, unaffected as well as affected, be studied. In small families or when individuals are not available this is not always possible. Another problem in fatal disorders is that the affected individuals may have died before DNA could be stored. It is thus good policy to 'store' DNA from key individuals, 20 ml of EDTA anticoagulated blood yields a sufficient quantity of DNA in most circumstances. Even if the disorder is not listed amongst those amenable to molecular genetic tests, it is quite reasonable to store blood samples from any individual with an inherited neurological condition against the day when such tests may be developed to offer an option for other family members. Most regional genetic centres have facilities for such storage.

Case illustrations

9.1 Dominant, not recessive gait disorder
9.2 Laughing 'Rett syndrome'
9.3 It's the way he stands and looks up at you

See Appendix for definitive diagnoses.

In addition to the following case illustrations, *see* 1.5, 2.3, 2.5, 3.1 and 10.4.

9.1 Dominant, not recessive gait disorder

A woman who had had walking difficulties since childhood, and who had been diagnosed as having juvenile spinal muscular atrophy, became worried that her 4-year-old daughter might be developing the same thing. She did not know how this could be possible, as she knew that spinal muscular atrophy was recessively not dominantly inherited. Her daughter had flat feet and minor foot drop, and absent or markedly diminished tendon reflexes.

Investigations (Child)
Nerve conduction. All motor conduction velocities were markedly slow, with prolonged distal latencies. For example, left common peroneal 21 metres per second, distal latency 7.0 ms.

Investigations (Mother)
The EMG had been reported as showing denervation on two occasions with 'stigmata of motor neurone involvement'. In fact, review of the data indicated that there was some fibrillation but no giant motor unit potential. The voluntary units were rather small. The evoked muscle action potentials were of moderately normal amplitude. What seemed to have been overlooked was gross slowing of motor conduction velocity to 16 metres per second in the lateral popliteal, with a distal latency of 16 ms.

Comment
In this family with type I hereditary motor and sensory neuropathy (HMSN I), the neurologists had evidently been misled by the second-hand report of the EMG findings, and had overlooked the gross nerve conduction abnormalities. Those who investigate children often begin with third-hand information, but it is important to get hold of the primary data upon which diagnostic inferences depend.

9.2 Laughing 'Rett syndrome'

A girl with normal (above average) head circumference was thought by her parents and health visitor to be normal in the first 6 months. At that stage she was sitting reaching for things and alert looking. By 10 months there was a 'fantastic change'. She seemed 'like another baby', not reaching and not attempting to do anything. She had ceased to vocalize. Head circumference fell to the 2nd percentile.

By the age of 3 years she had not progressed further. She laughed a great deal and was jerky when attempting to walk with one hand held.

Investigations
CT scan was normal.
EEG (Figure 9.2) showed bursts of 3–4 s high-voltage broad waves with sharp
   apex up to 300 μV in amplitude. These became more obvious with age.

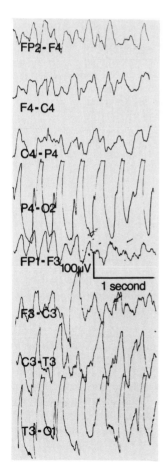

Figure 9.2 The EEG shows very high-voltage (over 400 μV) 3/s sharp components in posterior head regions with smaller (100 μV) spikes frequently associated. (The peaks of the sharp components have been truncated due to the recording technique.)

CSF protein 0.11 g/l with normal concentrations of biogenic amines.

Chromosome analysis. There was apparent loss of material at 15q 12 from one homologue of chromosome 15, and appropriate shortening on flow karyotype.

Comments
This girl was initially suspected of having Rett syndrome on the basis of loss of skills and fall-off in head circumference, but the later clinical evaluation indicated that she had Angelman's (happy puppet) syndrome. Two points are illustrated: (1) the diagnosis of Rett syndrome, for which there is no specific diagnostic test at the time of writing, should not be made in the first 3 years of life, and (2) the characteristic EEG with high-voltage, sharp components strongly suggests Angelman's syndrome, which can be confirmed in a proportion of cases by demonstrating the deletion within the long arm of chromosome 15 using targeted chromosome analysis, together with shortening of that chromosome on flow karyotyping.

9.3 It's the way he stands and looks up at you

A boy presented between 2 and 3 years of age. It was not clear if his gait was worse, but he repeatedly fell. His speech was not easily intelligible. He was said to have blanks, but it was that sometimes he appeared to look one way and then the other, and his mother said 'it's the way he stands and looks up at you', demonstrating a tilt downwards of the head. He had had frequent colds, spells of diarrhoea, and an attack of pneumonia at the age of 15 months.

On examination he had a hen-toed wide-based gait and tended to run rather than walk. His head tended to flop about from time to time and his eye movements were not appropriately directed. Although his tendon reflexes were brisk his plantar responses were flexor. His tonsils were flat and resembled tiddley-winks. He had no ordinary sized lymph nodes. He had a loose cough.

Investigations
EEG was normal.
Brain imaging was not done.
CSF protein 0.02 g/l.
Alphafetoprotein 35 μg/l.
Chromosome analysis: Normal male karyotype in the majority of cells. Four out of 15 cells showed chromosome breakage.
Serum IgA was absent.
Lymphocyte culture: Marked depression of lymphocyte function in all tests.

Comment
There were difficulties at first in distinguishing between a static and progressive motor disorder. His 'absences' were actually a result of his impaired saccadic eye movements. The clinical picture, however, suggested ataxia telangiectasia, so that the critical test of his alphafetoprotein level could be done at the outset. More detailed evaluation of his DNA repair disorder could be undertaken later.

Further reading

Artlett, C. F. (1986) Human DNA repair defects. *Journal of Inherited Metabolic Disease*, **9** (Suppl. 1), 69–84

Lamont, M. A., Dennis, N. R. and Seabright, M. (1986) Chromosome abnormalities in pupils attending ESN/M schools. *Archives of Disease in Childhood*, **61**, 223–226

McKusick, V. A. (1988) *Mendelian Inheritance in Man*, 8th edn. The Johns Hopkins University Press, Baltimore

Magenis, R. E., Brown, M. G., Lacy, D. A. *et al.* (1987) Is Angelman syndrome an alternate result of del (15) (q 11 q 13)? *American Journal of Medical Genetics*, **28**, 829–838

Martin, J. B. (1987) Molecular genetics: applications to the clinical neurosciences. *Science*, **238**, 765–772

Schinzel, A. (1988) Microdeletion syndromes, balanced translocations and gene mapping. *Journal of Medical Genetics*, **25**, 454–462

Chapter 10

Biochemistry

There is an increasing number of biochemical tests which may easily overwhelm the investigator. Some workers have advocated batteries of screening tests on economic or medicolegal grounds, but there are two main dangers of the 'screening' approach. One is that one will stop thinking about the diagnosis and imagine that the 'metabolilc screen' has excluded a detectable metabolic explanation for the disease. The second danger is that if enough tests are done, one of them may be 'abnormal' on grounds of chance alone.

Biochemical investigations may detect disorders reversible by a specific treatment, or more often genetic disorders of great family significance. Many of the disorders are progressive and in the initial decision about whether and what tests to do, one has to decide whether the condition of the child is static or progressive. If the answer is 'don't know', then investigations may have to proceed as if the disorder were progressive.

In this chapter we are going to deal, very briefly, with most of the biochemical tests currently used in the diagnosis of neurological disorders. CSF biochemistry has been discussed in Chapter 5.

Urine tests

'Side-room' urine tests

Urine is tested for protein and glucose, and reducing substances when galactosaemia or fructose intolerance is a clinical possibility. The authors do not normally use ferric chloride, dinitrophenyl hydrazine, or nitroprusside cyanide tests, although these are rapid and cheap methods of detecting phenylketonuria, maple-syrup urine disease, and homocystinuria. We do not recommend simple spot tests for mucopolysaccharidoses (glycosaminoglycans, GAGs) because disorders with excessive GAG excretion are too important to miss (*see* Table 10.1 for details). The sulphite test strip is easy to use but may miss disorders of molybdenum metabolism (or sulphite oxidase deficiency).

Table 10.1 Glycosaminoglycans (GAGs) in urine

GAG	Old name	Excreted in*
Chondroitin-4-sulphate	Chondroitin sulphate A	Normals
		Excess in Lowe, Zellweger
Chondroitin-6-sulphate	Chondroitin sulphate C	Normals
Dermatan sulphate	Chondroitin sulphate B	Hurler, Hurler–Schie, Hunter, Multiple sulphatase deficiency, Lowe, Zellweger
Heparan sulphate	Heparitin sulphate	Sanfilippo, Hurler, Hurler–Schie, Hunter, multiple sulphatase deficiency
Keratan sulphate	Keratosulphate	Some GM_1 gangliosidoses

* Non-neurological mucopolysaccharidoses excluded

Laboratory urine tests

Urine tests are listed (Table 10.2), with a note on important precautions for obtaining a specimen for useful analysis. For each test we give a thumbnail account of the main indications and a note on the interpretations, including the diagnosis most likely to be substantiated.

Blood biochemistry

Table 10.3 lists a number of the biochemical tests on serum or plasma which may be helpful in neurological investigation. The format is the same as for laboratory urine tests (Table 10.2).

Lysosomal disorders

Lysosomal enzyme deficiencies may be sought in serum and plasma (for example, hexosaminidase A and B), in leucocytes (white cell pellet) and in cultured fibroblasts. Summarized clinical/enzyme correlations appear in Table 10.4 and in the section on 'Regression with coarse facies' at the end of Chapter 25. The excretion of storage material as summarized in the 'Coarse facies' section and in Table 10.1 may suggest the group of enzyme deficiencies which needs to be further investigated. Sialic acid (N-acetylneuraminic acid or NANA) is a component of many of the stored compounds, and its excessive urinary excretion may reflect other lysosomal disorders than sialic acid storage disease (in which the enzyme deficiency is unknown): 'salla disease' or 'sialuria'. Rarely it is necessary to confirm neuronal storage by rectal biopsy. On the other hand, finding of stored material in a skin biopsy will lead to a search for the underlying enzyme deficiency.

Although it is evident that there is great variation in the severity of the neurological disorders which may result from a severe lysosomal

Table 10.2 Urine biochemistry

Test	Indications	Precautions	Interpretation
Amino acids	Mental handicap, acute encephalopathy, intermittent ataxia, suspect Lowe's syndrome, suspect mitochondrial disorder, acquired movement disorder	24-h sample not necessary. If unusual amino acid being sought (e.g. S-sulphocysteine in sulphite oxidase deficiency) discuss with laboratory	Relate to dietary input. The significance of minor deviations from 'normal' is uncertain. Abnormalities are found in aminoacidopathy, organic acidaemias, sulphite oxidase deficiency, renal tubular leak (including Wilson's disease)
Organic acids	Acute encephalopathy, 'near-miss' SIDS, movement disorder with acute exacerbations, hypotonia (± vomiting, rash, alopecia). Regression in infancy with large head and leucodystrophy on CT/MRI. Agenesis of the corpus callosum and other (cystic) malformations. Ataxia. Macrocephaly.	Preferably not on drugs or medium-chain triglyceride (MCT) oil. Best taken during acute illness. Freeze urine immediately	Negative result does not exclude disorder when the urine is obtained other than during the acute illness. Methods of analysis vary in their power of resolution and sensitivity, depending on whether GC alone, GC–MS, or FAB–MS and size of GC–MS column. Organic acidurias, fatty acid oxidation defects, N-acetylaspartic acid detected
Acylcarnitines	Acute metabolic encephalopathy	Excretion much increased by carnitine load (100 mg/kg) except when enzyme defect confined to brain	Specific acylcarnitines indicate particular disorders, e.g. octanoyl carnitine in MCAD deficiency, glutaryl carnitine in glutaric aciduria type I, best measured by FAB–MS
Porphyrins	Acquired motor neuropathy ± Convulsive seizures ± Abdominal colic (at puberty)	Random sample, then 24-h urine	Excess excretion leads to specific tests for acute intermittent porphyria
GAGs	Mental handicap ± Coarse features, corneal clouding, dysostosis. Speech deterioration. Behavioural difficulties	24-h collection obligatory if Sanfilippo possible	Mucopolysaccharidosis will be detected (see Table 10.1). Excess possible in Lowe and Zellweger syndrome and peroxisomopathies

Oligosaccharides	Mental handicap ± coarse features, corneal clouding, dysostosis. Dysmorphic neonate, hydrops. Myoclonus epilepsy	Random sample adequate	Easy on thin-layer chromotography. Mucolipidoses detected in particular
Orotic acid	Ill neonate. Vomiting–headache–impaired consciousness complex. Stroke	Random sample	If elevated = OTC deficiency. If in doubt, repeat after protein load under expert supervision
Copper	Acquired movement disorder, acquired behaviour disorder ± abnormal liver function	24-h urine. Meticulous attention to ensure copper-free containers and to prevent copper contamination	Elevation = Wilson's disease (false negative in 5%)
Bile acids	Suspect peroxisomopathy	Has to be arranged with reference laboratory in advance. Random sample – freeze immediately	Output of abnormal bile acids declines with age. May be negative after early infancy
Sulphite	Mental handicap with early epileptic seizures ± opisthotonus ± ectopia lentis. Or acquired deficits (e.g. infantile hemiplegia)	Random sample fresh, kept on ice (sulphite is unstable)	May be positive in molybdenum cofactor defiency or sulphite oxidase defiency. Stix tests not reliable
Thiosulphate	As for urine sulphite	Reliable in urine stored at room temperature up to 72 h	Positive in sulphite oxidase deficiency and molybdenum cofactor deficiency
Urate	Early seizures ± opisthotonus. Early acquired movement disorder with motor delay and high or high–normal plasma urate. Ataxic or spastic cerebral palsy ('dysequilibrium – diplegia')	24 h urine preferable	High output = Lesch–Nyhan or similar disorder. Low excretion = deficiency of molybdenum cofactor or purine nucleoside phosphorylase (more sensitive than plasma urate estimation)
HMMA, HVA	Acute or subacute cerebellar ataxia/myoclonus/opsoclonus	Special diet no longer usually indicated. 24 h urine preferred	Increase is consistent with occult neuroblastoma

Table 10.2 Urine biochemistry (continued)

Test	Indications	Precautions	Interpretation
Free sialic acid	Infants: coarse facies hepatosplenomegaly, profound inactivity, rapid course Infants: coarse facies (mild); hepatosplenomegaly, psychomotor delay (moderate) Later: mental handicap ± transient nystagmus (infancy), ataxia, dyskinesias, spasticity. Progression may not be obvious. Variable age of onset, degree of coarsening and mental handicap	Single urine. Screen for oligosaccharides may not detect free sialic acid	10–20-fold increase in sialic acid storage disease 100-fold increase in sialuria 5–10-fold increase in Salla disease and variants With the exception of sialuria, all show vacuolated lymphocytes and evidence of lysosomal storage on skin biopsy. Specific enzyme defect not yet identified in above disorders. False positives may be seen in other lysosomal disorders
Succinyl purines	'Autism', unexplained mental handicap	Random urine	TLC of urine sugars may show an abnormally situated ribose spot in adenylocyclase deficiency. A simple specific test for succinyladenosine is now available (Maddocks and Reed, 1989). Further analysis requires a purine reference laboratory

Table 10.3 Blood biochemistry

Test	Indications	Precautions	Interpretation
Albumin	When CSF protein significance is important	Discussion with laboratory may be necessary on techniques of albumin estimation	Allows calculations of CSF/serum albumin index, IgG albumin ratio, and IgG index with respect to blood-brain barrier defect and CNS infection
IgG	As above	—	See above Hypogammaglobulinaemia with persistent CNS viral infection
IgA	Acquired progressive encephalopathy Additional test in early acquired ataxia	—	May be absent in ataxia telangiectasia and with phenytoin therapy, low values common, non-specific
Calcium	Neonatal seizures. Unexplained seizures ± photophobia, mental handicap. Acquired dyskinesia. Developmental delay ± elfin face	—	Reduced in hypocalcaemia, true and pseudo-hypoparathyroidism Raised in idiopathic hypercalcaemia etc.
Copper	Steely hair, early seizures. Movement disorder ± behaviour disorder age 5 years or over	Ensure apparatus is completely copper free and avoid copper contamination	Reduced in Menke's disease. Reduced in Wilsons disease (not always)
Magnesium	Neonatal seizures		Reduced with disturbances of magnesium metabolism
Ammonia	Neonatal seizures ± vomiting. Acute encephalopathy. Vomiting–headache–impaired consciousness complex. Stroke	May be fasting or postprandial or at time of acute illness. Can be venous or arterial but with minimum disturbance. Separate immediately	Normal arterial level is higher than venous. Raised in urea cycle defects, some aminoacidopathies, organic acidurias, Reye's syndrome, sodium valproate therapy, illness with shock
Alpha-1-antitrypsin	Late neonatal intracranial haemorrhage	—	May be alpha-1-antitrypsin deficiency with PiZZ or PiSZ phenotype. ('Clotting screen' abnormal)
Caeruloplasmin	Early seizures, hypothermia, steely hair. Movement and/or behaviour disorder 5 years or older	—	Reduced in Menke's disease Wilson's disease (not always)
Alpha-fetoprotein	'Ataxic cerebral palsy'	—	Increased in all cases of ataxia telangiectasia

Table 10.3 Blood biochemistry (continued)

Test	Indications	Precautions	Interpretation
Thyroxine-binding globulin (TBG)	Mental handicap with hypotonia, neuropathy, retinopathy (see Recent Advances, page 236 Appendix II)	—	Reduced in carbohydrate deficient glycoprotein disease (disialotransferrin may be estimated)
Carnitine	Lipid myopathy. Acute metabolic encephalopathy.	—	Very low in primary carnitine transport defect. Low in various fatty acid oxidation disorders
Amino acids	Mental handicap. Acute encephalopathy. Intermittent ataxia. Progressive dystonia ± seizures/microcephaly/hypotonia in first year, i.e. possible tetrahydrobiopterin deficiency (see chapter 26)	Deproteinize plasma promptly if homocystinuria is a possibility. Increased pipecolic acid level may be missed by usual methods	Relate to dietary input. Uncertain significance of minor deviations from normal. Aminoacidopathies, most cases of glycine encephalopathy will be diagnosed. Reye's syndrome, mitochondrial disorders
Cholesterol	Developmental delay with retinal defect, sensorineural deafness, spinocerebellar ataxia. As TBG	Fasting	Reduced in generalized peroxisomal deficiency. Abetalipoproteinaemia (lipoproteins can then be investigated)
Very long-chain fatty acids (VLCFA)	Neonatal hypotonia and seizures. Delay, sensorineural deafness, pigmentary retinopathy. School-age regression	Special arrangements with laboratory	Neonatal and early childhood onset peroxisomal disorders Adrenoleucodystrophy
Urate	Early acquired movement disorder with motor delay, ataxic cerebral palsy ('dysequilibrium – diplegia')	—	High in Lesch–Nyhan or similar disorder. Low in molybdenum cofactor deficiency. Very low in purine nucleoside phosphorylase deficiency (confirm by red cell assay)
Hexosaminidase A and B (free)	Regression in infancy with startle. Progressive ataxia. Dementia ± seizures	Serum or plasma	GM_2 gangliosidosis (Tay-Sachs, Sandhoff – infantile and juvenile variants)

Lactate	Acute encephalopathy with increased anion gap. Suspicion of mitochondrial disorder (see below) intermittent ataxia/movement disorder. Suspicion of organic aciduria. Hypoglycaemia	Often recommended to be taken fasting, but better 1 h after a meal. Laboratory must be prepared. Minimal disturbance of child and immediate processing of specimen	The laboratory should be experienced. Increased in Reye's, Leigh's, biotinidase deficiency, PNDC, pyruvate dehydrogenase and decarboxylase deficiency, (and in illness, hypoxia, muscle movement, stress, and seizures). Significance enhanced if alanine level increased also
Pyruvate	As for blood lactate	Preferably 1 h after a meal	Relatively more increased in defects of pyruvate dehydrogenase complex.
Vitamin B_{12}	Chorea in infancy ± regression	—	Reduced in breast-feeding by mother on vegan diet
Vitamin E	Delay, with retinal defect and sensorineural deafness, spinocerebellar ataxia ± retinitis pigmentosa	—	Reduced in peroxisomal deficiency, abetalipoproteinaemia, selective vitamin E malabsorption
AST ALT	Acute encephalopathy. Before starting sodium valproate. Intractable partial seizures and myoclonus. Developmental delay with hypotonia	—	Very high in Reye's syndrome, acute hepatic failure, hypoxic ischaemic insults (including HSES). Increased in progressive neuronal degeneration of childhood with liver disease, Duchenne muscular dystrophy, MCAD deficiency, disialotransferrin syndrome, and other non-specific situations.
Creatine kinase	Language delay, mental handicap, delayed walking, toe walking, acquired muscle weakness. History of malignant hyperthermia. HSES	Test with minimal disturbance, preferably not after exercise or biopsy	Very high in Duchenne muscular dystrophy and in acute multiple-organ failure (e.g. in HSES). Increased in congenital muscular dystrophy (often), myositis (often), malignant hyperthermia
Biotinidase	Atypical seizures, regression, hypotonia ± skin rash ± alopecia. Remission on biotin trial (see Table 12.1)	Serum (assay not affected by coincident biotin therapy)	Biotinidase deficiency

Table 10.4 White cell lysosomal enzymes

Clinical clues	Precautions	Enzyme deficiency
Extra CNS storage (coarse face, corneal clouding, visceromegaly, dysostosis). Characteristic neurodegenerative disease (e.g. Krabbe's [1] metachromatic leucodystrophy [2]) unexplained dementia [3], ataxia [4], movement disorders [5], spinal muscular atrophy [6], myoclonus epilepsy [7]	Laboratory needs advance warning. Ensure laboratory uses validated methods (i.e. appropriate substrate) and includes the enzyme requested in their 'screen'. Beware inferences from 'heterozygote' levels	[2] If enzyme normal consider activator protein deficiency. Seek tissue confirmation. [3, 4, 5, 6] β-Galactosidase [3, 4, 5, 6] Hexosaminidase A + B [2, 3, 4, 5] Arylsulphatase A [1, 3, 4] Galactocerebroside -β-galactosidase [7] Neuraminidase

Note: Neurological presentations are numbered to match enzyme deficiency most likely to be detected

enzyme deficiency (hexosaminidase in particular), extreme caution is necessary when partial deficiency is found, particularly if it is in the 'heterozygote range'. In the case of some of the disorders, the prevalence of heterozygotes is quite high in the normal population. Considerations of sensitivity and specificity should prevent, for example, the diagnosis of metachromatic leucodystrophy in a child with primary generalized epilepsy or isolated dystonia and heterozygote levels of arylsulphatase A. These clinical presentations would be inappropriate indications for assay of this enzyme, but having obtained a low result, the clinician may feel bound to pursue the diagnosis by culturing fibroblasts and searching for sulphatide in urinary sediment and sural nerve biopsy. Such temptations should be resisted.

Mitochondrial disorders

With the explosion of knowledge about disorders of the mitochondria, definitive investigations have become complex and specialized. However, clinical clues can point towards a mitochondrial disorder, and fairly simple tests support the diagnosis sufficiently to proceed to specific investigations of mitochondrial function.

To a certain extent there is a relationship between the type of disease and the site of the metabolic defect along the pathway from the inner mitochondrial membrane transit to the termination of the respiratory chain, but there is considerable heterogeneity and for simplicity we will tend to lump rather than split.

Clinical clues to mitochondrial disorders

Myopathy with fatigue.

Infantile hypotonia with failure to thrive ($\pm$ congenital microcephaly).

Acute encephalopathy (with vomiting and fatty liver).

'Progressive neuronal degeneration of childhood' (hemiclonic and focal myoclonic seizures, regression, cerebral atrophy, $\pm$ terminal liver failure).

Leigh's disease picture (regression with hypotonia, oculomotor and respiratory disturbance).

Intermittent ataxia $\pm$ other neurological deficits.

Chronic encephalomyopathy of childhood (fatigue, pigmentary retinopathy, oculomotor disturbance, sensorineural deafness, ataxia, pyramidal signs, regression).

Kearns–Sayre syndrome (ptosis and ophthalmoplegia, pigmentary retinopathy, heart block, short stature).

MELAS picture (severe migraines, partial epileptic seizures, hemipareses). The acronym refers to Mitochondrial Encephalopathy with Lactic Acidosis and Stroke-like episodes.

MERRF picture (myoclonic epileptic seizures and repetitive myoclonus with progressive ataxia and regression in late childhood). The acronym is Myoclonic Epilepsy with Ragged Red Fibres.

Investigation results found in mitochondrial disorders

Combinations of the following abnormalities on investigation lend support:

EEG polyspikes on slow background.

Slow nerve conduction velocity.

CT scan findings of
cerebral atrophy
low densities in the neostriatum (putamen, especially)
low densities in brainstem and cerebellum
calcification in neostriatum (caudate and putamen).

CSF
protein elevation
lactate and pyruvate elevation.

ECG evidence of cardiac conduction defects (e.g. Wolff–Parkinson – White, heart block).

Muscle biopsy
ragged red fibres on trichrome staining (Gomori)
fat accumulation.

Liver biopsy
fat accumulation
fibrosis.

Blood biochemistry
  increased lactate and pyruvate
  increased alanine.
Urine biochemistry
  aminoaciduria
  Krebs cycle organic acids (e.g. fumarate, succinate)
  non-specific glycosaminoglycanuria.

Special mitochondrial investigations

Of the investigations listed above (listed as in order of discussion in this book, not in order of execution!) elevated blood or CSF lactate and/or pyruvate is the most suggestive supporting evidence of a mitochondrial disorder underlying a neurological disturbance, apart from the demonstration of ragged red fibres on muscle biopsy, which is diagnostic – although not specifying the precise mitochondrial defect.

If the combined clinical and investigational result is sufficiently suggestive, then discussion with one of the supraregional laboratories is needed on the practicalities of mitochondrial isolation from fresh muscle liver and fibroblasts. The most likely findings in neurological disorders are deficiency of the pyruvate dehydrogenase complex or of one of the components of the respiratory chain (especially complex IV or cytochrome c oxidase), but Krebs cycle defects (such as fumarase deficiency) are probably also not rare.

Peroxisomal disorders

Peroxisomes are now known to be of major importance for brain development, and deficiency of the peroxisomes themselves or of one of their enzymes may lead to striking neurological disorder.

Understanding of peroxisomal diseases has advanced with great rapidity and already all known inherited disorders are capable of antenatal diagnosis. We summarize the main clinical clues to peroxisomal disorders, the typical findings in neurological and general investigations, and the special tests which have to be done to confirm the diagnosis and allow genetic advice. 'Screening' tests presently available do not detect these disorders, so recognition of the wider clinical clues is important.

Clinical clues to peroxisomal disorders

Neonatal hypotonia (especially extreme hypotonia of the neck).
Neonatal seizures (refractory or phenytoin-responsive in a hypotonic
  baby).
Neonatal unresponsiveness (except reflex crying).
Retinal blindness ('Leber's amaurosis').

Sensorineural deafness.

Gross dysmorphic features of Zellweger syndrome type (high forehead, flat face, simian creases, simple genitalia).

Mild dysmorphism (large fontanelle with open metopic suture, absent ear lobules).

Hepatomegaly (± hepatic insufficiency).

Developmental delay with malabsorption features, retinopathy and sensorineural deafness.

Developmental delay with seizures and areflexia (peripheral neuropathy).

School age regression in a boy with previously normal development (± Addison's disease).

Investigation results found in peroxisomal disorders

In the neonatal and early manifesting disorders:

EEG trains of repetitive spikes shifting from side to side.
Slow nerve conduction (± EMG denervation).
Low or absent ERG.
BAEP gross abnormalities
   high threshold
   delayed wave V latency
   lack of response.
Ultrasound evidence of germinal layer cysts.
CT scan evidence of migration disorder
   pachygyria
   abnormal (e.g. parietal) sulci.
CT white matter hypodensity (with contrast enhancement in acute regression).
Patellar and other chondral calcification.
Bone age retardation.
Echogenic renal cortex on ultrasound.
Increased CSF protein.
Liver biopsy: hepatic fibrosis.
Clotting defect of hepatic type.
Increased AST and ALT.
Low cholesterol.
Low vitamin E.
Increased phytanic acid.
Urinary excretion of
   aminoacids
   glycosaminoglycans
   dicarboxylic acids.

In the regressing school-child:

VEP latency increase.
BAEP increased latency of wave V.
CT white matter hypodensity (especially around trigone posteriorly, but may be anterior around anterior horns).
CT streaky contrast enhancement of central white matter.
Increased CSF protein (albumin and globulin).
Biochemical evidence of adrenal insufficiency (reduced cortisol output, increased ACTH).

Special peroxisomal investigations

Once sufficient clinical and investigational clues have been assembled, special tests for peroxisomal disorders can be sought at specialized laboratories. These primarily test:

1. The size of the peroxisomal compartment – simply: are peroxisomes missing and all functions depressed, and
2. The integrity of the peroxisomal beta-oxidation pathway, which metabolizes very long-chain fatty acids (VLCFA) and also, in part, bile acids.

The tests of most direct help are as follows:

Very long-chain fatty acids (VLCFA) in plasma (and fibroblasts). VLCFA are increased in all disorders with absent or grossly diminished peroxisomes, and in all disorders of the VLCFA metabolic pathway. This is the only test necessary for confirmation of the diagnosis of adrenoleucodystrophy in the regressing schoolchild.

Bile acids. Abnormal bile acids are found in the urine, plasma and duodenal juice in infants with a lack of peroxisomes, and in those who have a defect in the terminal enzyme (thiolase) of the beta-oxidation pathway.

Dihydroxyacetone phosphate acyl transferase (DHAP-AT). This is estimated in fibroblasts (and in platelets). It is reduced in all cases of general lack of peroxisomes.

VLCFA oxidation. Assays are being developed for use in fibroblasts. When combined with DHAP-AT activity, this should prove to be a robust test for peroxisomopathy.

Liver biopsy with special studies. It is possible to demonstrate lack of peroxisomes by special histochemistry and electronmicroscopy, and enlarged peroxisomes in biochemical lesions of the beta-oxidation pathway, but such studies are no longer essential for diagnosis.

Immunoblot methods allow determination of the individual beta-oxidation enzymes, but as these enzymes may be totally inactive despite demonstrable protein, it cannot at present be said that liver biopsy is a necessary investigation.

Case illustrations

See Appendix for definitive diagnoses.

In addition to the following case illustrations, *see* 1.3, 2.5, 4.3, 5.3, 6.1, 7.2 and 7.3.

10.1 Not birth asphyxia

This girl, the first child of unrelated parents, was born at home after a 14 h labour. The cord was wrapped around the neck twice. The Apgar scores were 7 at 1 min and 9 at 5 min. She fed from the breast immediately after birth, but thereafter sucked poorly, did not cry or move her limbs, and was floppy. She was admitted to hospital at 72 h of age in a collapsed state with occasional gasps and unresponsiveness.

Investigations (1)
'Septic screens' of blood, urine and CSF were negative.
Urine ketones were negative.
Plasma urea was 9 mmol/l.
Plasma creatinine was 151 μmol/l.
Plasma ammonia was 60 μmol/l.
Plasma bicarbonate was 20.8 mmol/l.
Cerebral ultrasound was normal.
EEG (Figure 10.1) showed a burst-suppression pattern 'suggestive of severe hypoxic-ischaemic damage'.
CT brain scan 'showed ill-defined low-density areas in the white matter and frontal lobes consistent with regional cerebral ischaemia'.

Course
She required ventilatory support for 2 weeks and was started on nasogastric feeds. She remained profoundly hypotonic and unresponsive with stimulus-sensitive myoclonus and occasional hiccups.

Investigations (2)
Amino acids chromatography of plasma and CSF showed a plasma glycine level of 839 μmol/l and a CSF glycine of 140 μmol/l with a CSF:plasma ratio of 0.16 (normal 0.025 or less).

Comments
The evolution of symptoms and signs was consistent with a metabolic disorder; stimulus-sensitive myoclonus, hiccups and a burst-suppression EEG were

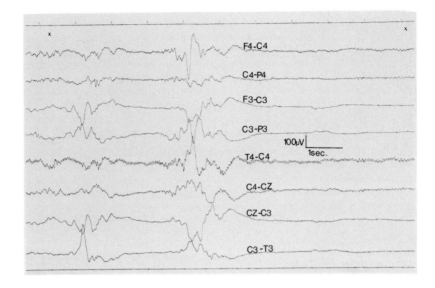

Figure 10.1   EEG at 5 days of age showing burst-suppression pattern.

strongly suggestive of non-ketotic hyperglycinaemia (glycine encephalopathy). There was no sound evidence of intrapartum asphyxia and the EEG and CT brain scan reports were misleading. This girl's parents withheld permission for liver biopsy for specific enzyme analysis.

10.2 Slow to sit up

The parents of this 11-month-old girl brought her up because she still could not sit. There had been no regression of development. She recognized her parents, but was not inquisitive. She had begun to use her hands, but still regarded them and flicked her fingers. Since the age of 2 weeks she had startled to sound. Occasionally in recent months her left eye had seemed to vibrate. On examination she was a placid, plump infant who jumped at sounds. The cherry-red of the macula was surrounded by pale bluish infiltrate on the retina. The trajectory of her head circumference was above that expected from her parental head size. The liver and spleen were not palpable.

Investigations
EEG was normal.
Biochemistry. Total isolated deficiency of leucocyte and fibroblast hexosaminidase A.

Comments
The clinical picture of Tay–Sachs disease was so typical that had the hexosaminidase A values been normal, diagnostic confirmation would have been undertaken by rectal biopsy and attempts made to confirm an absence of the activator protein of the malfunctioning hexosaminidase.

10.3 Crying baby

A 6-month-old boy was admitted with a history of crying constantly for 24 h, vomiting his feeds, and holding his head back. He was supposed to have been normal until the age of 4 months but did not get to the stage of reaching for objects or controlling his head. He was irritable on examination, with a head circumference on the same percentile as his father. Pupils had a sluggish reaction to a light, and he did not definitely follow it, but the optic discs were normal at that stage. He tended to lie in an asymmetric tonic neck reflex posture. Very strong toe jerks and extensor plantar responses were present, but all tendon reflexes were absent. There were no abnormalities outside the nervous system.

Investigations
EEG was within normal limits.
Flash visual evoked potentials: poorly reproducible with delayed latency.
Nerve conduction: motor conduction 13 metres per second in peroneal nerve, 4.8 metres per second in sural nerve.
CSF protein 1.6 g/dl; IgG 68 mg/l.
Beta-galactocerebrosidase using an artificial substrate and a fluorogenic method was normal.
Skin biopsy showed an excess of small, unmyelinated axons in the peripheral rims of Schwann cell processes. None of the Schwann cells contained abnormal materials.
Further white cells and fibroblasts were obtained and sent for analysis for galactocerebroside-beta-galactosidase using a natural substrate. The enzyme was absent.

Comments
The combination of neurological findings made the diagnosis of Krabbe's globoid leucodystrophy certain, but two measurements of the 'Krabbe's enzyme' gave a normal result. Once the correct methodology was used, the diagnosis was confirmed.

10.4 Not speaking at school

A 6-year-old boy was referred because he did not speak at school and appeared to have significant mild global delay. On questioning, his mother said that her brother had been unsteady on his feet from the age of 5 years, became confined to a wheel-chair, and had died at the age of 15; she did not know what his diagnosis was. At the time of presentation the subject of this case illustration had only subtle difficulty in getting himself off the floor.

Investigations
Creatine kinase (CK) 1777 U/l.
AST 323 U/l; ALT 34 U/l.
Needle biopsy of muscle (vastus lateralis) showed small areas of inflammatory infiltration in relation to necrotic muscle fibres, areas of 'regenerating' fibres, and many 'dystrophic' fibres.

Course
The patient transferred to a school for physically and mentally handicapped children, and took to a wheel-chair full-time at the age of 12.

Comments

Duchenne muscular dystrophy may present nowadays as language or global delay. The diagnostic power of a very high CK is further increased by the concurrent increase in AST and ALT. In this case an intragenic deletion was later detected (using probe cDMD 2b-3), together with a 'junction fragment' of DNA produced by the deletion. The presence of the junction fragment allows exact carrier detection and prenatal diagnosis.

10.5 Tadpole with hairy legs

This very nice, but shy, firstborn girl of unrelated parents presented at 15 months with failure to thrive and grow and was described by the referring paediatrician as resembling 'a tadpole with hairy legs'. She had persistent vomiting and soon needed to have all her nutrition by nasogastric tube. Motor skills seemed to arrest at the age of 10 months. She had impaired head control, ataxia with tremor, absent tendon reflexes, and occasional inconstant, brief occular oscillations.

Investigations (1)

EEG was normal.

Nerve conduction and EMG. Motor nerve conduction velocity was grossly slow at around 15 to 19 metres per second. Sensory action potentials were absent. EMG was unremarkable.

CT scan was normal.

Bone age retarded at 6 months at a chronological age of 15 months.

CSF protein 0.65 g/l.

Haematology. Lymphocytes containing lipid vacuoles were observed on one occasion.

Muscle biopsy was histologically normal. Special biochemistry was abnormal. *See below.*

Nerve biopsy showed demyelination.

General biochemistry: Marked generalized aminoaciduria, excretion of unidentified glycosaminoglycan on two occasions. Acid–base status usually normal, base excess −8 on one occasion. Plasma lactate 1.9 and 2.1 mmol/l. CSF lactate 6 mmol/l on one occasion.

Plasma pyruvate 77 and 131 μmol/l.

Lysosomal enzymes normal.

Special biochemical studies on muscle. Muscle histochemistry suggested a defect of cytochrome c oxidase, which was confirmed by direct analysis of muscle.

Course

Progress was fairly static until the age of $3\frac{1}{2}$ years, when she began to choke on her saliva and became much more shaky. Respiratory failure rapidly developed.

Investigations (2)

Pre-terminal CT (Figure 10.5) scan showed low-density areas in brain stem and cerebellum.

Neuropathology confirmed Leigh's disease.

Studies of mitochondria in brain, muscle, liver, heart and kidney showed cytochrome c oxidase deficiency.

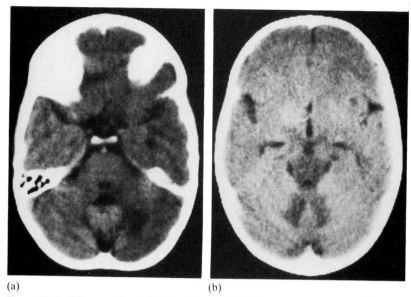

(a)   (b)

Figure 10.5 CT scans (a) and (b) show hypodensities in brain stem and cerebellum. The striatum was unaffected (not shown).

Comments
Despite the normal blood lactate and pyruvate, the diagnosis of Leigh's disease was suggested by the combination of ataxia and peripheral neuropathy and the aminoaciduria. CT abnormalities were late appearing. The features were, however, strong enough to stimulate the analysis of mitochondrial function and the discovery to cytochrome c oxidase deficiency. A young sister is now following the same course.

10.6 Very complicated migraine

An 18-year-old boy was reported by Montagna et al (*Neurology* 1988, **38**, 751–754). He had had diffuse, throbbing headache once or twice a week from age 5 years. At 9 years of age attacks of right-sided throbbing headache with vomiting lasted up to 10 days. At this time he also had bouts of vasomotor rhinitis and abdominal cramps, which responded temporarily to steroids. At age 12 years he had two generalized epileptic seizures during sleep and then the first of a series of right or left sensory and motor partial seizures associated with vomiting and followed by transient hemiparesis. Migrainous attacks continued to be associated with right- or left-sided partial seizures, which might culminate in partial epileptic status. Stepwise neurological and cognitive deficits ensued, and before his death in status epilepticus he had cortical blindness, ptosis, dysarthria, spasticity and continuous clonic activity of his left face and upper limb. There was also hyperlaxity of ligaments.

Investigations
EEG is not reported.
Motor and sensory nerve conduction velocities were slowed.

CT: from 12 years of age, temporary lucencies in one or other occipital region; later, extensive bilateral lucencies and cortical and cerebellar atrophy.

Blood lactate: 3.4 mmol/l.

Blood pyruvate: 145 μmol/l.

Muscle biopsy. Small lipid vacuoles surrounded by clusters of mitochondria. Ragged red fibres on trichrome stain.

Special biochemistry. Tests on isolated mitochondria did not reveal the basic defect in this boy, nor in his mildly affected mother.

Comments

A combination of features of migraine and epilepsy, with the accretion of neurological deficits, suggested a mitochondrial disorder. This was supported by the lactic/pyruvic acidosis and confirmed by the finding of ragged red fibres, although the precise mitochondrial defect was not elucidated.

10.7 Post-anaesthetic coma

A previously healthy 2-year-old with a history of mild speech delay was fasted in an adult hospital before anaesthesia to set a fractured radius and ulna. While looking at a book with her mother 20 h after her last food she had a tonic seizure, and was admitted to the intensive care unit extending, or at best flexing to pain.

Investigations (1)

Blood glucose 0.6 mmol/l before intravenous dextrose.

Urine ketones strong (3 +) positive.

Plasma urea 11.7 mmol/l.

Plasma bicarbonate 17 mmol/l.

Plasma ammonia 173 μmol/l.

ALT 68 U/l; AST 111 U/l.

Coagulation mildly deranged (prothrombin time 18 s, control 12 s.

Course

She did not respond to intravenous dextrose. She was intubated, paralysed and ventilated, and her intracranial pressure monitored by an intraventricular catheter (Figure 10.7). Great difficulty was experienced in maintaining an adequate cerebral perfusion pressure, but after 5 days she improved and was left with an increase in output speech impairment, a mild left lower limb spastic monoparesis, and intact intelligence.

Investigation (2)

Intracranial pressure varied from 15 to 50 mmHg.

CSF protein (ventricular) 0.5 g/l; 2 white cells per mm^3.

Plasma amino acids were normal.

Plasma salicylate 0.36 mmol/l.

Liver biopsy. Predominantly periportal macrovesicular fatty change with some centrilobular microvesicular fatty change. Glycogen was normal. Mitochondria and endoplasmic reticulum were normal on electronmicroscopy. Peroxisomes had not proliferated.

Urine organic acids were abnormal with a marked increase in 3-hydroxybutyrate together with the dicarboxylic acids, adipic, suberic and sebacic. The hydroxybutyric/adipic ratio was 2.4, suggesting relative hypoketosis. By gas

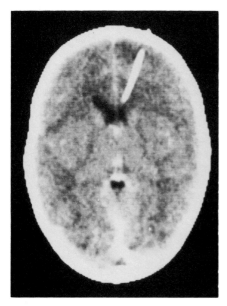

Figure 10.7   CT scan showing catheter in right lateral ventricle during intracranial pressure monitoring.

chromatography mass spectroscopy at one laboratory hexanoyl-glycine was detected, and at another laboratory suberyl-glycine.

Phenylpropionic acid loading led to the excretion of phenylpropionylglycine.

L-carnitine loading led to the excretion of very large amounts of octanoylcarnitine, which was present in smaller quantities before the load.

Comment
This was a severe, life-threatening metabolic encephalopathy from a specific fatty acid oxidation defect, medium-chain acyl-CoA dehydrogenase deficiency. Investigational 'greed' seems justified in these circumstances. Primarily neurological investigations which were also carried out here, such as EEG and CT scan, were not additionally helpful.

10.8 Irritability and arching in a 13-month-old boy

This boy was developing normally until 4 days after the onset of upper respiratory symptoms. He became listless and irritable and had a spell which consisted in rolling up his eyes and twitching his face. He was given intramuscular penicillin by his family doctor and was febrile on admission to the district hospital, with signs of otitis media. CSF analysis was normal. Over the next day he had a number of myoclonic jerks and was transferred to a paediatric unit. Shortly after admission he deteriorated and became irritable with neck extension, and held his head to one side. There was truncal hypotonia and brisk reflexes. He exhibited fluctuation in his blood pressure and required antihypertensive treatment. Blood pressure stabilized after a few days but he exhibited marked arching of the neck as if in pain, and had difficulty swallowing. He was examined by an otorhinolaryngologist who could find no abnormality. Thereafter the clinical picture evolved into a prominent dystonia. There were dystonic neck, facial and tongue movements with intermittent extension of the lower limbs. He remained lucid and did not have seizures. There was no response to various antiparkinsonian drugs. Feeding improved after several weeks, but he remained severely dystonic with poor head control and inability to sit several months later. There was significant decrease in dystonia following introduction of baclofen.

Investigations
EEG was normal.
Full blood count and blood film were normal.
ESR was normal.
X-ray of cervical spine and neck was normal.
CT brain scan was normal.
Myelogram was normal.
CSF was normal.
Acid-base status was normal.
Creatine kinase greater than 3000 U/l.
Plasma, urine and CSF amino acids were normal.
Plasma and CSF pyruvate and lactate were normal.
Plasma uric acid was normal.
Urine HMMA/HVA was normal.
Urine organic acid analysis revealed excess excretion of glutaric acid.
Assay of glutaryl-CoA dehydrogenase activity in cultured fibroblasts revealed
    no activity of this enzyme, confirming the diagnosis of glutaric aciduria type I.

Comment
This was a classical presentation of glutaric aciduria type I. Other diagnoses which were considered early on were acute striatal necrosis and neuroleptic malignant syndrome, but these were not relevant. Several weeks after the onset of symptoms the total picture became clear, and organic acids were analysed on the urine sample which was collected and frozen at the peak of the illness.

10.9 'Stroke' in a 15-month-old girl

This girl, an only child, had episodes of respiratory infection lasting a few days and associated with listlessness and vomiting for about 10 weeks before her admission to hospital. During one of these she stopped moving her left arm and developed vesicles on two fingers on her right hand and around the mouth. She was referred to the district hospital. She had a low-grade pyrexia and a left hemiparesis. Over a period of 48 h she became drowsy and was referred to the regional neurosurgical unit. A CT brain scan showed a large infarct in the right middle cerebral artery territory, with no shift of the midline structures. The provisional diagnosis was herpes encephalitis. She was started on intravenous acyclovir and dexamethasone. A lumbar puncture was performed which was normal, but the pressure was not recorded. Four hours later she had a respiratory arrest with unreactive pupils and extension to pain. She was ventilated and given mannitol, with return of pupil responses, respiratory effort and flexion to pain. A CT brain scan showed increased oedema on the right side, with obliteration of the right basal cistern and a wedge shaped infarct in the left frontal lobe. She had a few seizures over the next few days but made steady improvement and was weaned off ventilation one week later. She had a dense left hemiplegia with a left homonymous hemianopia and tremulousness.

Investigations (1)

EEG showed high-voltage slow activity on the left with relative suppression on the right.

Full blood count and blood film were normal.

Coagulation screen was normal.

Viral titres in CSF and plasma were negative.

Autoantibody screen was negative.

Immunoglobulins were normal.

Complement levels were normal.

Plasma amino acids ranged from normal to 'slightly elevated' glutamine and alanine.

Urine amino acids were normal.

Plasma ammonia was not measured during the first 2 weeks of the illness, but thereafter levels ranged from 14 to 204 μmol/l.

Transaminases. AST normal to 507 U/l; ALT normal to 517 U/l.

Plasma and CSF pyruvate and lactate were normal.

Urine orotic acid was normal (after acute illness).

Muscle histology was normal (no ragged red fibres were seen on trichrome stain).

In view of the elevated ammonia level a protein load was administered and samples taken at 0, 2, 4 and 8 h for ammonia, amino acids and urinary orotic acid estimation.

This revealed:

Time	Plasma ammonia
Baseline	63 μmol/l
2 h	99 μmol/l
4 h	75 μmol/l
8 h	40 μmol/l

Plasma amino acids were normal and urine orotic acid excretion was verbally reported 'normal'.

Course

She was started on a low-protein diet pending the formal report on the urine orotic acid excretion during the protein load, and was dismissed home. Two months later she returned and her mother reported that although she was making progress in terms of her motor development and symbolic understanding, she continued to have episodes of vomiting lasting 24 h or so, and was 'not right'.

Investigations (2)

Plasma ammonia 255 μmol/l.

Plasma amino acids: marked elevation of glutamine and alanine.

CSF amino acids: marked elevation of glutamine.

On review of the previous investigations it transpired that orotic acid was not measured in the 8 h sample after the protein load, and when this was analysed the orotic acid was found to be fifteen times above the normal range. Liver ornithine transcarbamylase was reduced to 20%.

Comments
The story prior to the development of stroke and the events during the acute encephalopathy strongly suggested a metabolic encephalopathy rather than an 'acute hemiplegia' or pure herpes encephalitis. This was supported by elevation of plasma ammonia, transaminases, glutamine and alanine. This case emphasizes the importance of obsessive attention to detail when performing metabolic studies, and adequate discussion with laboratory colleagues who might not be aware of the critical importance of such results.

Further reading

Aukett, A., Bennett, M. J. and Hosking, G. P. (1988) Molybdenum cofactor deficiency: an easily missed inborn error of metabolism. *Developmental Medicine and Child Neurology*, **30**, 531–535

Aula, P., Autio, S., Raivio, K. O. *et al.* (1979) 'Salla disease' a new lysosomal disorder. *Archives of Neurology*, **36**, 88–94

Burk, R. D., Valle, D., Thomas, G. H. *et al.* (1984) Early manifestations of multiple sulfatase deficiency. *Journal of Pediatrics*, **104**, 574–578

Carroll, J. E., Roesel, A., Du Rant, R. H. *et al.* (1986) Urinary sialic acid screening in neurologic disorders *Pediatric Neurology*, **2**, 67–71

Di Mauro, S., Bonilla, E., Zeviani, M. *et al.* (1987) Mitochondrial myopathies. *Journal of Inherited Metabolic Disease*, **10**, 113–128

Garcia Silva, M. T., Aicardi, J., Goutières, F. and Chevrie, J. J. (1987) The syndrome of myoclonic epilepsy with ragged-red fibres. Report of a case and review of the literature. *Neuropediatrics*, **18**, 200–204

Gordon, B. A., Gordon, K. E., Hinton, G. G. *et al.* (1987) Tay-Sachs disease: B[1] variant. *Pediatric Neurology*, **4**, 54–57

Jaeken, J., Eggermont, E. and Stibler, H. (1987) An apparent homozygous x-linked disorder with carbohydrate-deficient serum glycoproteins. *Lancet*, **2**, 1398

Jaeken, J. and Van der Berge, G. (1984) An infantile autistic syndrome characterised by the presence of succinylpurines in body fluids. *Lancet*, **2**, 1058–1061

Jenkins, H. R., Leonard, J. V., Kay, J. D. S. *et al.* (1982) Alpha-1-antitrypsin deficiency bleeding diathesis and intracranial haemorrhage. *Archives of Disease in Childhood*, **57**, 722–723

Johnson, W. G. (1981) The clinical spectrum of hexosaminidase deficiency. *Neurology*, **31**, 1453–1456

Kretzschmar, H. A., De Armond, S. J., Koch, T. K. *et al.* (1987) Pyruvate dehydrogenase complex deficiency as a cause of subacute necrotising encephalopathy (Leigh's disease). *Pediatrics*, **79**, 370–373

Kristiansson, B., Andersson, M., Tonnby, B. and Hagberg, B. (1989) Disialotransferrin developmental deficiency syndrome. *Archives of Disease in Childhood*, **64**, 71–76

Lipkin, P. H., Roe, C. R., Goodman, S. I. and Batshaw, M. L. (1988) A case of glutaric acidemia type 1: effect of riboflavin and carnitine. *Journal of Pediatrics*, **112**, 62–65

Maddocks, J. and Reed, T. (1989) Urine test for adenylosuccinase deficiency in autistic children. *Lancet*, **1**, 158–159

Matalon, R., Michals, K., Sebesta, D. *et al.* (1988) Aspartoacylase deficiency and n-acetylaspartic aciduria in patients with Canavan disease. *American Journal of Medical Genetics*, **29**, 463–471

Montagna, P., Gallassi, R. Medori, R. *et al.* (1988) MELAS syndrome: characteristic migrainous and epileptic features and maternal transmission. *Neurology*, **38**, 751–754

Page, T., Nyhan, W. L. and Morena de Vega, V. (1987) Syndrome of mild mental retardation, spastic gait and skeletal malformations in a family with partial deficiency of hypoxanthine–guanine phosphoribosyltransferase. *Pediatrics*, **79**, 713–717

Parnes, S., Karpati, G., Carpenter, S. *et al.* (1985) Hexosaminidase – A deficiency presenting as atypical juvenile onset spinal muscular atrophy. *Archives of Neurology*, **42**, 1176–1180

Paton, B. C. and Poulos, A. (1987) Normal dolichol concentration in urine sediments from four patients with neuronal ceroid lipofuscinosis (Batten's disease). *Journal of Inherited Metabolic Disease*, **10**, 28–32

Pavlakis, S., Phillips, P. C., Di Mauro, S. and Rowland, L. P. (1984) Mitochondrial myopathy, encephalopathy, lactic acidosis and strokelike episodes: a distinctive clinical syndrome. *Annals of Neurology*, **16**, 481–488

Petty, R. K. H., Harding, A. E. and Morgan-Hughes, J. A. (1986) The clinical features of mitochondrial myopathy. *Brain*, **109**, 915–938

Prick, M. J. J., Gabreels, F. J. M., Renier, W. O. *et al.* (1981) Progressive infantile poliodystrophy, associated with disturbed pyruvate oxidation in muscle and liver. *Archives of Neurology*, **38**, 767–772

Renlund, M. (1984) Clinical and laboratory diagnosis of Salla disease in infancy and childhood. *Journal of Pediatrics*, **104**, 232–236

Roe, C. R., Millington, D. S., Maltby, D. S. and Kinnebrew, P. (1986) Recognition of medium-chain acyl-CoA dehydrogenase deficiency in asymptomatic siblings of children dying of suddent infant death or Reye-like syndromes. *Journal of Pediatrics*, **108**, 13–18

Shih, V. H., Abroms, I. F., Johnson, J. *et al.* (1977) Sulfite oxidase deficiency. *New England Journal of Medicine*, **297**, 1022–1028

Simmonds, H. A., Fairbanks, L. D., Morris, G. S. *et al.* (1987) Central nervous system dysfunction and erythrocyte guanosine triphosphate depletion in purine nucleoside phosphorylase deficiency. *Archives of Disease in Childhood*, **62**, 385–391

Stephenson, J. B. P. (1988) Inherited peroxisomal disorders involving the nervous system. *Archives of Disease in Childhood*, **63**, 767–770

Stevens, R. L., Fluharty, A. L. Kihara, H.*et al.* (1981) Cerebroside sulfatase activator deficiency induced metachromatic leukodystrophy. *American Journal of Human Genetics*, **33**, 900–906

Van de Kamp, J. J. P., Niermeijer, M. F., von Figura, K. and Giesberts, M. A. H. (1981) Genetic heterogeneity and clinical variability in the Sanfilippo syndrome (types A, B and C). *Clinical Genetics*, **20**, 152–160

Wiliken, B., Don, N., Greenaway, R. *et al.* (1987) Sialuria: a second case. *Journal of Inherited Metabolic Disease*, **10**, 97–102

Wolf, B., Grier, R. E., Allen, R. J. *et al.* (1983) Phenotypic variation in biotinidase deficiency. *Journal of Pediatrics*, **103**, 233–237

Ylitalo, V., Hagberg, B., Rapola, J. *et al.* (1986) Salla disease variants. Sialoylaciduric encephalopathy with increased sialidase activity in two non-Finnish children. *Neuropediatrics*, **17**, 44–47

Zinn, A. B., Kerr, D. S. and Hoppel, C. L. (1986) Fumarase deficiency: a new cause of mitochondrial encephalomyopathy. *New England Journal of Medicine*, **315**, 469–475

Chapter 11

Antiepileptic drug level monitoring

Adequate therapeutic effect without toxicity is often helped by monitoring the concentrations of antiepileptic drugs in body fluids. The wise use of these levels needs more than the data provided in Table 11.1. This chapter gives a brief guide to principles. Ideally, a therapeutic level is the concentration of the drug in body fluids below which epileptic seizures may recur and above which epileptic seizures will be prevented. A drug which has these properties is described as level-dependent. In the case of level-dependent drugs, the therapeutic level as defined may vary with the body fluid utilized, and will certainly vary between one person and another and one seizure type and another. If an individual has more than one variety of seizure, then for a particular drug the therapeutic level for one seizure may be considerably higher than that for the other.

The so-called toxic level for a given drug also varies between individuals. Although it may be at the level given in the Table it may on occasion be considerably lower or higher. If in an individual with a particular type of seizure a toxic level is reached without abolition of the seizures, then no therapeutic level can be obtained. On the other hand, if the toxic level for a given drug is higher than usual in a particular individual with an apparently resistant epileptic seizure type, then it may be possible to reach a therapeutic level which is above the usual therapeutic range.

Saliva is a convenient fluid for measurement of phenytoin and ethosuximide in particular and can be obtained from infancy onwards without the use of citric acid (which has been blamed for errors in drug measurement). Some children, however, actually prefer giving a sample of blood to spitting into a container.

Some notes about the individual drugs follow.

Phenobarbitone

It is likely that the range is wider than that given in the Table, but progressive decline in consciousness occurs the higher the concentration in body fluids, and it is probable that milder toxicity (attention deficit or waking up during the night) may occur at levels well below the top of the therapeutic range.

Table 11.1 Antiepileptic drug monitoring

	Common therapeutic ranges: Blood	Common therapeutic ranges: Saliva	Toxic Levels*
Phenobarbitone	45–130 μmol/1 (10–30 μg/ml)	?	Blood > 180 μmol/1 (40 μg/ml)
Phenytoin	40–80 μmol/1 (10–20 μg/ml)	4–8 μmol/1 (1–2 μg/ml)	Blood > 80 μmol/1 (20 μg/ml) Saliva > 8 μmol/1 (2 μg/ml)
Carbamazepine	17–50 μmol/1 (4–12 μg/ml)	?	Blood > 34 μmol/1 (8 μg/ml)
Ethosuximide	300–1500 μmol/1 (40–200 μg/ml)	300–1500 μmol/1 (40–200μ μg/ml)	Blood and saliva: > 1200 μmol/1 (160 μg/ml)
Sodium valproate	Not level-dependent	Not level-dependent	Not level-dependent

* See text

Phenytoin

Phenytoin is a model level-dependent drug, but difficulties arise because of its inhibition of its own metabolism at high levels. Saliva levels are commonly useful in young children. The saliva concentration tends to be between 1/6th and 1/10th of the blood concentration. Some children with refractory secondary generalized epileptic seizures arising from cerebral malformations need concentrations above the usual therapeutic ranges for adequate seizure control. In this situation saliva levels can be measured weekly (or even more often). Some of these children seem to be able to tolerate saliva levels of 9–12 µmol/l for long periods.

Saliva levels, or the more technically difficult measurement of free phenytoin in plasma, are necessary when phenytoin is given with a drug such as sodium valproate, which displaces it from its protein binding.

Carbamazepine

This is certainly a level-dependent drug, but there are difficulties because all active metabolites are not normally measured. The authors tend to titrate this drug against toxic symptoms rather than rely upon measured levels. If levels are measured, it will be found that quite low levels are associated with toxicity at the start of treatment, but much higher levels tolerated later.

Ethosuximide

This is a level-dependent drug in which there is no binding to plasma proteins and so the saliva level equals the blood level. The toxic level (in the sense of the level at which adverse neurological symptoms develop) varies considerably between individuals. The therapeutic range is much wider than usually stated in that some individuals need high concentrations to abolish their absences or other ethosuximide-responsive seizures. Obviously this can only apply to those in whom the toxic level is even higher.

Sodium valproate

Levels of this drug are often measured and 'therapeutic ranges' quoted, but it is not established that sodium valproate is a level-dependent drug. A measurement may be made to check compliance, and on rare occasions to document the level in severe toxicity, but level measurements (as opposed to mg/kg dose levels) do not seem helpful in clinical practice.

Other drugs

Measurement of benzodiazepine levels are possible in some centres but in general do not seem helpful. Acetazolamide level is not practical but the acid-base status can be monitored as a measure of toxicity. Corticosteroids, as used in epileptic encephalopathies, probably are not level-dependent.

Monitoring in acute situations

Those who use phenytoin loading in status epilepticus will need repeated and rapid phenytoin analysis, but will also need continuous ECG and blood pressure monitoring if doses of up to 30 mg/kg (albeit slowly) are employed.

Indications for drug monitoring

In this list ↑ indicates that the sample should be taken when the level is expected to be at its peak, ↓ indicates that the sample should be obtained when the level is expected to be at its trough, and * indicates that the sample should be obtained at the time of an 'unexpected' seizure.

1. *Neonates.* (↑ ↓) Metabolic handing and fluctuations of levels tend to be considerable in the first weeks of life.
2. *The child is too young to show toxic symptoms* (↑).
3. The child is too handicapped to show toxic symptoms (↑). This and the preceding are situations in which carbamazepine levels may be of value.
4. *Suspicion of toxicity* (↑).
5. *When the therapeutic ratio is low*, that is, when the level required for seizure control is very close to the level at which toxic symptoms are manifest. However, with carbamazepine in the older child who is not physically handicapped the authors prefer to go by symptoms rather than measured level.
6. *Phenytoin therapy*, in all patients. The higher the level, the more frequent must be the sampling.
7. *Interfering drugs.* When more than one drug is needed for seizure control or when other drugs are being given which may alter the metabolism of the drug in question.
8. *Compliance* (*). A random level can also be done at the time of a consultation but on the whole only a zero level of a drug indicates that it is not being taken.
9. *Persistence of seizures* despite proper therapy (* ↓).
10. *'Breakthrough' after previous control* (* ↓). The metabolic handling of drugs may alter over the years and of course children get heavier, but it is always important to confirm that 'relapse' after a seizure-free interval is genuine, as opposed, for example, to convulsive syncope or psychic pseudoepileptic seizures.
11. *Before stopping an apparently ineffective treatment* (↓).

12. *Before stopping a drug in supposed complete remission*. There is an arguable indication for this practice, in that if the same seizures later recur, one knows the (maximum) therapeutic level.

Summary

Time and money should not be wasted in monitoring drug levels when this is not helpful. However, when monitoring is necessary the laboratory must be prepared to perform frequent analyses, accept saliva when appropriate, and provide answers within hours rather than days.

Further reading

Vajda, F. J. E. and Aicardi, J. (1983) Reassessment of the concept of a therapeutic range of anticonvulsant plasma levels. *Developmental Medicine and Child Neurology*, **25**, 660–671

Chapter 12

Diagnosis by therapeutic trial

An important part of neurological investigation is the diagnostic therapeutic trial, especially as a positive response commonly allows sustained
improvement. Table 12.1 lists some of the more important diagnostic
trials in which the administered agent is more or less specific. The list
could be expanded to include trials of other vitamins such as riboflavin
or thiamine in mitochondrial disorders (e.g. lipid myopathy) and
vitamin B_{12} in acidosis (methylmalonic acidaemia).

'Therapeutic trial' of antiepileptic drugs is *not* to be recommended as
part of the diagnosis of epilepsy.

Further reading

Goutières, F. and Aicardi, J. (1985) Atypical presentations of pyridoxine-dependent
seizures: a treatable cause of epilepsy in infants. *Annals of Neurology*, **17**, 117–120
Ouvrier, R. A. (1978) Progressive dystonia with marked diurnal fluctuation. *Annals of
Neurology*, **4**, 412–418
Wolf, B., Grier, R. E., Allen, R. J. *et al.* (1983) Phenotypic variation in biotinidase
deficiency. *Journal of Pediatrics*, **103**, 233–237

Table 12.1 Therapeutic trials

Test	Indications	Precautions	Interpretation
Pyridoxine			
1. Intravenous	Intractable neonatal epileptic seizures with EEG spikes	Have naloxone available in case of opiate reaction. Give 50 mg while EEG running	Spikes cease in pyridoxine dependency but exceptions occur
2. Oral	Intractable epilepsy of unknown origin, any type, onset up to age 18 months, especially if bouts of status	Oral pyridoxine 100 mg/day–48 h minimum	Abolition of seizures may indicate pyridoxine responsiveness. Several trials may be necessary for this to be convincing
Edrophonium	Floppy neonate, Suspect myasthenia	Consider: 1. Video recording procedure 2. Nerve stimulation during 1 mg (neonate) to 5 mg subcutaneously or i.m. observing change in muscle	Most varieties of myasthenia respond. Neostigmine 0.1 mg/kg i.m. with atropine allows longer period of evaluation
Biotin	Developmental delay, hypotonia, especially progressive ± myoclonic jerks ± seizures ± alopecia ± rash (no need to demonstrate acidosis or organic aciduria)	Oral 10 mg daily for 1 week – continue if symptoms remit	Remission suggests biotinidase deficiency: confirm by enzyme assay in serum (no need to stop biotin)
L-dopa	'Toe-walking', 'spastic' diplegia', dystonia, fluctuating or otherwise, juvenile Parkinsonism	CSF homovanillic acid may be estimated beforehand but not essential. Low dose e.g. 100 mg/day used, titrating to response	Marked reduction of dystonia indicates dopa responsiveness

Part 2

Disorders or diseases

Chapter 13

The neonate

The neonate is fragile. Selection of investigations has to be careful and conservative, even more so than in the case of the older child.

Neurological tests in the newborn

Brief comments about the application of neurological tests to the newborn follow.

Electroencephalography

The EEG varies markedly with gestational age between waking, quiet sleep and active sleep. Interpretation is not possible unless gestational age and sleep/wake state is known. 'Standard' EEGs are of limited value. Cassette EEG recording is in some ways more satisfactory, but in available systems it is not easy to observe the current EEG except by using a special modification which displays the signal transiently on a TV screen. Power spectral analysis systems allow frequency changes to be observed and so can detect sleep cycles and seizures, but normally do not have a facility for the observer to see the current raw EEG, and the recordings are not easy to interpret. The cerebral function analysing monitor (CFAM) has the advantage of being able to write out raw EEG whether at regular intervals or on demand. An important distinction has to be made between the discontinuous EEG of the normal premature baby in quiet sleep (tracé alternans) and pathological burst-suppression (suppression-burst) of serious consequence. In brief, the suppression in the latter situation is 'flatter' and longer and less likely to be altered by sensory stimuli or change in sleep/wake state.

Nerve conduction and EMG

Nerve conduction velocity mirrors gestational age, but the test is rarely of clinical value except in the diagnosis of the rare severe cogenital hypomyelinating polyneuropathy. More valuable is the actual muscle potential response to nerve stimulation, since this may be the main abnormality in a floppy baby with severe spinal muscular atrophy. EMG may be difficult to interpret, particularly in the more immobile baby.

Evoked potentials

All the types of evoked potential can be elicited from the neonatal brain, but in practice only the brain-stem auditory evoked potential has unquestioned value in the detection of auditory impairment.

Electroretinogram (ERG)

This is easily recordable in the term neonate using surface, foil or contact lens electrodes, and is helpful in the diagnosis of certain genetic disorders (see Table 3.1).

Skull X-ray

This is of limited value except when there is suspicion of fractures or craniosynostosis.

Cranial ultrasound

Ultrasound is excellent for the demonstration of fluid–parenchyma interfaces, and the greatest value of the technique is that it may be safely repeated as often as necessary. It has limitations in part because of the variability of operators. Misleading information may be obtained even in the best hands. For example, the presence of haemorrhages which are easily seen has little prognostic importance, whereas periventricular leucomalacia with its severe consequences is often sonically invisible.

CT scan

The necessity for moving the baby makes this a much more traumatic examination for the neonate than ultrasound. Furthermore, the normal appearances, which vary with gestational age, make for difficulties in interpretation. For example, large areas of the white matter have a normally 'hypodense' appearance which may be misinterpreted as abnormal. CT scan is superior to ultrasound in defining lesions in the brain parenchyma, subdural and subarachnoid spaces, and posterior fossa.

Magnetic resonance imaging

MRI brain imaging is superior to CT scan in demonstrating the posterior fossa and recent infarcts but transport, long scan time, and difficulties in monitoring the infant make it unsuitable for sick neonates. When combined with plain spine X-rays it is ideal for evaluation of infants with suspect spinal cord lesions, e.g. trauma and malformations.

CSF pressure

Debate continues as to whether non-invasive methods of pressure measurement are reliable for clinical monitoring. The recently described modification of the fontanometer method is promising but requires confirmation. Normal values have been established for neonates (0.0.–5.7 mmHg., mean 2.8 mmHg.) by direct measurement.

Newer tests

Doppler studies attempt to measure flow velocity in cerebral arteries. Research methods for studying flow, oxidation and metabolism include infrared transmission spectroscopy, NMR spectroscopy, and PET scanning. The clinical value of such studies is not yet known, but the potential is exciting.

Asphyxia looms large in the neurology of the newborn, but the real value of investigations in determining the severity and the outcome is not clear. Moreover, what appears to be related to asphyxia may have another explanation. The same applies to prematurity, and indeed to neonates with dysmorphic features and apparent malformation syndromes. The following clinical settings illustrate the approach to investigations.

Clinical settings

Seizures

(a) Seizures in a well neonate

Glucose, calcium and magnesium determinations and correction of deficits are routine. Pyridoxine load (50–100 mg) will always be given if seizures persist. True partial epileptic seizures which persist and are confirmed by EEG may indicate a malformation detectable on CT if not on ultrasound.

(b) Seizures in an ill neonate

Lumbar puncture will be performed as part of a 'septic screen' to determine if there is pyogenic meningitis or subarachnoid haemorrhage. Other clinical clues may suggest prenatal infection, but in any case it is important to have virus cultures and blood for initial titres. Ultrasound will reveal intracerebral haemorrhage but may miss subdural haemorrhages; a subdural tap with a short bevelled needled may be less traumatic for the baby than a trip to the CT scanner. Routine prophylaxis should prevent haemorrhage due to vitamin K deficiency, but the admittedly rare explanation of alpha-l-antitrypsin deficiency is often not sought. Continuous EEG recording should determine whether the seizures are epileptic or not. Many of the tonic and 'subtle' episodes in ill neonates which were previously thought to be epileptic seizures are no longer recognized as such.

If the EEG shows a burst suppression pattern (with 'flat' interludes between high-voltage discharges), and particularly if something resembling a hiccup occurs with each high-voltage burst, then blood and CSF glycine estimation must be done to confirm *glycine encephalopathy*. In this disorder ('non-ketotic hyperglycinaemia') the diagnostic finding is an increased CSF : plasma glycine ratio of 0.1 or more, against a norml of 0.025 or less. Liver biopsy can then be obtained and frozen for specific enzymatic studies. If the degree of illness is out of proportion to the severity of, say, putative asphyxia, and particularly if there are metabolic clues (hypoglycaemia, low urea, acidosis or alkalosis) then plasma ammonia, plasma and urinary amino acids, plasma pyruvate and lactate, and urinary organic acids and orotic acid should be estimated immediately. Protein restriction and vitamin therapy may be given pending the results.

Repeated EEG or, more simply, continuous EEG by for example CFAM gives an additional measure of the progress of the neonate with a metabolic disorder.

Optic nerve hypoplasia with hypopituitarism (with or without agenesis of the septum pellucidum) may present with seizures due to hypoglycaemia. Clinical clues are prolonged jaundice, nystagmus and optic hypoplasia. Cerebral ultrasound and/or CT scan may show absence of the septum pellucidum; tests of hypothalamic–pituitary function will clarify.

(c) Unexplained refractory seizures

These should prompt consideration of the following disorders.

Certain peroxisomal disorders presenting with neonatal seizures may have very little in the way of dysmorphic features, and may need special investigations for confirmation (*see* Chapter 10). Clinical clues in the neonatal period include extreme nuchal hypotonia, large metopic suture, and markedly delayed bone age with or without patellar calcification. Additional suggestive evidence is obtained by electroretinography and brain-stem auditory evoked responses, both of which are likely to be severely impaired.

Molybdenum cofactor deficiency usually presents with seizures and opisthotonus ± dysmorphism in the first month. Very low plasma and urinary urate will prompt analysis of urinary sulphite, sulphate and

S-sulphocysteine, and plasma and urinary xanthine and hypoxanthine, followed by specific enzyme assay in fibroblasts.

Brain malformations, especially migration disorders, may not have much in the the way of dysmorphism nor be detectable on cerebral ultrasound. In lissencephaly the characteristic EEG will not be seen until later in the first year, and diagnosis depends on CT or MRI scan.

The dysmorphic neonate

Chromosomes are routinely evaluated in the dysmorphic neonate, and attempts made at syndrome identification. Prometaphase banding should be delayed for a few months. However, in a number of rare metabolic disorders affecting the nervous system the neonate may have a dysmorphic appearance and a non-metabolic malformation may be mistakenly diagnosed. Coarsening of the facial features, gum hypertrophy, hepatosplenomegaly, unexplained illness, and the features earlier detailed of a peroxisomopathy (Chapter 10) are clues which should stimulate further testing. Mucolipidosis I (sialidosis), mucolipidosis II (I-cell disease), multiple sulphatase deficiency, fumarase deficiency, and glutaric aciduria type II are examples. Investigations include skeletal survey, lysosomal enzymes including neuraminidase, and urinary oligosaccharides and organic acids. Defective ERG and BAER will suggest a peroxisomal disorder and the special biochemical investigations required (*see* Chapter 10).

Arthrogryposis multiplex congenita

In a small number of cases the cause will be clinically apparent in the infant (e.g. trisomy 18, neural-tube defects) or the mother (e.g. myotonic dystrophy). However, more often there are no clinical clues to aetiology, and the following tests should be considered in an attempt to establish a neurogenic or myogenic basis for the disorder: creatine kinase, EMG, nerve conduction studies, muscle histology, chromosomes, and cerebral ultrasound.

Floppy neonate with feeding and/or respiratory difficulties

As in the case of seizures in the neonate, it is easy to attribute floppiness or weakness to preceding perinatal asphyxia. Clinical clues however may point to other aetiologies and investigations are then confirmatory. For example, facial diplegia and inability to suck in the neonate may be due to congenital myotonic dystrophy or one of the congenital myopathies; if the right diaphragm is markedly elevated, the diagnosis of congenital myotonic dystrophy is further supported; if the baby's mother is unable to bury her eyelashes on request, the diagnosis is virtually certain. Formal confirmation of that diagnosis would be by EMG of the mother, in the first dorsal interosseous muscle of the hand.

The approach of thinking about 'where is the lesion?' is helpful and may be translated into four clinical settings:

1. Ill, floppy baby

Investigations will be microbiological tests, including CSF examination, brain ultrasound, plasma ammonia, plasma and urine amino acids, and urine organic acids. Particularly if epileptic seizures are present, tests directed towards defects of peroxisomal fatty acid oxidation will be in order (*see* Chapter 10).

Intrapartum cervical cord injury may present as an ill, floppy baby mistakenly thought to be asphyxiated without an additional lesion. (*See below* under 'Weakness sparing the face').

2. Axial hypotonia without limb weakness

The Prader–Willi syndrome will be suggested by the increased stickiness of the saliva. Investigation by chromosome analysis using prometaphase banding, looking for the 15 q 12 deletion is not helpful in adding confidence to imparting the diagnosis to the parents at an early stage, since this study is technically difficult in the neonate.

Peroxisomal very long-chain fatty acid defect investigations are as detailed elsewhere (Chapter 10).

Brain malformations occasionally present in this way. Ultrasound and/or CT scan may clarify.

3. General weakness

Myasthenia. When maternal myasthenia is present, little difficulty arises. *Investigations*: The intravenous edrophonium (Tensilon) test does not always give a clear-cut response. The use of neostigmine is preferable, giving longer time to observe changes in the baby. EMG should be carried out with repetitive nerve stimulation at various rates. A marked decrement of the action potential should be detected at 2 Hz.

Botulism. In this situation the weakness will not develop until the age of 10 days or later. *Investigations*: The EMG response to repetitive nerve stimulation is the opposite from that seen in myasthenia, with an incremental response, the action potential increasing by more than 20% at high stimulation rates (20–50 Hz). The EMG itself may show 'myopathic' features, but this is not evidence of a primary muscle disease. Microbiological evidence of infection with Clostridium will confirm the diagnosis.

Congenital dystrophies and myopathies. *Investigations*: Maternal examination and EMG confirms myotonic dystrophy as indicated previously. Elevated serum creatine kinase is not helpful in the first 10 days of life but if found later will assist in the recognition of some cases of congenital muscular dystrophy. EMG is of limited value in supporting the diagnosis. The best confirmatory test is needle biopsy of muscle using a 4 mm Bergstrom needle, the specimen being processed for histochemistry and electronmicroscopy. The procedure may be performed in an incubator under local anaesthetic.

If one is thinking through these investigations, confusion should not usually arise, but it has to be borne in mind that on the one hand a brain imaging abnormality in the form of ventricular dilatation may be found in conditions in which the major involvement is in the muscle (such as in myotonic dystrophy and centronuclear myopathy), and on the other hand muscle biopsy abnormalities may be detected in disorders in which the major disturbance is in the brain (such as the Warburg syndrome with type II lissencephaly and hydrocephalus, and in peroxisomal deficiency disorders).

4. Weakness sparing the face

While facial weakness may be not very obvious in some of the above conditions such as congenital muscular dystrophy, in the following three groups of disorders, weakness above the neck is more often absent.

Cervical cord damage. Pre- or intrapartum injury or cervical cord arteriovenous malformation or congenital cord tumour are possibilities. Neonates with intrapartum cervical cord damage will be ill at birth and often develop temporary generalized oedema. Birth asphyxia may coexist and lead to diagnostic confusion. Careful clinical and neurological examination should define the site of the lesion in these various cases. *Investigations*: Although there is little data at present, it is likely that MR imaging of the cervical cord will be the ultimate investigation of choice in these circumstances. CT myelography is good at showing the lesion, but does not alter management.

Spinal muscular atrophy (Werdnig–Hoffman disease). *Investigations*: EMG may not be particularly helpful. It may be normal, silent (due to absence of muscle contraction), or show unusual spontaneous activity generated by motor units discharging at 5–15 Hz at rest. Fibrillations and large long-duration polyphasic motor unit potentials may not be present early on. More helpful is an examination of the motor action potential in nerve conduction studies. The muscle action potential is likely to be either absent or greatly diminished due to loss of anterior horn cells. The motor nerve conduction velocity may be delayed. Muscle biopsy can at first appear entirely normal, or all the fibres may be very small (about 10 μm in diameter). An important contribution of muscle biopsy is to allow the recognition of a completely different diagnosis.

Peripheral neuropathy. Demyelinating peripheral neuropathy is exceedingly rare in the neonate. Congenital hypomyelinating neuropathy presents with severe hypotonia, feeding and respiratory difficulties, and often limb deformities. *Investigations*: Motor nerve conduction velocity will be markedly less than that expected for gestational age ($<$ 5 metres per second). CSF protein is elevated. Sural nerve biopsy shows virtual absence of myelin.

Prediction of neurological handicap

Studies of neurological investigations in the neonate seldom address the question of handicap prediction in terms of sensitivity, specificity and positive or negative predictive value. In the difficult domain of the preterm infant, evaluation of the available evidence suggests that the cranial ultrasound finding of persistent ventricular dilatation (at term-corrected age) is a simply obtained predictor of cerebral palsy, with a low false-positive rate. However, normal ultrasound findings do not imply normal neurodevelopmental outcome.

In the term infant, difficulties in outcome prediction most often arise in the context of suspected hypoxic-ischaemic encephalopathy. Various electrophysiological, imaging, and cerebral artery Doppler studies are sensitive predictors of handicap, but lack specificity.

The optimal choice of investigations for aiding neurological prediction remains to be determined.

Case illustrations

See 1.5, 4.1, 8.2 and 10.1.

Further reading

Adams, C., Babyn, P. S. and Logan, W. J. (1988) Spinal cord birth injury: value of computed tomographic myelography. *Pediatric Neurology*, **4**, 105–109

Archer, L. N., Levens, M. I. and Evans, D. H. (1986) Cerebral artery doppler ultrasonography for prediction of outcome after perinatal asphyxia. *Lancet*, **2**, 1116–1118

Banker, B. Q. (1986) Congenital deformities. In *Myology, Basic and Clinical*, (ed. G. Engel and B. Q. Banker), McGraw–Hill Book Co., New York, pp. 2109–2159

Bennett, M. J., Pollitt, R. J., Laird, J. M. *et al.* (1987) Lethal multiple acyl-CoA dehydrogenase deficiency with dysmorphic features. *Journal of Inherited Metabolic Disease*, **10**, 95–96

Bozynski, M. E. A., Nelson, M. N., Genaze, D. *et al.* (1988) Cranial ultrasonography and the prediction of cerebral palsy in infants weighing $\leqslant$ 1200 grams at birth. *Developmental Medicine and Child Neurology*, **30**, 342–348

Burch, M., Fensom, A. H., Jackson, M. *et al.* (1986) Multiple sulphatase deficiency presenting at birth. *Clinical Genetics*, **30**, 409–415

Hislop, J. E., Dubowitz, L. M. S., Kaiser, A. M. *et al.* (1988) Outcome of infants shunted for post-haemorrhagic ventricular dilatation. *Developmental Medicine and Child Neurology*, **30**, 451–456

Kaiser, A. M. and Whitelaw, A. G. L. (1986) Normal cerebrospinal fluid pressure in the newborn. *Neuropediatrics*, **17**, 100–102

Mehta, A., Wright, B. M. and Shore, C. (1988) Clinical fontanometry in the newborn. *Lancet*, **1**, 754–756

Mizrahi, E. M. (1987) Neonatal seizures: problems in diagnosis and classification. *Epilepsia*, **28** (Suppl 1), S46–S55

Roesel, R. A., Bowyer, R., Blankenship, P. R. and Hommes, F. A. (1986) Combined xanthine and sulphite oxidase defect due to a deficiency of molybdenum cofactor. *Journal of Inherited Metabolic Disease*, **9**, 343–347

Scher, M. S., Bergman, I., Ahdab-Barmada, M. and Fria, Th. (1986) Neurophysiological and anatomical correlations in neonatal non-ketotic hyperglycinemia. *Neuropediatrics*, **17**, 137–143

Volpe, J. J. (1987) *Neurology of the Newborn*, 2nd edn, W. B. Saunders Co, Philadephia

Chapter 14

Floppy baby

In this chapter we deal with the investigation of infants and very young children whose dominant feature is floppiness or hypotonia. Some aspects of the very earliest presentation have been dealt with in Chapter 13, The Neonate. A prime example is the Prader–Willi syndrome, in which hypotonia declines steadily with age during the first year of life. The most common setting for milder hypotonia is the child with one of the familial variants of normal motor development, in particular the bottom-shuffler. Such cases were previously called benign congenital hypotonia. No investigations are indicated. Another relatively common situation where hypotonia may dominate is Down's syndrome, where the diagnosis is obvious on other grounds. In the various conditions with prominent pathological hypotonia, the nature of the disorder may be suspected from the history and the non-neurological features, and the site of the lesion from careful clinical neurological examination. We now list these disorders with reference to the site of the lesion, and conclude with a discussion of the investigations in disorders in which several mechanisms are involved.

Brain

Atonic cerebral palsy and profound mental handicap

This is a common situation. Tendon reflexes are present if carefully elicited. Some of these children have a history of severe hypoxic ischaemic damage and presumption of lesions in basal ganglia and/or brain stem, but imaging investigations such as high-resolution CT scan may not add important information. High-resolution imaging is indicated to look for malformations and other prenatal deformations, since some will have a substantial genetic recurrence risk and some will not. Chromosome studies are indicated, despite the low yield. Other investigations which may be considered depend upon the level of responsiveness and are discussed elsewhere in the section on 'Unresponsive infants' in Chapter 18.

Ataxic cerebral palsy

Congenital cerebellar disorders may be suspected by clinical features such as jerky pursuit eye movements. CT scan may show cerebellar hypoplasia, and MRI will show the details of this more precisely. Other disorders which are mainly manifest later in childhood are discussed in the chapter on 'Peculiar Gait' (20).

Cord

The site and extent of cord lesions should be determined by neurological examination, but very extensive indolent spinal cord tumours may prove difficult. MR imaging will be the investigation of choice, with CT metrizamide myelography a more invasive alternative.

Anterior horn cell

Spinal muscular atrophy

Werdnig–Hoffmann disease. To a very great degree this diagnosis is clinical, but it is important not to get it wrong. Some detailed investigations are in order, but it is worth explaining to the parents that one is not waiting for the last investigation result (which is commonly the muscle biopsy report) to give positive evidence of the disease. It is better to indicate that one is adding some additional pieces to the jig-saw puzzle and that the only really important results of investigations will be the unexpected discovery of a disorder which is either treatable or has a much better prognosis.

Investigations: EMG may be a valuable diagnostic aid in experienced hands. In the study of Packer *et al.* (1982) on hypotonic infants under the age of one year, neurogenic disorders (of which 20 out of 21 were Werdnig–Hoffmann disease) were retrospectively diagnosed by EMG with a sensitivity and specificity of about 90% and a predictive value of 95%. In that study the criteria of neurogenic EMG abnormality were reduced interference pattern, early recruitment of large motor units, long duration potentials, and increased incidence of spontaneous activity. That study did not find the presence of fibrillation potentials of diagnostic help, these being present also in infants with myopathic disorders. The longer duration motor unit potential with decreased interference patterns on effort were the most sensitive indicators of anterior horn cell disease. Others have found regularly recurring motor unit activity every 5–15 seconds. Motor units may be small and short or longer and larger but are not giant.

Motor nerve conduction may be slightly slow, but more likely is a reduction in the amplitude of the muscle evoked potential which may be absent in the more severely affected infant. The authors would recommend needle or conchotome biopsy in all cases in which there is sufficient muscle bulk, primarily to exclude alternative specific diagnoses. In practice, the muscle biopsy appearance may be normal early on in the condition, may show groups of small fibres, or may show a uniform appearance of small fibres in the specimen obtained. If the nerve conduction velocity undertaken at the time of the EMG is markedly rather than mildly reduced, then the CSF should be examined for protein elevation and the question of the alternative diagnosis of polyneuropathy explored.

Intermediate spinal muscular atrophy. EMG and muscle biopsy findings are similar in this variant, which is usually distinguishable by the timing of onset of symptoms (after 6 months; the patient achieves sitting but fails to stand or walk). There is emerging evidence that EMG or muscle biopsy evidence of reinnervation indicates a better prognosis. Motor nerve conduction velocity is normal. ECG shows baseline tremor (due to limb muscle fasciculation) in most cases.

Peripheral nerve

Hereditary neuropathies

Hereditary motor and sensory neuropathy may very rarely present at this age. Motor nerve conduction velocity will be very slow with prolonged distal latencies. CSF protein may be increased. Tests for metachromatic leucodystrophy (*see below*) are indicated if there is any diagnostic doubt.

Congenital hypomyelinating neuropathy has a clinical appearance closely resembling Werdnig–Hoffmann disease but on investigation, nerve conduction velocity is markedly slow. Sural nerve biopsy shows impaired myelination. Milder forms of this disorder probably exist.

Riley–Day syndrome. This sensory neuropathy syndrome should be completely diagnosable on clinical grounds alone. An absent flare response to intradermal histamine (0.03 ml of 1:1000 histamine phosphate) will support the diagnosis, although it is not pathognomonic (*see* Chapter 6).

Chronic (relapsing) polyneuropathy

This should be differentiated clinically from a hereditary motor and sensory neuropathy by the more obviously acquired nature of the symptoms. CSF albumin and IgG will be increased. Nerve conduction velocities will not be as slow, conduction block is likely to be present, the muscle action potential may be reduced and the sensory action potential absent. It is extremely rare for this disorder to present in infancy, but being treatable it must not be forgotten.

Metachromatic leucodystrophy

In due course the mechanism is mixed (that is to say, there is more than one site of the lesion). Children may present at the end of the first year with predominant hypotonia and virtually a pure polyneuropathy. CSF protein rises and the motor nerve conduction velocity reaches a plateau and then slows progressively. Leucocyte and fibroblast arylsulphatase A deficiency and renal epithelial intracellular metachromatic granules will confirm the diagnosis.

Krabbe's disease

These infants may be briefly hypotonic when peripheral neuropathy dominates. CSF protein is elevated, nerve conduction velocity is very slow, galactocerebroside-beta-galactosidase is absent in leucocytes, using a natural substrate.

Neuromuscular junction

Myasthenia

Familial infantile myasthenia is most likely to present as a floppy baby. If in doubt about the results of the edrophonium (Tensilon) test, neostigmine (Prostigmin) 0.5 mg with atropine should clarify. The decremental muscle action potential response to repetitive nerve stimulation which is reversed by neostigmine will provide further confirmation. Single-fibre EMG and more complex muscle studies can be considered if the diagnosis has not been clarified by the previous method.

Botulism

See 'The Neonate' (Chapter 13).

Muscle

Myotonic dystrophy

When a case of the congenital type presents in this way, maternal EMG myotonia will confirm the diagnosis.

Congenital muscular dystrophy

The creatine kinase will often be increased to moderate levels up to about 1000 units per litre. EMG may show myopathic features. Muscle biopsy shows a rather mild appearing 'dystrophy' with much fat and fibrous tissue between muscle fibres. In a proportion of cases CT scan shows a remarkable hypodensity of central white matter with or without functional cerebral impairment. The brain findings in autosomal recessive congenital muscular dystrophies vary to a considerable degree in different parts of the world, with different CT scan findings.

Infantile myositis

This rare disorder is treatable by corticosteroids, so diagnosis is important. However, the diagnosis is more often suggested as a possibility by the histopathologist when the true diagnosis is congenital muscular dystrophy showing more than usual inflammatory changes around the muscle fibres.

Congenital myopathy

Although to a certain extent the diagnosis of some of the congenital myopathies may be suggested by clinical features, diagnosis is by needle or conchotome biopsy of muscle, processed for light microscopy, histochemistry and electronmicroscopy. If a disorder of glycogen metabolism is suggested, the various enzymes which may be deficient in one or other glycogenosis can then be determined.

Tendoskeletal

Neurological examination will be normal in the various conditions which may masquerade as a floppy baby, such as congenital laxity of the ligaments, forms of Ehlers–Danlos syndrome, and osteogenesis imperfecta. Neurological investigations are not indicated.

Mixed mechanisms

Brain–eye–muscle disorders

Warburg (congenital hyrocephalus with ocular abnormalities) and other similar syndromes will be confirmed by defective electroretinogram, CT scan, and muscle biopsy appearance.

Lowe's syndrome

The dysmorphism with corneal and lens changes should allow recognition. Renal tubular leak, including amino acids and glycosaminoglycan (chondroitin-4-sulphate), and cytoplasmic membrane-bound electron-lucent vacuoles on skin biopsy confirm the diagnosis.

Peroxisomopathies

See section on peroxisomal disorders in Chapter 10.

Pompe's disease

In glycogenosis type II, hypotonia may be as profound as in the above three groups of conditions, with involvement of brain, anterior horn cells, and muscles. The waxy appearance of the skin should suggest the diagnosis, supported by the ECG, which includes short PR interval, high R waves, and T-wave inversion. Needle biopsy of muscle shows the expected increase in glycogen, and the diagnosis is confirmed by enzyme assay of acid maltase in leucocytes. EMG may show changes of denervation because of anterior horn cell involvement, but this investigation is superfluous (*see* Case 6.1).

Mitochondrial disorders

Central nervous system, peripheral nerve, and muscle may be involved in various disorders of the electron transport chain. Findings on investigation are sometimes subtle and inconstant. Investigational abnormalities include increased blood lactate and pyruvate, renal tubular leak including amino acids, elevated CSF protein and lactate, slow motor and sensory nerve conduction, low densities in basal ganglia on CT scan, and in some cases ragged red fibres on needle biopsy of muscle stained by Gomori trichrome. Special studies of mitochondria confirm the diagnosis, which may be further clarified by studies of the mitochondria in cultured fibroblasts.

Neuroaxonal dystrophy

Sometimes it can be difficult to show that this is actually a progressive disorder, and parents might distort the history so that the child seems to be a 'floppy baby' of unknown cause. A mixture of subtle eye movement abnormalities and upper and lower motor neuron signs suggest the diagnosis. Confirmation by investigation is difficult. EMG shows signs of denervation with normal nerve conduction velocity and normal CSF protein. The EEG shows diffuse fast (beta) activity but this does not necessarily appear before the age of 2 years. Skin and conjunctival biopsies may show dystrophic axons with spheroids, but such tests may be negative in definite cases. Nerve or open muscle end-plate biopsy are alternatives. Brain biopsy using esterase stain as well as electronmicroscopy can further establish the diagnosis, but the condition of the child is for a long time such that this procedure may not be thought justifiable.

Metabolic

Extrinsic

Rarely, infants are poisoned chronically without the physician's knowledge, to a state of fluctuating floppiness. Toxicological investigations are in order.

Intrinsic

Biotinidase deficiency is the best known of the organic acidurias leading to dominant hypotonia. The therapeutic potential makes investigation by urinary organic acid analysis and plasma biotinidase essential when such a diagnosis is possible.

Other organic acidaemias such as methylmalonic acidaemia which may be B_{12} responsive, may present with hypotonia, vomiting, and failure to thrive before fulminant acidosis develops.

A potentially important autistic syndrome due to a novel purine disorder (adenylosuccinase deficiency) is described in Chapter 18. A urine test is available.

In carbohydrate deficient glycoprotein disease, first described by Jaeken, hypotonia is associated with fat pads on the buttocks and convergent strabismus and cerebellar atrophy. The CSF protein is increased later. Blood thyroid binding globulin (low) is the simplest screening test. Low disialotransferrrin confirms.

(*Hypothyroidism* is an important treatable metabolic cause of hypotonia, but other features dominate the clinical picture.)

Non-specific

In many other systemic disorders presenting in infancy, such as malabsorption or renal tubular acidosis, hypotonia may be a prominent feature. Investigations will depend on the general clinical examination.

Summary

A large proportion of the available neurological investigations is necessary in the total range of children who present as floppy babies. Systematic clinical analysis is therefore necessary to limit the investigations to those most likely to help in curative therapy, interim management, and genetic advice.

Case illustrations

See 2.1, 6.1, 10.2 and 10.5

Further reading

Axelrod, F and Pearson, J. (1984) Congenital sensory neuropathies. Diagnostic distinction from familial dysautonomia. *American Journal of Diseases of Children*, **138**, 947–958

Bordarier, C., Aicardi, J. and Goutières, F. (1984) Congenital hydrocephalus and eye abnormalities with severe developmental brain defects: Warburg's syndrome. *Annals of Neurology*, **16**, 60–65

Di Mauro, S., Bonilla, E., Zeviani, M. *et al.* (1987) Mitochondrial myopathies. *Journal of Inherited Metabolic Disease*, **10**, 113–128

Echenne, B., Arthuis, M., Billard, C. *et al.* (1986) Congenital muscular dystrophy and cerebral CT scan anomalies. *Journal of the Neurological Sciences*, **75**, 7–22

Fukuyama, Y., Osawa, M. and Suzuki, S. (1981) Congenital progressive muscular dystrophy of the Fukuyama type – clinical, genetic and pathological considerations. *Brain and Development*, **3**, 1–30

Goebel, H. H., Zeman, W. and De Myer, W. (1976) Peripheral motor and sensory neuropathy of early childhood simulating Werdnig–Hoffmann disease. *Neuropädiatrie*, **7**, 182–195

Guzzetta, F., Ferrier, G. and Lyon, G. (1982) Congenital hypomyelinating polyneuropathy. Pathological findings compared with polyneuropathies starting later in life. *Brain*, **105**, 395–416

Hagberg, B. and Westerberg, B. (1983) The nosology of genetic peripheral neuropathies in Swedish children. *Developmental Medicine and Child Neurology*, **25**, 3–18

Jaeken, J., Eggermont, E. and Stibler, H. (1987) An apparent homozygous x-linked disorder with carbohydrate-deficient serum glycoproteins. *Lancet*, **2**, 1398

McMenamin, J. B., Becker, L. E. and Murphy, E. G. (1982) Congenital muscular dystrophy: a clinicopathologic report of 24 cases. *Journal of Pediatrics*, **100**, 692–697

Moosa, A. and Dubowitz, V. (1976) Motor nerve conduction velocity in spinal muscular atrophy of childhood. *Archives of Disease in Childhood*, **51**, 974–977

Packer, R. J., Brown, M. J. and Berman, P. H. (1982) The diagnostic value of electromyography in infantile hypotonia. *American Journal of Diseases of Children*, **136**, 1057–1059

Pasternak, J. F., Fulling, K., Nelson, J. and Prensky, A. L. (1982) An infant with chronic relapsing polyneuropathy responsive to steroids. *Developmental Medicine and Child Neurology*, **24**, 504–510

Ramaekers, V. T. L., Lake, B. D., Harding, B *et al.* (1987) Diagnostic difficulties in infantile neuroaxonal dystrophy. A clinicopathologic study of eight cases. *Neuropediatrics*, **18**, 170–175

Thompson, C. E. (1982) Infantile myositis. *Developmental Medicine and Child Neurology*, **24**, 307–313

Thompson, C. E. (1985) Pitfalls in muscle biopsy of hypotonic children. *Developmental Medicine and Child Neurology*, **27**, 675–677

Wolf, B., Grier, R. E., Allen, R. J. *et al.* (1983) Phenotypic variation in biotinidase deficiency. *Journal of Pediatrics*, **103**, 233–237

Chapter 15

Abnormal head size

The need for further investigations in a child with an abnormally sized head is influenced by the head size of the parents, the head size of the child at birth, the trajectory of head growth on the head circumference chart, and the presence or otherwise of neurodevelopmental disorder or dysmorphic features.

When parents and child are plotted on a 0–18 year head circumference chart, the child's head circumference should not normally be on a higher percentile than the parent with the larger head, nor smaller than the parent with the smaller head. Dominantly inherited large and small heads occur without additional abnormality, but there is also a dominantly inherited microcephaly with normal CT scan and mild intellectual retardation.

The size of the head at birth and the trajectory thereafter give some clue as to the process underlying the abnormal head size, in that a change in percentile may indicate a progressive process. However the distinction is not clear and one can have either an acceleration or a deceleration in head growth with an apparently static disorder.

The explanation may be deduced from the clinical appearance of the child so that syndrome identification will be followed by lysosomal enzyme studies or chromosome analysis, depending on the appearance. The presence of marked neurodevelopmental difficulties will merit further investigation irrespective of the head size, and several of the cerebral malformations can have large, normal, or small head circumferences.

Small head

If microcephaly is defined as a head circumference of more than three standard deviations below the mean, then a good 25% will have autosomal recessive inheritance, so diagnosis is important.

Small head present at birth

The principal investigations are:

3-view skull X-ray. This will demonstrate extensive synostosis (if this diagnosis cannot be made clinically). Only gross intracranial calcification may be detected.

Maternal phenylalanine level.

Throat swab and urine culture for viruses (rubella and CMV) obtained within the first 2 weeks of birth. Negative IgM titres do not necessarily exclude such infections.

Chromosome karyotype.

Ultrasound imaging of brain. Evidence of gross malformation or destructive changes may be detected.

In cases where the diagnosis is not certain we would follow up with an EEG and CT scan after about 6 months. MRI would be requested if the CT seemed abnormal but if the exact abnormality were not clear.

When there is failure to thrive, with or without epileptic seizures, investigations for a mitochondrial disorder should be considered (*see* Chapter 10).

Microcephaly evolving in infancy

The precise clinical details will influence the choice of investigations, but the following are commonly necessary:

Amino acids, for missed phenylketonuria in particular.

Organic acids, looking for the pattern seen in biotinidase deficiency.

Plasma biotinidase.

Chromosomes, including prometaphase banding and flow karyotyping for chromosome 15, for Angelman syndrome.

EEG, looking for high-voltage alpha-frequency (or beta-frequency) activity in general or focal pachygyria, or posterior spike wave in Angelman syndrome or less specific abnormalities. The appearance of burst-suppression or hypsarrhythmia will not be expected in the absence of considerable developmental impairment.

CT scan. Various malformations or destructive lesions may be evident. Features of tuberous sclerosis would only be expected if there had already been a considerable period of epileptic activity.

CSF. Lymphocytosis may indicate Aicardi–Goutières syndrome. Blood and CSF glucose (see Recent advances) Appendix II.

Acquired microcephaly with apparent neurodevelopmental regression

Both pathologically static and truly degenerative disorders may present in this manner.

EEG may detect hypsarrhythmia which underlies the regression in various malformations. CT scan will verify.

No tests are available for confirming the diagnosis of Rett syndrome in a girl, but development will never have been totally normal.

The electroretinogram (ERG) is an essential investigation when infantile neuronal ceroid lipofuscinosis is suspected. However, the amplitude of the ERG may be slow to decline. The authors do not regard urinary dolichol estimation as of value. Electronmicroscopic granular inclusions in skin or conjunctiva may not be detected, and rectal biopsy may be necessary (Case 3.1).

Macrocephaly

Macrocephaly should probably be regarded as a head circumference of three or more standard deviations above the mean. Many take the cut-off point as two standard deviations, or even regard a head size over the 90th percentile as large, so that many normal heads are investigated. The commonest cause of a large head is familial 'megalencephaly'.

Large head at birth

Brain ultrasound will normally clarify the explanation for the large head in so far that it will indicate which structures or fluid spaces are enlarged. Additional CT scanning is indicated if unexplained hydrocephalus has been detected. CT is also indicated when it is uncertain whether there is holoprosencephaly or a giant percallosal cyst, since the latter may be amenable to treatment. It is important to recognize the benign nature of the extracerebral fluid collections which may be detected on imaging the child with a large brain.

Toxoplasma titres are indicated in unexplained hydrocephalus.

A rare cause of enlargement of the head due to obstructive hydrocephalus is the Warburg syndrome. Hydrocephalus is usually apparent at birth, but occasionally may not be clinically obvious for some months. The ocular findings and unresponsiveness from birth will suggest the diagnosis, which is important because of its autosomal recessive inheritance. Investigations show: *electroretinogram*: flat; *CT scan*: lissencephaly with white matter hypodensity; *muscle biopsy* ; myopathy; and *brain biopsy* (carried out at time of ventricular shunting procedure): four-layered cortex.

Large head appearing later

Other clinical features may suggest further investigations. For example, external signs of tuberous sclerosis or neurofibromatosis may be present in a child with evolving megalencephaly. Evidence of storage disease (corneal clouding, visceromegaly or dysostosis) may direct investigations into one or other lysosomal enzyme deficiency. Delayed bone age will suggest hypothyroidism.

A large brain with excessive external cerebrospinal fluid on ultrasound or on CT scan is one of the more common clinical problems. This may be seen sporadically or in the context of familial megalencephaly. In the absence of regression a conservative approach is indicated without excessive CT imaging.

Aqueduct stenosis with or without a slow growing tumour may lead to accelerated head growth over years, and investigation is by CT with or without MR imaging. In osteopetrosis the head size is often increased, with wobbly eyes and progressive visual loss. Ultrasound or CT scan will not be informative (the lateral ventricles may be slightly large) but X-ray of any bone will confirm the diagnosis (*see* Case 4.10).

Enlarging head with irritability and crying and loss of interest and vision is a feature of Canavan's disease. CT shows striking hypodensity of all cerebral white matter. There is aspartoacylase deficiency in fibroblasts and n-acetylaspartic aciduria. A large head may be associated with other organic acidurias.

Spasticity and seizures and an enlarging head and a somewhat similar CT scan appearance are found in Alexander's disease, which so far can only be diagnosed by brain biopsy.

It is often a necessary prerequisite to CT scanning that the physician recognizes the possibility of a disorder which may need prompt treatment. It is worth emphasizing that in chronic increased intracranial pressure in the younger child, an enlarging head and (once the anterior fontanelle has closed) a cracked-pot percussion note over the coronal sutures are more reliable signs than the appearance of the optic disc.

Case illustrations

See 1.5, 3.1, 4.3, 9.2 and 10.2

Further reading

Bordarier, C., Aicardi, J. and Goutières, F. (1984) Congenital hydrocephalus and eye abnormalities with severe developmental brain defects: Warburg's syndrome. *Annals of Neurology*, **16**, 60–65

Hamza, M., Bodensteiner, J. B., Noorani, P. A. and Barnes, P. D. (1987) Benign extracerebral fluid collections: a cause of macrocrania in infancy. *Pediatric Neurology*, **3**, 218–221

Jaworski, M., Hersh, J. H., Donat, J. *et al.* (1986) Computed tomography of the head in the evaluation of microcephaly. *Pediatrics*, **78**, 1064–1069

Matalon, R., Michals, K., Sebesta, D. *et al.* (1988) Aspartoacylase deficiency and n-acetylaspartic aciduria in patients with Canavan disease. *American Journal of Medical Genetics*, **29**, 463–471

Chapter 16

Wobbly-eyed baby

The baby who seems not to see well or has apparent nystagmus or whose eyes wobble for reasons as yet unexplained will commonly be referred by the paediatrician to the ophthalmologist or to the paediatric neurologist, but it is helpful to have some kind of plan of investigation. It is convenient to go through the additional clinical pictures which may suggest further specific tests.

Wobbly eyes as an isolated finding

The younger the baby, the more difficult it is to be sure that this is so. However, if the neurological examination suggests congenital brainstem nystagmus (for example normal optokinetic nystagmus in the vertical plane while absent in the horizontal), then no further investigations are indicated.

Wobbly eyes and visual defect

Additional clinical features may clarify the situation.

Photophobia or Optic nerve hypoplasia

Albinism will be obvious. Ocular albinism less so. In total colour-vision defect or achromatopsia (in which, as in albinism, the visual acuity improves under subdued lighting) ophthalmological referral is essential, and diagnosis may be by red-light flicker ERG as a test of cone function. It must be re-emphasized that if such children are tested only with standard ERG and VEP they may be thought to have an optic-nerve defect because of the reduced VEP amplitude which in fact reflects loss of macular cone output. A similar situation obtains in osteopetrosis (*see below*) in the early stage before the ERG becomes flat. In neurologically normal babies, optic nerve hypoplasia may occur as an isolated finding or in association with hypothalamic hypopituitarism. In all cases, high-resolution CT scan is desirable not just to see the dimensions of the optic nerves, but to document abnormalities of midline structures around the third ventricle. Endocrinological tests are indicated when there is a midline CT abnormality or a history of neonatal jaundice and/or hypoglycaemia.

Optic atrophy

In the absence of signs of neurofibromatosis, optic atrophy is rare as an isolated finding in infancy. While high-resolution CT may be indicated to look for a mass lesion near the chiasm, osteopetrosis must be excluded by X-ray of any bone. Commonly the eyes in this condition look normal.

Eyes appear normal

A normal fundoscopic appearance may be seen in three situations: congenital retinal blindness, osteopetrosis, and cortical blindness. Pure Leber's congenital amaurosis is detected by the extinction of the flash ERG. In the severe form of osteopetrosis clinical clues to the cause of the wobbling eyes may be minimal, without hepatosplenomegaly or overt skeletal deformity. Flash ERG is at first normal, but the VEP amplitude is low due to cone dystrophy. Later the ERG becomes flat. CT scan will be unhelpful, but X-ray of any bone confirms the diagnosis. In cortical blindness, for example that due to prenatal occipital infarction, posterior spike wave is expected on EEG, with loss of occipital parenchyma on CT scan.

Wobbly eyes, neurological defect and *some* vision

A number of unrelated disorders have motor rather than sensory defects of eye movement, with additional neurological impairment.

Neonatal onset burst of panting tachypnoea may signify Joubert's syndrome, in which CT scan will show aplasia of the cerebellar vermis. Some infants with Joubert's syndrome also have a retinal defect (*see below*).

An appearance resembling dystonic cerebral palsy with rapid pendular eye movements and without, at that stage, clear visual defect may, in a boy, indicate sudanophilic X-linked leucodystrophy or Pelizaeus–Merzbacher disease. The same sort of rotatory nystagmus with a more slowly progressive spasticity is another manifestation of this disorder. Diagnosis is by the characteristic appearance of white matter on T2 weighted MR imaging.

Acquired chaotic or oscillatory nystagmus accompanied by acquired cerebellar ataxia or myoclonus may be described as 'dancing-eyes syndrome'. Investigations are in order to detect an extracerebral occult neuroblastoma by urinary homovanillic acid excretion and general imaging studies. Vision is normal.

Associated failure to thrive with feeding difficulty or respiratory irregularity and areflexia suggests one of the forms of Leigh's disease. Mitochondrial investigations are indicated (*see* Chapter 10).

Wobbly eyes, neurological defect, low vision

Acquired prenatal encephalopathies of various kinds may produce this clinical picture. Third-trimester hypoxic-ischaemic encephalopathy (for example after death of an identical twin *in utero*, or in association with isoimmune thrombocytopenic purpura), or premature delivery may be followed by optic-nerve hypoplasia. In the case of the premature infant, retrolental fibroplasia may complicate matters further. Second-generation CT scan is adequate to show cerebral defects in the more gross of these acquired encephalopathies, but high-resolution CT scan is necessary to detect the late effect of periventricular leucomalacia.

A number of rare autosomal recessive disorders present in this manner, and all have a very low ERG as one of the investigational findings. Epileptic seizures or hypotonia may be early features of both the Warburg syndrome and of various peroxisomal disorders in which there is a defect of the oxidation of very long-chain fatty acids. In Warburg's syndrome the diagnosis will be suggested by the ophthalmoscopic finding of retinal aplasia and other ocular abnormalities (such as microphthalmia, or corneal or lenticular opacities). High-resolution CT scan will demonstrate the lissencephaly with associated white-matter hypodensity and obstructive hydrocephalus. Muscle biopsy may show dystrophic or myopathic changes. In the group of peroxisomal disorders, many neurological and extraneuronal abnormalities are present, and are further discussed in Chapter 10. Joubert's syndrome with prominent panting tachypnoea may be associated with congenital retinal blindness with or without peroxisomal dysfunction. Finally, non-specific Leber's amaurosis may be associated with other cerebral malformations (and also with renal dysplasia), so that 'cortical blindness' should not be assumed when a baby with an abnormal brain appears not to see.

Case illustrations

See 4.2, 4.10, 8.2 and 10.2

Further reading

Bordarier, C., Aicardi, J. and Goutières, F. (1984) Congenital hydrocephalus and eye abnormalities with severe developmental brain defects: Warburg's syndrome. *Annals of Neurology*, **16**, 60–65

Boulloche, J. and Aicardi, J. (1986) Pelizaeus–Merzbacher disease: clinical and nosological study. *Journal of Child Neurology*, **1**, 233–239

Costin, G. and Murphree, L. (1985) Hypothalamic–pituitary function in children with optic nerve hypoplasia. *American Journal of Diseases of Children*, **139**, 249–254

King, M. D., Dugeon, J. and Stephenson, J. B. P. (1984) Joubert's syndrome with retinal dysplasia: neonatal tachypnoea as the clue to a genetic brain–eye malformation. *Archives of Disease in Childhood*, **59**, 709–718

Pavone, L., Gullotta, F., Grasso, S. and Vannucchi, C. (1986) Hydrocephalus, lissencephaly, ocular abnormalities and congenital muscular dystrophy. A Warburg syndrome variant. *Neuropediatrics*, **17**, 206–211

Stephenson, J. B. P. (1988) Inherited peroxisomal disorders involving the nervous system. *Archives of Disease in Childhood*, **63**, 767–770

Chapter 17

The child who is not speaking

Speech may not develop, or be slow to develop, or may develop and then be lost.

Speech that has not developed adequately

The solution to this common problem usually depends on clinical evaluation including specialist help from the speech therapist and the psychologist. Deafness, sensorineural or otherwise, is of obvious importance, but once deafness has been diagnosed that is not the end of the evaluation, as cognitive defects may coexist, as in congenital rubella and CMV infection.

If in the absence of deafness there is a defect both of language comprehension and symbolic understanding, then investigations are in order as discussed in Chapter 18, Mental handicap, but creatine kinase estimation and chromosome studies with folate-deficient medium will detect the most common causes (Duchenne muscular dystrophy and fragile X syndrome).

Even if the language comprehension defect is an isolated one, it is worth estimating creatine kinase.

Acquired loss of speech

Once again deafness is a common cause, in this case being acquired as with pyogenic meningitis. This should not present diagnostic difficulties unless the ataxia from labyrinthine damage is regarded as cerebellar rather than vestibular. Very gradual fall off after initial slowing of speech and language development is the picture of Sanfilippo disease, and suspicion of this warrants 24-h urine collection for heparan sulphate.

Special tests are not at the time of writing available to clarify the diagnosis of Rett syndrome (loss of purposeful hand movement, agitated behaviour, and jerky unsteadiness in a girl with a previous developmental ceiling of about 10 months) nor disintegrative psychosis (acquired autistic behaviour with loss of symbolic understanding in a boy – or rarely a girl – with previous supposedly normal development). Acquired loss of speech may be attributed to elective mutism or to acquired deafness when this is in fact unsubstantiated, the actual diagnosis being Landau–Kleffner syndrome.

Landau–Kleffner syndrome

Otherwise called epileptic aphasia or epileptic auditory agnosia, this disorder need not be associated with any overt epileptic seizures, and if it is they may be few and trivial, often being hemifacial–salivatory as in benign focal epilepsy of childhood. The only helpful test is the EEG which shows frequent spike complexes. The spikes are commonly bilateral, although on the whole not symmetrical and they may be more frequent on one side, particularly on the left. Their site is in mid-head regions near or posterior to the Rolandic strip. The frequency of these spikes is usually such that there is no difficulty in seeing many of them during a standard recording session. The importance of recognizing this condition or group of conditions lies not only in the help the diagnosis gives to the child's family and educational management, but also because in some cases abolition of the EEG spikes by corticosteroids leads to simultaneous improvement in auditory interpretation and language comprehension.

Of the various other disorders which are discussed later in Chapter 25 on Regression, late infantile neuronal ceroid lipofuscinosis in particular may present with loss of speech, but ataxia and dementia are usually apparent at this time, and seizures develop later.

Case illustrations

See 1.4 and 10.4

Further reading

Beaumanoir, A. (1985) The Landau–Kleffner syndrome. In *Epileptic Syndromes in Infancy, Childhood and Adolescence* (ed. J. Roger, C. Dravet, M. Bureau, F. E. Dreifuss and P. Wolf). John Libbey, London, pp. 181–191

Chapter 18

Mental handicap and autism

Mental handicap

The diagnosis of the cause of mental handicap is within the province of paediatric neurology, but it is beyond the scope of this book to discuss all known possibilities. It is important that prenatal infections be diagnosed in the neonatal period, otherwise these cases may continue to be regarded as 'unknown'. Static disorders with dysmorphic features may be recognized with the help of computer programs set up for this purpose.

In this chapter we try to give some help with a choice of tests for investigating mental handicap when the diagnosis is not obvious. Microcephaly is discussed in Chapter 15, and other clinical situations elsewhere. If from clinical data one is able to obtain a clue to the most probable disorder, then one can move to the appropriate test in the first instance. The type of test is listed in the succeeding Tables, along with the disorders detected by that test, and comment on the interpretation of the finding. The mentally handicapping disorders have been divided firstly into those in which retardation is profound and development minimal, often with seizures and either hypotonia or spasticity (Table 18.1), secondly into those with severe isolated mental retardation (Table 18.2) and, thirdly mild mental handicap (Table 18.3). The divisions are somewhat arbitrary, and overlaps occur.

Finally we discuss neurological investigations in 'autism', under some clinical presentations.

Two aspects should be emphasized; first the frequency of fragile X as a 'cause', secondly the large number of children in whom diagnosis is currently impossible.

Autism

Much research is under way into the biological basis of autism and autistic behaviour. A few remarks are in order on the present state of neurological investigations.

Table 18.1 Profoundly retarded, poorly responsive

Investigation	Disorders detected	Comment
EEG	Lissencephaly	Very high voltage in the alpha or beta range. Less obvious in first months, may have intermittent suppression and be reported as 'modified hypsarrhythmia'
	Glycine encephalopathy	Suppression-burst EEG: hiccups associated with the spike bursts
	Ohtahara's (early infantile epileptic) encephalopathy	Burst suppression, but no increase in CSF glycine and normal blood : CSF glycine ratio
ERG	Leber's, Joubert's	Flat ERG and cerebral malformation
	Peroxisomopathy	Various defects of VLCFA beta-oxidation
BAEP	CMV, rubella	Should have been diagnosed by virus culture in neonatal period
	Peroxisomopathy	Defects of beta oxidation
High-resolution CT scan	Various malformations	Migrational and other defects
	White-matter hypoplasia	Loss of white matter in all areas
	Prenatal destructive lesions	Loss of white matter around the trigone in periventricular leucomalacia, or muiltiple holes, or hydranencephaly after prenatal death of monozygotic twin, etc.
Chromosome G-banding	Trisomies, deletions	Well-known defects should have been detected by morphological appearance, but this test is indicated in case something novel turns up
Plasma amino acids	Tetrahydrobiopterin deficiency	Phenylalanine raised, followed by studies of pterin metabolism. Should be detected by neonatal screening
Plasma uric acid	Molybdenum cofactor deficiency	Refractory seizures, spastic quadriplegia. Very low uric acid. Excess excretion of sulphite, thiosulphate and s-sulphocysteine on urine amino acid analysis. Sulphite stick test may be negative
DHAP–AT VLCFA urine and plasma bile acids	Peroxisomopathy	*See* Peroxisomal disorders, Chapter 10

Table 18.2 Severe mental handicap

Investigation	Disorder detected	Comment
'Routine' EEG	Angelman's syndrome	Posterior high-voltage rhythmic 3–4/s, sharp components on passive eye closure
	Pachygyria	High-voltage alpha/beta frequency activity
CT brain scan	Malformations	Low yield – more likely if handicap very severe. Tuberous sclerosis findings possible if spasms/epilepsy already evident
T_3, T_4, TSH	Hypothyroidism	Diagnosis should be obvious if handicap severe
Chromosomes: G banding	Various chromosomal disorders	Diagnostic finding unlikely unless child dysmorphic or (less so) has severe epilepsy
Chromosomes: low-folate medium	Fragile X	Test girls also; dysmorphism may be slight. Essential investigation unless another sound explanation is obtained
Chromosomes: prometaphase for 15	Angelman's (happy puppet) syndrome	EEG should indicate diagnosis before morphology (Prader-Willi syndrome with similar site deletion will be evident on neonatal history)
Plasma amino acids	PKU and homocystinuria	May have been missed or not tested for in neonatal period
Plasma amino acids in mother	Maternal PKU	Usually microcephaly
Urine amino acids	Homocystinuria	Plasma amino acids may be normal
24-h urine for heparan sulphate	Sanfilippo disease	Dysmorphism may be slight and progression so slow that mental handicap diagnosed
24-h urine for free sialic acid	Salla disease	May not have dysmorphism or prominent motor signs early on
Skin biopsy for lysosomal inclusions	Salla disease	Progression of disorder may be minimal

Overtreatment of epilepsy, for example with high-dose clonazapam in infancy, may give a false appearance of severe mental handicap for which there is no test, except that if the dose of the drug is reduced then the mental handicap is reversed.

In 'pure' autism the yield from neurological investigations is low. There is recent evidence that MR imaging may show small cerebellar roof nuclei. The importance of this finding to management is not yet clear.

When language disorder is prominent, particularly if comprehension is fluctuating, then standard EEG looking for spike complexes in

Table 18.3 Mild mental handicap

Investigation	Disorder detected	Comment
'Routine' EEG	Landau–Kleffner variants	Asymmetrical spike-and-wave complexes in mid-head regions. Language comprehension difficulty predominates. History of regression may not be obvious
	Unexpected absences	Symptomatic bursts of regular spike and wave may have been overlooked
Chromosomes: low-folate medium	X-linked mental retardation	Fragile X. This is an essential investigation unless another sound explanation has been obtained, in girls as well as boys
Creatine kinase	Duchenne muscular dystrophy	Language difficulty may predominate. Cognitive and language difficulties may be the presenting feature in preschool children before the weakness becomes apparent
	Female Duchenne carriers	Some of these girls are mentally handicapped
Plasma calcium	Pseudohypoparathyroidism	Moon face, but phenotype subtle. Calcifications on CT
Plasma and urine amino acids	Homocystinuria	May be vitamin responsive (other aminoacidopathies are not likely to present as isolated mental handicap)

head regions is indicated, and sleep EEG may show continuous slow spike-and-wave in quiet sleep.

Search for fragile X using a low-folate medium in chromosome karyotyping is important (despite the low yield) because of the genetic implications.

With additional mental handicap, or evidence of dementia, neurological investigations are more likely to yield diagnostic results.

Mental handicap with autistic behaviour

Infantile spasms

Miscellaneous disorders in which infantile spasms feature are a common antecedent to autistic behaviour. Of these, tuberous sclerosis may at first be overlooked. EEG spikes are likely to be asymmetrical. The subependymal calcified nodules on CT scan usually confirm.

New purine disorder

A well-defined autistic syndrome with static profound mental handicap has been described by Jaeken and Van den Berge (1984). These children, boys or girls, are hypotonic from infancy and have very little mental development. They have 'autistic' behaviour from the age of a few months. They tend to have only brief eye contact, and have repetitive stereotypies, laughing to themselves or grinding their teeth. They do not have any dysmorphism, they are normocephalic and they do not have epilepsy. Investigations revealed normal EEG, VEP, BAEP, SEP, EMG, and NCV. CT scans showed hypoplasia of the cerebellum, especially of the vermis, in all children. The CSF protein was reported as low, being 0.11–0.17 g/l but in fact this level is normal (*see* Appendix). Other studies, of skeletal maturation, general imaging, standard biochemistry, and chromosome analysis were normal. Specialized biochemistry showed abnormal purines in CSF and urine, and the enzyme adenylosuccinase was absent on renal biopsy. A new urine test is available as outlined in Chapter 10. We have detailed the initial description of this disorder because it has been sufficient to allow the retrospective detection of several other affected children, with the condition, which is probably autosomal recessive and not excessively rare.

Regressive disorders

Regressive disorders will be discussed elsewhere (Chapter 25) but three examples for which tests are available deserve mention. If hypsarrhythmia is not accompanied by obvious infantile spasms the regression may seem unexplained, but routine EEG should easily clarify.

Untreated phenylketonuria, if missed in the neonatal period, may be detected by estimation of plasma amino acids.

Infantile neuronal ceroid lipofuscinosis may manifest at the end of the first year and in the second year as apparent autism, and declining retinal function may be misinterpreted as gaze avoidance. Support for the diagnosis needs serial EEG to show declining amplitude, CT to confirm atrophy, and histopathological evidence of autofluorescent material and granular membrane-bound inclusions on electronmicroscopy of buffy coat cells, skin, or rectum.

Case illustrations

See 1.2, 1.3, 1.5, 3.1, 4.1, 4.4, 4.6, 9.2 and 10.4.

Further reading

Aicardi, J. (1986) *Epilepsy in Children*, Raven Press, New York

Aukett, A., Bennett, M. J. and Hosking, G. P. (1988) Molybdenum cofactor deficiency: an easily missed inborn error of metabolism. *Developmental Medicine and Child Neurology*, **30**, 531–535

Aula, P., Autio, S., Raivio, K. O. *et al.* (1979) 'Salla disease' a new lysosomal disorder. *Archives of Neurology*, **36**, 88–94

Boyd, S. G., Harden, A. and Patton, M. A. (1988) The EEG in the early diagnosis of Angelman (Happy Puppet syndrome). *European Journal of Pediatrics*, **147**, 508–513

Chattha, A. S. and Richardson, E. P. Jr (1977) Cerebral white matter hypoplasia. *Archives of Neurology*, **34**, 137–141

Gastaut, H., Pinsard, N., Raybaud, Ch. *et al.* (1987) Lissencephaly (agyria–pachygyria): clinical findings and serial EEG studies. *Developmental Medicine and Child Neurology*, **29**, 167–180

Jaeken, J. and Van der Berge, G. (1984) An infantile autistic syndrome characterised by the presence of succinylpurines in body fluids. *Lancet*, **2**, 1058–1061

Renlund, M. (1984) Clinical and laboratory diagnosis of Salla disease in infancy and childhood. *Journal of Pediatrics*, **104**, 232–236

Simmonds, H. A., Fairbanks, L. D., Morris, G. S. *et al.* (1987) Central nervous system dysfunction and erythrocyte guanosine triphosphate depletion in purine nucleoside phosphorylase deficiency. *Archives of Disease in Childhood*, **62**, 385–391

Stephenson, J. B. P. (1988) Inherited peroxisomal disorders involving the nervous system. *Archives of Disease in Childhood*, **63**, 767–770

Van de Kamp, J. J. P., Niermeijer, M. F., von Figura, K. and Giesberts, M. A. H. (1981) Clinical heterogeneity and clinical variability in the Sanfillippo syndrome (types A, B and C). *Clinical Genetics*, **20**, 152–160

Winter, R. M., Baraitser, M. and Douglas, J. M. (1984) A computerised data base for the diagnosis of rare dysmorphic syndromes. *Journal of Medical Genetics*, **21**, 121–123

Chapter 19

'Cerebral palsy'

In this chapter we discuss the investigations which might be helpful in various categories of true cerebral palsy (disorders of posture and movement due to static lesions of the developing brain) and in a number of those conditions which may mimic cerebral palsy more or less closely.

Investigations in cerebral palsy are mainly indicated for genetic purposes, but a precise diagnosis can allow improved management and in some cases dramatic clinical benefit in a child previously judged to have cerebral palsy.

Spastic diplegia and tetraplegia

In the absence of a clear-cut aetiology, the appearance of a defined lesion on CT scan is comforting with respect to correctness of diagnosis. Destructive lesions and malformations may be visible. If the CT seems to be abnormal but it is not clear what is amiss, then MR imaging may clarify the lesion. It is important to consider spinal-cord tumours when pure paraplegia is present, and proceed to spine imaging and perhaps sensory evoked potentials.

Hyperekplexia may masquerade as tetraplegia in the first months of life. The babies may be very stiff and irritable, with thumbs in palms. Gradual improvement and the demonstration of an excessive transient startle response on EEG with surface EMG will support the diagnosis.

Early manifesting *Duchenne muscular dystrophy* is commonly mis-diagnosed as diplegia when neurological examination is insufficiently detailed. Creatine kinase and cDNA studies confirm the diagnosis (muscle biopsy is often not necessary – *see* p. 177).

Dopa-sensitive dystonia (Segawa's syndrome) may simulate diplegia when tip-toe gait is present at the onset of walking and when diurnal fluctuation with evening worsening is absent or subtle. Ideally, the condition should be diagnosed by finding a reduced CSF homovanillic (HVA) concentration. In practice, HVA estimations may be difficult to obtain, and a trial of L-dopa (*see* Chapter 12) is indicated when this treatable disorder is a diagnostic possibility. The CT scan will be normal.

Familial spastic paraparesis has attracted no diagnostic tests at the time of writing.

Aicardi-Goutières syndrome may for a while simulate spastic tetraplegic cerebral palsy in early infancy (*see* p. 211).

Purine nucleoside phosphorylase (PNP) deficiency may initially present as a symmetrical or asymmetrical tetraparesis before evidence of T-cell deficiency is apparent. Diagnosis is suggested by extremely low plasma uric acid, further supported by extremely low urine uric acid and confirmed by PNP assay in red cells.

Leigh's disease may rarely present as a static paraparesis or ataxia but deterioration with infection is usual. The initial investigation is plasma and CSF pyruvate and lactate.

Spastic hemiplegia

CT scan of the brain is indicated when the explanation is not clear, to define the extent of the loss of cerebral tissue, and when the distinction between a static and a progressive lesion is uncertain.

Spinal-cord tumour in the cervical region may also masquerade as spastic hemiplegia, so spinal imaging is indicated when careful neurological examination makes this a realistic possibility.

Athetoid dystonic and atonic 'cerebral palsy'

Prader–Willi syndrome may initially lead to confusion because of the axial atonia and dystonic postures of the limbs. When positive, chromosome 15 studies will support the diagnosis.

Sandifer's syndrome, while it may itself complicate cerebral palsy later on, may masquerade as dystonic cerebral palsy early in life. The neck-twisting movements can be confirmed as resulting from gastro-oesophageal reflux by barium swallow and pH studies (possibly aided by radionuclide milk scan or oesophagoscopy), the diagnosis being further confirmed by the reversal of symptoms when gastro-oesophageal reflux is abolished by clinical management. It should be borne in mind that although bethanechol will commonly reverse reflux and thus 'cure' the dystonia, this drug may itself rarely lead to idiosyncratic dystonia.

Pelizaeus–Merzbacher disease in its classical X-linked form may masquerade as severe cerebral palsy due to perinatal asphyxia. Dystonic features may be prominent, with early rotatory nystagmus, optic atrophy, and often laryngeal stridor. EEG and CT scan are commonly normal, although the latter may show mild 'atrophy'. Visual evoked potentials and brain-stem auditory evoked responses are markedly diminished. MR imaging has been reported to show extensive abnormality of white matter on T2 weighted images so that the white matter looks 'white' rather than 'dark'. Diagnosis is important for genetic purposes.

Lesch–Nyhan syndrome is commonly diagnosed as cerebral palsy, because of the initial choreoathetosis at the end of the first year. Not only serum uric acid should be obtained, but also urine to determine if the urate:creatinine ratio is increased. Confirmation is by demonstrating a defect of red cell hypoxanthine–guanine phosphoribosyl transferase.

Glutaric aciduria type I should not cause diagnostic difficulty because the athetoid or dystonic state usually appears during or after some sort of febrile illness, but being potentially treatable, this diagnosis is important. Only a few laboratories may have the methods available to detect excess glutaric acid in the urine, at any rate when the child is not acutely ill. If the diagnosis is feasible, fibroblasts must be obtained and the specific enzyme glutaryl-CoA dehydrogenase assayed.

Ataxic cerebral palsy

Of all the varieties of cerebral palsy, this one is perhaps most likely to be diagnosed when in fact there is a progressive neurological disorder. However, the converse is equally possible. Once again, it is helpful to have satisfactory brain imaging (commonly CT) to demonstrate a presumptive static lesion such as cerebellar hypoplasia.

Of the treatable disorders which may sometimes masquerade as ataxic cerebral palsy, any form of hydrocephalus and indolent cerebellar tumour will be detected on the CT scan.

The progress of *ataxia telangiectasia* may be sufficiently slow to make this enter the differential diagnosis. The impaired saccadic eye movements and tiddley-wink tonsils will suggest the diagnosis, which is confirmed by a raised serum alphafetoprotein, and given added precision by the finding of chromosomal breakage and DNA repair abnormalities in cultured fibroblasts.

Metachromatic leucodystrophy may for a while confuse and is investigated as in Chapters 20 and 25.

Hexosaminidase A and B deficiency may present in this sort of way in one of its many guises. Cerebellar ataxia dominates and progression may be minimal. The enzyme deficiency will be first detected in leucocytes, and then further studies may be performed on fibroblasts.

Salla disease and variants. Steady development with prominent ataxia makes this an important diagnostic consideration. No consistent abnormalities are found in the various neurological investigations. Diagnosis is by finding increased (5–10-fold) free sialic acid in urine. Skin and conjunctival biopsies are expected to show cytoplasmic membrane-bound inclusions on electronmicroscopy.

Summary

Most cases of 'cerebral palsy' will have cerebral palsy, but it is important not to let this label prevent reconsideration of the diagnosis and appropriate investigations when the course is atypical.

Case illustrations

See 1.3, 5.3, 8.2 and 9.3.

Further reading

Aicardi, J. and Goutières, F. (1984) A progressive familial encephalopathy in infancy, with calcifications of the basal ganglia, and chronic cerebrospinal fluid lymphocytosis. *Annals of Neurology*, **15**, 49–54.

Boulloche, J. and Aicardi, J. (1986) Pelizaeus–Merzbacher disease: clinical and noso-logical study. *Journal of Child Neurology*, **1**, 233–239

Costeff, H., Gadoth, N., Mendelson, L. *et al.* (1987) Fluctuating dystonia responsive to levodopa. *Archives of Disease in Childhood*, **62**, 801–804

Deonna, T. (1986) Dopa-sensitive progressive dystonia of childhood with fluctuations of symptoms – Segawa's syndrome and possible variants. *Neuropediatrics*, **17**, 81–85

Haslam, R. H. A. (1975) Progressive cerebral palsy or spinal cord tumour. Two cases of mistaken identity. *Developmental Medicine and Child Neurology*, **17**, 232–237

Lingham, S., Wilson, J. and Hart, E. W. (1981) Hereditary stiff-baby syndrome. *American Journal of Diseases of Children*, **135**, 909–911

Nanayakkara, C. S. and Paton, J. Y. (1985) Sandifer syndrome: an overlooked diagnosis? *Developmental Medicine and Child Neurology*, **27**, 816–819

Ouvrier, R. A. (1978) Progressive dystonia with marked diurnal fluctuation. *Annals of Neurology*, **4**, 412–418

Shanks, D. E. and Wilson, W. G. (1988) Lobar holoprosencephaly presenting as spastic diplegia. *Developmental Medicine and Child Neurology*, **30**, 383–386

Simmonds, H. A., Fairbanks, L. D., Morris, G. S. *et al.* (1987) Central nervous system dysfunction and erythrocyte guanosine triphosphate depletion in purine nucleoside phosphorylase deficiency. *Archives of Disease in Childhood*, **62**, 385–391

Stutchfield, P., Edwards, M. A., Gray, R. G. F. *et al.* (1985) Glutaric aciduria type I misdiagnosed as Leigh's encephalopathy and cerebral palsy. *Developmental Medicine and Child Neurology*, **27**, 514–518

van Erven, P. M. M., Gabreels, F. J. M., Ruitenbeek, W. *et al.* (1987) Mitochondrial encephalomyopathy. Association with an NADH dehydrogenase deficiency. *Archives of Neurology*, **44**, 775–778

Ylitalo, V., Hagberg, B., Rapola, J. *et al.* (1986) Salla disease variants. Sialoylaciduric encephalopathy with increased sialidase activity in two non-Finnish children. *Neuropediatrics*, **17**, 44–47

Chapter 20

Peculiar gait

The first question is whether the peculiar gait seems to have a neurological basis. In many cases there are orthopaedic explanations, or benign variants of gait of no serious significance. The normal neurological examination, including running, getting off the floor and standing with eyes closed, together with intact tendon reflexes and flexor plantar responses, will be reassuring in this regard. It is extremely valuable to be able to tell from the history that the gait disorder is either static or progressive, but unfortunately it is quite often not possible to be certain. However, in this situation one can either wait and follow up, or undertake tests on the presumption that a progressive disorder may be present.

A more limited range of possibilities exists when there are clearly marked fluctuations or intervals of complete normality. Diurnal fluctuation occurs in Segawa's disease (discussed below) and intermittent ataxia may be a feature of inborn errors of metabolism (notably variants of maple syrup urine disease, isovaleric acidaemia, biotinidase deficiency, and urea cycle defects). Blood ammonia, lactate and pyruvate, plasma and urinary amino acids, and urinary organic acids may be measured during attacks.

It is helpful to attempt to clarify whether the disorder is one of weakness or spasticity or ataxia or dystonia. Difficulties arise with this oversimplified classification because more than one pattern of neurological abnormality may occur in the same disorder, and the type of abnormality may also vary within one disorder. For example, children with neuropathy may be weak on the one hand, and on the other may present with predominant ataxia.

Weakness

Duchenne muscular dystrophy (DMD)

Children with DMD who have not already presented with language delay will have a history of difficulty with running and climbing.

Toe-walking and the pattern of weakness should indicate the diagnosis. Early on, very brisk ankle jerks may suggest diplegia. EMG shows myopathic changes. Diagnosis is confirmed by creatine kinase (CK) of several thousand units per litre, and appropriate X p 21 deletion using intragenic cDNA probes (see Case 10.4). Muscle biopsy (with dystrophin assay) is reserved for those without detectable cDNA deletions.

Inflammatory myopathy

Juvenile dermatomyositis, when of insidious onset, may present in this way and is an important diagnosis, being eminently treatable. The diagnosis is essentially clinical, based on the triad of misery, violaceous rash (which may be subtle) and proximal weakness. Creatine kinase and/or muscle histology may be normal in up to one-third of cases, but EMG is invariably abnormal, showing features of myopathy and denervation. Creatine kinase is of no value in monitoring response to steroid treatment.

Rarely Coxsackie B infections may be chronic and confined to muscle. They may be sufficiently florid to manifest as myositis with appropriate biopsy findings, but may be more subtle. CK levels may be very high. Diagnosis is suggested by a persistently raised Coxsackie B IgM and confirmed by the presence of enteroviral RNA in the muscle biopsy. More than one needle or conchotome biopsy may have to be taken to detect this abnormality.

Becker muscular dystrophy

It has been until recently very difficult to distinguish more severe cases of Becker dystrophy from milder cases of Duchenne muscular dystrophy. It now seems that while the protein dystrophin is absent from Duchenne muscle, it is present but in reduced quantity in most cases of Becker dystrophy.

Other forms of muscular dystrophy

The pattern of weakness, CK, muscle histology, and application of gene probes may help in diagnosis.

The congenital myopathies

These are usually recognized long before a question of disturbance of gait arises and are distinguished by electronmicroscopy of biopsied muscle.

Spinal muscular atrophies (SMA)

Mild SMA may be confused with DMD, although there are various clinical differences. The CK may be mildly elevated but never to a range of several thousands. Confusion has occurred when intermediate elevations of 1000 IU are obtained. Such a value probably implies some form of dystrophy, not Duchenne. In electrophysiological testing, ECG commonly shows baseline tremor, signifying fasciculation; motor nerve conduction velocity is normal, muscle action potential may be reduced; EMG shows changes of denervation with reinnervation. Needle biopsy of quadriceps may show changes suggestive of denervation and reinnervation. Leucocyte enzymes: hexosaminidase A and B may be deficient in certain families, when other neurological features are present.

Distal spinal muscular atrophy

This disorder resembles hereditary motor and sensory neuropathy (HMSN II, *see below*) but has less upper-limb weakness, relative preservation of tendon reflexes, and normal clinical sensory examination. Motor nerve conduction velocity, sensory nerve conduction velocity, and sensory action potentials are normal; EMG shows evidence of chronic partial denervation.

Hereditary motor and sensory neuropathy types I and III

There is dispute as to whether HMSN I and HMSN III are different disorders. We will refer to them as HMSN I. CSF protein may be elevated but is usually not examined. Creatine kinase is normal. Motor conduction velocity is markedly delayed, with prolonged distal latency. Sensory conduction velocity is delayed or the action potential may not be recordable. EMG is normally not required, but will show changes of partial denervation.

Metachromatic leucodystrophy may closely resemble HMSN I. If in doubt, the range of tests for this disorder should be done, i.e. urine renal tubular cell metochromatic granules, and leucocyte and fibroblast arylsulphatase A.

Hereditary motor and sensory neuropathy type II

In this condition the motor nerve conduction velocity is normal or only slightly slow, the sensory conduction velocity is also normal or only slightly delayed, the sensory action potential may be small or absent. EMG shows evidence of chronic partial denervation in distal muscles. Sural nerve biopsy is usually not necessary in HMSN and should be reserved for those children with atypical findings and a negative family history.

Chronic relapsing polyneuropathy

This disorder may fluctuate little and have insidious onset. Findings on nerve conduction (Chapter 2), together with the increased CSF IgG and total protein will usually indicate the diagnosis without need for nerve biopsy.

Spinal dysraphism

Differences in the size and shape of the feet and/or superficial changes over the lumbar–sacral region will indicate this type of malformation. Spine X-ray will usually but not always be abnormal. CT myelography and/or MR examination will clarify the diagnosis.

Ataxia

Minor epileptic status

Drooling and alterations of behaviour and mentation should give a clue to this situation, which is confirmed by standard EEG showing continuous high-voltage, usually irregular, generalized spike and slow wave activity.

Chronic phenytoin intoxication

Disabling ataxia is still unfortunately seen in children with epilepsy on phenytoin therapy. Blood phenytoin level will be diagnostic. Occasionally when drug combinations are being used a high free phenytoin level is sufficient to cause ataxia without the total level being increased, but saliva estimation should clarify this. Otherwise formal free phenytoin estimation may be assayed in plasma.

Cerebellar hypoplasia

As in the case of the floppy baby, jerky ocular pursuit suggests this pathology, which CT (or better, MR imaging) will clarify.

Obstructive hydrocephalus

For this to present as a gait problem in the absence of a cerebral tumour the duration of the block is likely to have been long and the head size will be increased, with a cracked-pot percussion note. Lateral skull X-ray will confirm split sutures, and CT scan confirm the hydrocephalus. Small areas of calcification near the pineal gland may indicate that a tumour rather than simple aqueduct stenosis is responsible for the hydrocephalus.

Posterior fossa tumour

Symptoms of additional difficulties above the neck (vomiting, head tilt etc.) will prompt CT with contrast enhancement.

Basilar impression

Basilar impression or platybasia is an important treatable cause of ataxic gait. Clues may be neck pain and extensor plantar responses. Lateral skull X-ray with specific attention to the odontoid will allow the diagnosis, which may be missed if only brain CT scan is done.

Friedreich's ataxia

The willowy appearance of these children and the combination of neurological features makes the diagnosis virtually certain. It should be noted that they do not usually have pes cavus at presentation. The diagnosis is confirmed by (a) absent sural sensory evoked potentials, and (b) thickened septum on echocardiogram.

Ataxia telangiectasia

The peculiar head turning due to eye movement control defect suggests this disorder when conjunctival or ear-lobe telangiectasia are absent in early childhood. Alphafetoprotein increase confirms the diagnosis. Chromosomal aberrations and abnormal cellular responses to ionizing radiation are found in cultured fibroblasts; these tests are not necessary for diagnosis but are likely to have important implications for genetic counselling and prenatal diagnosis.

Hereditary motor and sensory neuropathies (see above)

Metachromatic leucodystrophy

Presentation with neuropathy may simulate ataxia, including Friedreich's ataxia (See Case 7.2).

Other neurometabolic disorders

Juvenile Sandhoff disease and juvenile GM 1 gangliosidosis may present with ataxia. Hexosaminidase A and B and beta-galactosidase determinations will clarify the diagnosis.

Abetalipoproteinaemia

A history of previous malabsorption will suggest this diagnosis. Neurological deficits should no longer occur now that it is known that vitamin

E administration will prevent their development. Diagnosis is by the finding of low serum cholesterol and total lipids and absent serum beta-lipoproteins.

Refsum's disease

The clinical features which include a demyelinating neuropathy should be clear enough to prompt phytanic acid estimation.

Hypothyroidism

This may present with various gait disturbances: thyroid function studies confirm the diagnosis.

Mitochondrial cytopathy

Affected children may have prominent disturbance of gait, but other clinical signs will suggest the diagnosis (Chapters 10 and 25).

Spasticity

Spastic diplegia

Spastic diplegia is a common outcome of survivors of low birthweight premature birth. If the perinatal history is normal and if one or other parent does not have extensor plantar responses (as in hereditary spastic paraplegia) a CT scan may be justified. A specific malformation such as lobar holoprosencephaly may be detected.

Basilar impression (platybasia)

Platybasia, discussed above, usually presents with dominant ataxia.

Spinal cord tumour

Cervical cord tumours may simulate diparesis or even hemiparesis. Progression, pain, fixed neck position, and upper limb signs will suggest the need for myelography/MR imaging.

Tumours at lower levels may be associated with scoliosis or back stiffness. They are particularly difficult to diagnose in a child who is already mentally handicapped for another reason (*see* case 4.6). Motor nerve stimulation may be impossible in the lower limbs with normal responses in upper limbs. Plain spine X-ray, carefully examined, is the first investigation, followed by CT myelography or MR imaging.

Segawa's disease (dopa-sensitive dystonia)

This may masqerade as spastic diplegia – see below.

Down's syndrome; Hunter's syndrome

Deterioration in gait which includes spastic paraparesis may occur in children with these disorders, due to lesions at the foramen magnum. Careful cervical spine X-rays may clarify the situation in Down's syndrome; in Hunter's syndrome MR imaging may be helpful.

Dystonia

Dystonia with diurnal fluctuations (Segawa's disease)

This disorder may present so early that it masquerades as a congenital diparesis. The characteristic history of normality in the morning (after sleep) and progression as the day goes on may be absent. It has to be suspected in a young child who variably walks on the toes in a rather diplegic manner without unequivocal extensor plantar responses. Testing for this disorder is by trial of L-dopa in small doses.

Torsion dystonia; hysteria

Either one may be mistaken for the other and specific non-clinical tests are not available. If Segawa's disease seems possible, testing by L-dopa trial is very worthwhile.

Case illustrations

See 1.3, 2.2, 2.3, 2.5, 3.2, 4.6, 4.8, 4.9, 5.3, 7.2, 9.1, 9.2, 9.3 and 10.4.

Further reading

Adams, C. and Green, S. (1986) Late onset hexosaminidase A and hexosaminidase A and B deficiency: family study and review. *Developmental Medicine and Child Neurology*, **28**, 236–243

Bowles, N. E., Dubowitz, V., Sewry, C. A. and Archard, L. C. (1987) Dermatomyositis, polymyositis and Coxsackie-B-virus infection. *Lancet*, **1**, 1004–1007

Buchtal, F. and Behse, F. (1977) Peroneal muscular atrophy (PMA) and related disorders. 1. Clinical manifestations as related to biopsy findings, nerve conduction and electromyography, *Brain*, **100**, 41–66

Dalakas, M. C. and Engel, W. K. (1981) Chronic relapsing (dysimmune) polyneuropathy: pathogenesis and treatment. *Annals of Neurology*, **9**, 134–145

Deonna, T. (1986) Dopa-sensitive progressive dystonia of childhood with fluctuations of symptoms – Segawa's syndrome and possible variants. *Neuropediatrics*, **17**, 81–85

Goel, K. M. and King, M. (1986) Dermatomyositis – polymyositis in children. *Scottish Medical Journal*, **31**, 15–19

Guzzetta, F., Ferriere, G. and Lyon, G. (1982) Congenital hypomyelinating polyneuropathy. Pathological findings compared with polyneuropathies starting later in life. *Brain*, **105**, 395–416

Harding, A. E. and Thomas, P. K. (1980a) Hereditary distal spinal muscular atrophy. *Journal of the Neurological Sciences*, **45**, 337–348

Harding, A. E. and Thomas, P. K. (1980b) The clinical features of hereditary motor and sensory neuropathy types I and II. *Brain*, **103**, 259–280

Hoffman, E. P., Fishbeck, K. H., Brown, R. H. *et al.* (1988) Characterisation of dystrophin in muscle biopsy specimens from patients with Duchenne's or Becker's muscular dystrophy. *New England Journal of Medicine*, **318**, 1363–1368

Ouvrier, R. A., McLeod, J. G., Morgan, G. J. *et al.* (1981) Hereditary motor and sensory neuropathy of neuronal type with onset in early childhood. *Journal of the Neurological Sciences*, **51**, 181–197

Parnes, S., Karpati, G., Carpenter, S. *et al.* (1985) Hexosaminidase–A deficiency presenting as atypical juvenile onset spinal muscular atrophy. *Archives of Neurology*, **42**, 1176–1180

Teodori, J. B. and Painter, M. J. (1984) Basilar impression in children. *Pediatrics*, **74**, 1097–1099

Chapter 21

Febrile seizures

What is a febrile seizure?

Febrile seizures are common and will come into the ambit of almost all doctors dealing with children. Considerable difficulty and controversy surrounds the question of which tests are appropriate, and in which circumstances, when a child has a seizure with fever. Although much is yet to be learned about febrile seizures, it is important to recognize the complexity of the subject, so that one can individualize the investigations in a specific patient. It is important neither to make blanket recommendations such as that all children with a first febrile seizure should have a lumbar puncture, nor to deprive the child with pyogenic meningitis or herpes encephalitis his lumbar puncture just because the potentially lethal infection happens to present as his second or third febrile seizure.

The nature of the seizure itself

Most febrile seizures are convulsions; that is to say, they include clonic and/or tonic components. Asymmetrical or lateralized clonic convulsions may have various explanations, but a simple partial or complex partial seizure with fever suggests that the child has at best an epilepsy or an underlying structural brain disorder. Postictal hemiparesis may predict the later appearance of epilepsy with complex partial seizures, but may also indicate an acute encephalopathy such as HSV-1 (Herpes simplex) encephalitis. A short tonic seizure with recovery of the ability to localize stimuli to the face (in the terminology of the Glasgow coma scale) may be a common and benign type of febrile seizure. However, tonic convulsions with persisting impairment of consciousness, and particularly when associated with the loss of ability to localize and only a flexion response to pain, indicate either high intracranial pressure or a metabolic disorder affecting the brain stem. It is believed that failure to localize pain implies a significant encephalopathy, commonly with increased intracranial pressure, and it is one's impression that failure of the child to recover sufficiently to recognize his parents as well as to localize within an hour makes an encephalopathy, such as with meningitis or encephalitis, more likely.

Differential diagnosis of seizures with fever

To understand the rationale for the selection of investigations in febrile seizures it is necessary to run over the rather complex differential diagnosis. It is important not to fall into the trap of imagining that 'febrile seizure' or 'febrile convulsion' is a specific diagnosis when a child presents acutely to a doctor. The following diagnostic possibilities exist, these being not mutually exclusive.

1. The convulsion is not a seizure in either of the accepted senses of an epileptic or anoxic seizure, being a rigor or, for example, an hallucination.
2. The seizure is a febrile syncope similar to a syncope suffered by adults with influenza and fever.
3. The seizure reflects the presence of a gene for one or other type of epilepsy, and may predict to a certain extent the occurrence of that type of epilepsy in later childhood. For example, the febrile seizure may predict absence epilepsy or epilepsy with generalized tonic–clonic seizures or benign focal epilepsy of childhood with Rolandic spikes or epilepsy with complex partial seizures.
4. The febrile seizure may be the beginning of polymorphous epilepsy, otherwise called severe myoclonic epilepsy of infancy.
5. The seizures may reflect static focal pathology. This may be overt with obvious neurological signs in a baby, or covert. The latter is thought to be the basis of many cases of lateralized febrile seizures with later epilepsy and complex partial seizures.
6. The febrile seizures when they are focal may represent the onset of a chronic progressive pathology, such as progressive neuronal degeneration of childhood (PNDC) or the chronic focal encephalitis of Rasmussen. An important situation is the coincidental tonic febrile seizure as the presenting symptom of a posterior fossa tumour.
7. The febrile seizures may be a manifestation of an acute encephalopathy due to central nervous system infections. This may for example be due to virus invasion or pyogenic or tuberculous meningitis. If there is focal brain pathology the seizure accompanying the febrile illness will tend to be lateralized, whereas if there is generalized brain swelling, a tonic non-epileptic seizure with failure to localize pain may be the consequence.
8. A febrile seizure may be a manifestation of a metabolic encephalopathy, the encephalopathy having been precipitated by the catabolism of the febrile illness. In this case the febrile seizure will often be a tonic non-epileptic one with loss of ability to localize, but lateralized seizures are also possible.

As an overview, it is likely that the vast majority of febrile seizures are related to virus infections and have a wholly benign outcome. Hence, it follows that for most patients no investigations of any kind are necessary. In some children investigations are absolutely essential, and to clarify who gets which test, and when, we have listed seven questions which might be asked about a child, and indicated which investigations might provide helpful answers in each case.

Investigations related to the question being asked

1. Is there a treatable disorder?

Whether a child is having his first, second, third or fourth seizure with fever, he or she may have a bacterial infection, as shown in cultures of the throat or urine or blood or stool. Much more seriously he may have pyogenic meningitis, or tuberculous meningitis, or HSV 1 encephalitis. The physician has to think – has to make a judgement – as to whether these disorders might realistically be present in each case, whatever the age and however many febrile seizures have occurred previously. If the child is not localizing to pain, then a serious encephalopathy is present and high intracranial pressure must be suspected. If meningitis is strongly suspected, it can be treated while either mannitol is given to restore localization to pain before lumbar puncture, or the CSF can be obtained by the ventricular route. Clinical clues should point to the correct investigations for other non-infective treatable disorders. Hepatomegaly and hypoglycaemia will prompt organic acid analysis in urine, whereas a history of 2 or 3 weeks of altered behaviour will prompt an emergency CT scan.

2. Is there evidence of an acute encephalopathy?

It is usually not necessary, but may be of interest and of value in epidemiological studies, to do investigations which clarify the nature of an acute encephalopathy even though no specific therapy is available for it. Particularly if seizures are prolonged and the neurological illness striking, it will be helpful to the family and to the doctor to have information about the aetiology and mechanism. The EEG is not particularly helpful. It is likely to contain an excess of slow activity which could be explicable by so many factors that inferences cannot be drawn. Possibly a normal EEG in the acute phase suggests absence of a significant encephalopathy. Blood and CSF studies may indicate the presence of albeit untreatable viral infections, such studies including the CSF IgG index and the CSF alpha-interferon. It is an old observation that some febrile seizures are associated with neutropenia, which is itself associated with roseola infantum (exanthum subitum), and it is a recent finding that human herpes virus 6 is linked to this disorder. (HHV–6) infection will be another aetiological virus which can be identified. Discovering a virus which has invaded the central nervous system will suggest that there has been a genuine encephalopathy. Skull X-ray will not help with this question, and is not indicated in febrile seizures.

3. Is there evidence of a pre-existing static lesion?

If either the neurodevelopmental state of the child does not appear to be normal, or if there have been recurrent hemiclonic febrile seizures on the same side, then further investigation may be performed, but not in the acute stage. CT scan may help here in discovering otherwise occult tuberous sclerosis.

4. Is there evidence of an underlying progressive disorder?

The most important coincidentally present progressive disorder, a posterior fossa tumour, has already been mentioned in section 1 'Is there a treatable disorder?'. A distinctly elevated CSF protein without increase of cells is commonly the first clue to progressive neuronal degeneration of childhood with hepatic involvement presenting as an atypical long febrile seizure. These features may prompt mitochondrial studies (Chapter 10). No tests are available for chronic focal encephalitis at the present time. Later imaging will show progressive focal atrophy.

5. Will the febrile seizures recur?

No tests are available to answer this question. The EEG is not helpful.

6. Can one predict later epilepsy?

In most instances the answer is no, and in most instances the EEG is of no help in predicting whether epilepsy will occur later or not. If, however, there have been non-convulsive epileptic seizures of partial or complex partial type with a fever, or if for reasons discussed in section 3 evidence of a pre-existing static lesion has been determined, then the probability of epilepsy will be extremely high.

Summary of investigations

Most children will require no investigation.

The febrile illness is best investigated in the same way as it would be if the seizure had not occurred. CSF should be examined whenever meningitis or HSV 1 encephalitis is suspected, provided the child localizes to pain.

EEG is not helpful once seizures have stopped, but if seizures persist it may point towards an alternative diagnosis.

The value of brain imaging is limited to serious acute encephalopathies and the out-patient follow-up of children with neurodevelopmental abnormalities or recurrent seizures on one side.

Case illustrations

See 4.4, 4.5, 5.1 and 5.3.

Further reading

Aicardi, J. (1986) Febrile convulsions. In *Epilepsy in Children*, Raven Press, New York, pp. 212–232

Dravet, C., Roger, J. and Bureau, M. (1985) Severe myoclonic epilepsy of infants. In *Epileptic Syndromes in Infancy, Childhood and Adolescence* (ed. J. Roger, C. Dravet, M. Bureau, F. E. Dreifuss and P. Wolf) John Libbey, London, pp. 58–67

Harding, B., Egger, J., Portmann, B. and Erdohazi, M. (1986) Progressive neuronal degeneration of childhood with liver disease. *Brain*, **109**, 181–206

Piatt, J. H., Hwang, P. A., Armstrong, D. C. *et al.* (1988) Chronic focal encephalitis (Rasmussen syndrome): six cases. *Epilepsia*, **29**, 268–279

Wallace, S. J. (1988) *The Child with Febrile Seizures*. John Wight, Bristol.

Yamanishi, K., Okuno, T., Shiraki, K. *et al.* (1988) Identification of human herpes virus 6 as a casual agent for exanthem subitum. *Lancet*, **1**, 1065–1067

Chapter 22

Epilepsy and non-febrile seizures

The diagnosis of paroxysmal disorders is made, on the whole, by the history, the investigations being confirmatory. The first question is differential diagnosis. Not all seizures are epileptic. They may be anoxic or toxic or metabolic or psychic ('pseudo') or hypnic (sleep disorders), or of miscellaneous mechanism.

Although this differential seems complex, in practice the situation is often simple. For example, if a normal child has a predominantly tonic seizure when standing in assembly at school, then the diagnosis is convulsive syncope mediated via the vagus nerve, that is, a type of anoxic seizure, and no investigations are necessary. If a child has a jerking seizure in front of a visual display unit of the computer at school, then the diagnosis is photic or pattern-sensitive epilepsy, and the only test that may be helpful is EEG with intermittent light or pattern stimulation.

We will discuss some of the better known clinical situations.

Epileptic seizures

Partial seizures

A Rolandic seizure characterized for example by occurrence during the night, one-sided twitching or spasm of the face, and excessive salivation, in a normally intelligent neurologically intact, child will suggest benign focal epilepsy of childhood. The only necessary investigation is a standard EEG, which will show one-sided or independent bilateral Rolandic spike and wave complexes often in clusters. CT scan is not indicated.

Other types of partial or partial complex seizure may need further imaging studies, whether or not there is secondary generalization in the form of a spasm or myoclonic or tonic or tonic-clonic seizure. A second-generation CT scan will pick up the lesions of tuberous sclerosis in most cases; high-resolution CT scans or MRI may be necessary to recognize small epileptogenic tumours or the more subtle cerebral malformations. If genetic questions arise and tuberous sclerosis is a clinical possiblity, CT scan is indicated without further question. If not, it may be reserved for those in whom the seizures are refractory or in whom neurological signs progress. Time-consuming and complex studies, including prolonged cassette EEG recording, cable telemetry with video recording, SPECT, MRI, and possibly recording with depth electrodes, will be necessary if neurosurgical treatment of the focal origin of epilepsy is a serious possibility.

Epilepsia partialis continua, manifest for instance as a continuous twitching of the corner of the mouth or the shoulder, may not have a discernible cause, but may be a manifestation of progressive neuronal degeneration of childhood, focal encephalitis of unknown origin (Rasmussen's), measles encephalitis in immunosuppressed children, or focal cortical dysplasia. Investigation is difficult. Increased CSF protein characterizes progressive neuronal degeneration of childhood, with later disturbance of liver function and increased lactate (mitochondrial studies indicated, Chapter 10). Focal encephalitis and focal cortical dysplasia may only be apparent on brain biopsy.

In a particular type of partial epileptic seizure, the gelastic seizure, high-resolution imaging is indicated. When there is early onset of such giggling or laughing seizures with mental handicap and behavioural deterioration, with (or without) early precocious puberty, high-resolution CT, or better, MR imaging, is necessary to demonstrate the underlying hamartoma of the tuber cinereum, which may be surgically accessible.

Startle epilepsy. In this carbamazepine-responsive disorder of mildly handicapped individuals, episodes may be reproduced during routine EEG by auditory startle. Desynchronization occurs during the brief tonic phase. CT scan will show a lateralized abnormality such as a porus.

Generalized seizures

Neonatal seizures are discussed elsewhere (Chapter 13) but myoclonic seizures of very early life are mentioned here. EEG shows suppression-burst and this appearance should prompt CSF glycine estimation, organic acid analysis of urine, and CT scan (see also Recent advances page 235).

Infantile spasms are an indication for CT scans in all patients unless the predisposition is obvious, as in Down's syndrome. As in the case of all refractory seizures, a short pyridoxine trial is indicated. Rarely, biochemical studies will help, for instance ammonia, CSF glycine, and mitochondrial and peroxisomal investigations (Chapter 10).

Children with epilepsy of mixed type, including atypical absences, falls and tonic seizures, the so-called Lennox–Gastaut syndrome, will show slow spike wave on EEG, and fast bursts of 10 Hz spike-like activity, especially in sleep. CT may reveal specific pathology such as that of tuberous sclerosis.

Simple absences can normally be distinguished from complex partial seizures by history, and may be induced by hyperventilation in the clinic. Standard EEG, or EEG with split-screen videotape, allows the absences to be precisely recorded and may give an indication as to whether the absences are in fact 'secondary' to a focal lesion. However, at the present time this does not greatly influence management.

Myoclonic epilepsy. The characteristic EEG appearance is a poly-spike and wave burst. In the case of myoclonic epilepsy of adolescence, multiple poly-spikes (fast spikes 18–20/s) tend to occur before the wave which is associated with a jerk. This appearance may only be induced if all-night sleep deprivation has preceded the morning EEG. If the EEG shows striking asymmetries in a myoclonic epilepsy of a younger child, the epilepsy may be secondary, generalized from a focal lesion, and CT scan should be considered to detect tuberous sclerosis.

'Grand mal'. There are probably multiple explanations for gener-alized tonic-clonic epileptic seizures. One example will be given. Early-morning tonic-clonic seizures occurring in late childhood or adolescence may be manifestations of the same disorder described above as myoclonic epilepsy of adolescence. Sleep deprivation, as in that condition, is likely to induce poly-spike and wave burst (especially runs of fast spikes at 18–20/s preceding 3–5/s wave or spike and wave). The importance of this investigation is that whereas a secondary, generalized tonic-clonic seizure, preceded by a transient aura, would be expected to respond to carbamazepine, the primary generalized epilep-sy revealed by sleep deprivation will not respond to carbamazepine but will respond to sodium valproate.

Light, pattern, eyelid closure, and self-induced seizures. EEG with photic stimulation (stroboscopic activation) and pattern stimulation will show spikes or spike and wave induced under these circumstances in photic and pattern-sensitive epilepsy. In some patients, spike wave is induced by voluntary eye closure. In others, self-induced seizures are induced by slow eye closure, particularly when watching television. The fact that seizures are being self-induced may be recognized by the shape of the rather slow voluntary eye closure seen as a biological artefact before the induction of spike wave on the EEG.

Progressive myoclonic epilepsy. These disorders are considered last as they have a completely different need for investigation. First of all it is necessary to be sure that there actually is a progressive myoclonic epilepsy rather than temporary deterioration associated with the seiz-ures or the therapy. In the case of true progression a number of complex investigations are necessary, including lysosomal and mitochondrial studies and biopsy sampling (*see* Chapter 25).

Anoxic seizures

Vagal or vasovagal attacks. Although ocular compression in the young child or the sight of blood or other emotional stimulus in the older child, may reproduce such episodes, normally no such investigations are necessary. Should a spontaneous episode occur during 'routine' EEG, the diagnosis will be missed unless an ECG channel is simultaneously in operation.

Congenital heart disease and intermittent pulmonary hypertension should not cause any diagnostic problem if the child is physically examined.

Paroxysmal ventricular tachycardia or ventricular fibrillation. The clinical situation is a story of syncope or anoxic seizures on excitement, during exercise or during sleep. The ECG will usually show a prolonged QTc with or without a prominant U wave. It may be necessary to induce tachycardia and determine if the QT interval declines at the same rate as the R-R interval. This is a difficult diagnostic area requiring consultation with cardiologists involved in 'pacing' studies.

Compulsive Valsalva manoeuvres occur in mentally handicapped or autistic children and may easily be mistaken for absences or more major generalized epileptic seizures. If the child can be connected to EEG/ECG/respiratory polygraphy, the diagnosis should soon become clear as the episodes are usually very frequent. The amplitude of the QRS complex characteristically declines by 50% during each Valsalva.

Prolonged expiratory apnoea or breath-holding does not normally present an investigational problem. It is not normally necessary to attempt to reproduce one of these episodes under polygraphic control. Rarely, this type of apnoea may be associated with a posterior fossa abnormality, either a malformation or a brain-stem tumour. Therefore in a patient with atypical features or neurological regression, a high-resolution CT scan or sagittal MR may be necessary, together with tests of vagal function (see Autonomic Tests, Chapter 6). It should be emphasized that only very exceptionally will such studies be indicated.

Meadow's syndrome. When it becomes apparent that the onset of tonic seizures with apnoea and bradycardia only occurs in the presence of the child's mother, then some form of covert surveillance is indicated. The simplest method of making this diagnosis is to attach a 7-channel EEG, 1-channel ECG cassette recorder and allow the child to be privately with the mother after 48 hours constantly monitored supervision. The sequence of movement and muscle potentials followed by simultaneous slowing of the EEG and ECG is characteristic of suffocation. Hidden video cameras may allow visual evidence of the act, but organizing this presents considerable difficulties.

Intermittent increased intracranial pressure. Such a situation will not often lead to diagnostic confusion. CT scan will usually clarify.

Brain-stem malformation. When increased intracranial pressure occurs in addition, anoxic seizures may appear more readily. MR imaging is ideal for evaluating such cases.

Toxic

Seizure-like episodes of toxic origin do not lead to a long-lasting diagnostic difficulty unless a mother is intermittently poisoning her child. However, in the acute situation a number of drugs may lead to clusters of tonic seizures. Investigations such as blood carbamazepine level may provide a solution.

Metabolic

Hypoglycaemia. Details of the history should suggest this possibility. The primary investigation is measurement of the blood glucose at the time of a seizure. Failure to respond to intravenous glucose may indicate a general mitochondrial disorder such as Reye's syndrome, or a selective one such as a fatty acid oxidation defect. Urine should be frozen for prompt analysis of organic acids. If the child is large and pigmented, the cortisol and ACTH level should be measured at the same time and cortisol replacements given pending confirmation of the diagnosis of ACTH unresponsiveness.

Hypocalcaemia. This is rarely a diagnostic problem beyond the neonatal period. Physical signs such as keratitis may suggest the diagnosis of hypoparathyroidism. The ECG channel obtained while running the EEG will show prolonged QT interval and U waves. Total and ionized calcium in blood will confirm the biochemical situation.

Hyperammonaemia is not expected to induce epileptic seizures beyond the neonatal period, but rather vomiting and decline in consciousness. However, urea cycle disorders, especially OTC deficiency, may be associated with tonic seizures and/or acquired neurological deficits (*see* Case 10.9). Orotic aciduria, which may require a protein load for its demonstration, is the diagnostic marker for OTC deficiency.

Biotinidase deficiency may lead to seizures in infancy, but these are likely to be symptomatic epileptic seizures. Biotinidase estimation should probably be limited to children in whom clinical clues such as lack of hair, skin rash, and developmental delay suggest the possibility, or in whom a trial of biotin has led to seizure remission.

Psychic

Hysterical pseudoseizures may sometimes be induced during an EEG by suggestion. No EEG changes are expected when these non-organic seizures occur, but in the differential diagnosis it must be borne in mind that partial or partial-complex epileptic seizures on occasion do not have any EEG accompaniments when using scalp EEG in the conventional manner.

Hypnic

When sleep disorders are difficult to diagnose, then some form of all-night sleep recording using a number of EEG channels and polygraphy, preferably with the techniques of polysomnography, is indicated. This is a labour-intensive investigation involving constant observation of the child, and the prior use of cassette EEG monitoring is almost always worthwhile.

Miscellaneous

Sandifer syndrome. The 'fits' in this disorder are tonic distortions of the neck. Diagnosis may require barium swallow, oesophageal pH studies, radionuclide milk scan, or oesophagoscopy.

Intussusception. The colic in this condition may mimic infantile spasms or (opistho)tonic seizures. Plain X-rays of the abdomen, and barium enema confirm the diagnosis.

Summary of investigations

1. Clinical methods should suggest
   (a) The general category of seizure mechanism (e.g. epileptic, anoxic etc.)
   (b) The specific seizure type within that category.
2. Electrophysiological tests will often help to confirm the provisional diagnosis of 1(b), most so in the case of epileptic seizures.
3. Tests of the structural integrity of the brain (e.g. CT scan) are confined to (a) children who have epileptic seizures of partial type (focal origin) and other features suggesting a lesion (pathology), or (b) extensive neurodevelopmental disorder.
4. Special investigations not of a primary neurological nature (biochemical etc.) are mainly indicated in epilepsies (a) of early infancy, and (b) when there is unequivocal evidence of progressive non-focal neurological deterioration.

Case illustrations

See 1.1–1.6, 4.1, 4.4, 4.5, 5.1, 7.1, 8.1, 9.3, 10.6.

Further reading

Aicardi, J. (1986) *Epilepsy in Children*, Raven Press, New York
Asconape, J. and Penry, J. K. (1984) Some clinical and EEG aspects of benign juvenile myoclonic epilepsy. *Epilepsia*, **25**, 108–114
Boyd, S. G., Harden, A., Egger, J. and Pampiglione, G. (1986) Progressive neuronal

disease of childhood with liver disease (Alper's disease): characteristic neurophysio-logical features. *Neuropediatrics*, **17**, 75–80

Delgado-Escueta, A. V. and Enrile-Bascal, F. (1984) Juvenile myoclonic epilepsy of Janz. *Neurology (Cleveland)*, **34**, 285–294

Gastaut, H., Broughton, R. and De Leo, G. (1982) Syncopal attacks compulsively self-induced by the Valsalva manoeuvre in children with mental retardation.. *Electro-encephalography and Clinical Neurophysiology*, **35** (Suppl.), 323–329

Gastaut, H., Zifkin, B. and Rufo, M. (1987) Compulsive respiratory stereotypies in children with autistic features: polygraphic recording and treatment with fenfluramine. *Journal of Autism and Developmental Disorders*, **17**, 391–406

Piatt, J. H., Hwang, P. A., Armstrong, D. C. *et al.* (1988) Chronic focal encephalitis (Rasmussen syndrome): six cases. *Epilepsia*, **29**, 268–279

Southall, D. P., Lewis, G. M., Buchanan, R. and Weller, R. O. (1987) Prolonged expiratory apnoea (cyanotic 'breath-holding') in association with a medullary tumour. *Developmental Medicine and Child Neurology*, **29**, 789–793

Werlin, S. L., D'Souza, B. J., Hogan, W. J. *et al.* (1980) Sandifer syndrome: an unappreciated clinical entity. *Developmental Medicine and Child Neurology*, **22**, 374–378

Wolf, B., Grier, R. E., Allen, R. J. *et al.* (1983) Phenotypic variation in biotinidase deficiency. *Journal of Pediatrics*, **103**, 233–237

Chapter 23

Headache

Acute headache

The history and the physical signs in children with acute headache commonly lead towards the diagnosis without the need for specific neurological investigations. Small retinal haemorrhages may indicate either acute intracerebral haemorrhage or sudden rise in intracranial pressure secondary to a posterior fossa tumour. In either of these cases CT scan is the first investigation.

Chronic or paroxysmal headache

Ideally one should be able to separate by history the various types of headaches which have a duration of weeks, months or years, although in the younger child this may not be possible.

The typical story of migraine with complete normality in between headaches does not require any further investigations. This is the only common condition in this section.

If the physician is not happy with the diagnosis of migraine, then a lateral skull X-ray is a reasonable investigation, but other tests are indicated in particular clinical settings.

Brain tumours may present with intermittent headache or headache that is steadily or intermittently progressive. Clinical clues on examination are: head larger than either parent, cracked-pot percussion note over the coronal suture, head tilt, papilloedema or optic atrophy, or inability to stand on one leg for 5 s from age 3 years onwards. Additional clues in the history would be any type of regression or failure of intellectual or physical development. In any of these circumstances one proceeds to a CT scan. A skull X-ray may be unjustifiably reassuring.

In apparent hemiplegic migraine one has to consider whether it is truly the diagnosis. If the attacks are always on the same side, angiography or MRI have to be considered to exclude vascular malformations. Residual focal neurological signs after an attack with cerebral involvement indicates rather full brain imaging (SPECT and/or MR), seeking evidence of moya-moya disease, and at least some mitochondrial function tests (*see* Chapter 10), initially blood lactate and pyruvate. Lactic acidosis suggests MELAS (Mitochondrial Encephalopathy with Lactic Acidosis and Stroke-like episodes).

In migraine, vomiting when it occurs normally follows after a considerable interval the onset of the headache. If vomiting precedes paroxysmal headache, four conditions should be considered.

1. Cerebral tumour. Investigation – CT scan.
2. Partial epileptic seizure – EEG (for example cassette EEG) attempting to capture the seizure. CT scan if response to medication (carbamazepine) is not complete.
3. OTC deficiency. In intermittent hyperammonaemia secondary to ornithine transcarbamylase deficiency, vomiting may precede headache, but is commonly associated with some impairment of consciousness. Investigation – blood ammonia and orotic acid excretion during attack.
4. MELAS. Lactic acidosis is a clue to this disorder (*see* Case 10.6).

Cough-induced headache may indicate a disorder of the cervicomedullary junction. If the headache can be reproduced by having the child perform a Valsalva manoeuvre, then MRI of the region in question is indicated.

Chronic lymphocytic meningitis may manifest as chronic headache. Investigation is by lumbar puncture after CT scan. In addition to well-known chronic infections, detected by microbiological methods, consideration has to be given to other imaging methods if chemical meningitis from ruptured dermoid cyst is a possibility. Further, some cases of chronic headache with lymphocytic meningitis without detectable cause respond dramatically to corticosteroid therapy.

In many other types of headache, neurological investigations are not helpful and other approaches, for example dental investigation, may be more appropriate.

Case illustrations

See 1.2 and 10.6.

Further reading

Lewis, D. W. and Berman, P. H. (1986) Vertebral artery dissection and alternating hemiparesis in an adolescent. *Pediatrics*, **78**, 610–613

Montagna, P., Gallassi, R., Medori, R. *et al.* (1988) MELAS syndrome: characteristic migrainous and epileptic features and maternal transmission. *Neurology*, **38**, 751–754

Nightingale, S. and Williams, B. (1987) Hindbrain hernia headache. *Lancet*, **1**, 731–734

Chapter 24

Acute encephalopathy

This chapter is about children who present with an apparently short history with altered consciousness, often focal neurological signs and seizures. They do not all have a true acute encephalopathy in the sense of a new pathology, but at the onset one does not know; hence the range of tests which need to be applied. Most of these children present a long way from paediatric neurointensive care units and most of them present outside working hours. Clinical observations, investigations and treatment have to be carried out in parallel. Coincident fever is possible in virtually all situations, but may be absent in encephalopathies of infective origin.

In many situations the cause will be already apparent from a history and examination (for example blocked shunt in hydrocephalus, meningococcal septicaemia in the presence of fulminant purpura).

In all cases the clinician will have to make some sort of guess about the intracranial pressure (ICP), knowing that if the child is flexing to pain rather than localizing to pain the cerebral perfusion pressure (CPP) is likely to be too low. Since the CPP approximates to the difference between the arterial pressure and the ICP, measurement of the arterial pressure by a reliable method is mandatory.

Conditions which may present as acute encephalopathy are listed with comment on recognition and key investigations.

Infections

Pyogenic meningitis or septicaemia (when the presence or absence of meningitis is not clear).

The question of importance is whether or not it is essential to obtain CSF, and if so is it safe to get it by the lumbar route? Provided blood culture is done and treatment (e.g. penicillin plus chloramphenicol) started immediately, such a decision can be deferred.

Brain abscess

This is almost unheard of with a history of less than 2 weeks. CT scan with contrast will be diagnostic.

Tuberculous meningitis

This is also uncommon with a history of less than 2 weeks. The CSF will have increased protein, lymphocytes, and possibly neutrophils, a low but not extremely low glucose, and often increased pressure. CT may show ventricular dilatation. The mycobacteria may not be visible in the stained CSF, and there is no guarantee that culture will be positive several weeks later. If Mantoux is not positive at 1:1000 or 1 : 100, BCG can be given; an accelerated response indicates active tuberculosis.

Herpes simplex encephalitis

Acyclovir will be started as soon as this disorder is thought of. However, it is important to recognize the significance of the tests which may aid diagnosis, otherwise acyclovir treatment may be abandoned too early, with devastating results. The initial CSF usually shows some abnormality, which may include protein elevation, some lymphocytes, some neutrophils, and some red cells. Alpha-interferon is already increased in the first CSF specimen, but the CSF herpes simplex titre is usually negative. Attempting to culture the herpes simplex virus from the CSF is not helpful.

The EEG, unlike in the adult situation, does not often show repetitive stereotyped high-voltage lateralized complexes. The EEG will certainly be too slow, often asymmetrical, often with focal slow. CT scan is usually normal at onset, but may show small low-density areas with associated haemorrhage, which may be mistaken for vascular infarcts or a consequence of trauma. The site of the CT lesions, if any, are as often parietal as temporal.

Recent evidence suggests that imaging by SPECT will be abnormal on presentation, with grossly increased focal perfusion. A repeat CSF herpes simplex titre has to be obtained approximately 14 days later to detect an increase. A repeat CT scan (or the first if it was not possible at the onset of the disease) is desirable to show the extent of any lesions.

It follows from the late appearance of much of the specific diagnostic evidence of herpes encephalitis, that once acyclovir treatment is begun it should never be stopped before the full 10-day course has been completed, unless an alternative and exclusive diagnosis has been established unequivocally.

Other encephalopathy or encephalitis

CSF alpha-interferon, evidence of CSF IgG synthesis, positive viral cuture from CSF, stool or throat swab, and in blood, will be of evidence in various other viral infections, for example Coxsackie B. Diagnosis of acute viral encephalitis some weeks after treatment for acute lymphoblastic leukaemia may be difficult because antibody responses are impaired.

Toxoplasma

This cause of encephalitis will be missed unless blood serology is repeated over several weeks.

Malaria

Diagnosis depends on thinking of this cause. Anaemia is usual if encephalopathy is severe.

Parainfections

When meningoencephalitis or encephalomyelitis complicates the well-known infectious fevers of childhood (varicella, etc.) diagnostic difficulties do not usually arise. In the case of mumps, the usual situation is a lymphocytic meningitis (sometimes with moderate lowering of the glucose) and isolation of the mumps virus from the CSF. However, some cases following mumps have focal cerebral deficits without meningitis and without culture of the mumps virus from the CSF, but with elevated protein and oligoclonal bands.

Mycoplasma pneumoniae infections (clues: rash, otitis, pneumonia) may trigger an acute disseminated encephalomyelitis with very prominent blood neutrophil leucocytosis and lymphocytes in the CSF.

Acute disseminated encephalomyelitis

Acute disseminated encephalomyelitis without apparent cause is worth recognition because it is steroid responsive. The CSF findings may be similar to those in herpes encephalitis, but the clinical findings of cerebellar and eye movement disturbances, optic neuritis, and spinal cord involvement if present will allow differentiation. A prolonged latency of the VEP supports the diagnosis. MRI scan may show multiple white matter lesions.

Bilateral striatal necrosis

Bilateral striatal necrosis (possibly of parainfectious origin) may present days after an apparently mild infection, often with seizures and coma. The clinical picture of extreme axial hypotonia, tight flexion of the limbs, little spontaneous movement or expression, inability to suck or swallow, and grimacing, monotonous cry and hyperextension to stimuli suggest the diagnosis. The CSF may show lymphocytosis with elevated protein, and hypodensities in the caudate and lenticular nuclei are seen on CT brain scan. Viral titres (including mumps), plasma and CSF pyruvate, and lactate and urinary organic acids should be measured in such patients.

Vascular and haematological conditions

Intracranial haemorrhage

An abrupt history usually makes this obvious. The ECG monitor may show arrhythmias secondary to subarachnoid bleeding. It is better to get a CT scan than to confirm subarachnoid haemorrhage by lumbar puncture, which probably should not be undertaken unless a neuro-surgeon is involved.

Subdural haemorrhage. This may be suggested by flattening of the EEG on one side, and is better confirmed by CT than by needle puncture.

'Stroke'

Hypertensive encephalopathy will already have been recognized.

Most apparent 'strokes' will not in fact be acquired vascular lesions but will be related to a temporary predominantly unilateral disturbance associated with an infection or with a prolonged seizure. Congenital malformations may present in this way, no weakness having been noted previously. CT scan is indicated in all cases, looking for unexpected structural lesions.

The condition with stenoses at the circle of Willis, known as moya-moya disease, is difficult to diagnose at the time of the first stroke, but once it is thought of it may be diagnosed by angiography. If available, SPECT may show characteristic low-flow areas, and MRI clusters of flow voids, in this disorder.

At least four metabolic disorders may present with stroke. *Homocystinuria* can be confirmed by plasma and urine amino acids. There is an argument for measuring (or repeating) the blood lactate, once the acute state has passed, to detect the condition known as MELAS (Mitochondrial Encephalopathy with Lactic Acidosis and Stroke-like episodes). Further evidence for this diagnosis will then come from muscle biopsy (ragged red fibres on the trichrome stain). *Sulphite oxidase deficiency* (a very rare disorder) may present as acute hemiplegia and seizures without lens subluxation or choreoathetosis. Diagnosis is suggested by the finding of increased urinary thiosulphate and confirmed by deficient enzyme activity in cultured fibroblasts. Stroke is a rare but important presentation of *urea cycle defects*, in particular OTC deficiency. If such a diagnosis seems plausible, quantitative orotic acid excretion measurement is essential, whether or not the plasma ammonia is raised at the time that the child is seen (*see* Case 10.9).

Sickle-cell disease should not pose diagnostic problems (using the *in vitro* sickling test), provided it is thought of in a child of the appropriate race who has acute encephalopathy, often with seizures and stroke-like neurological deficits. These children should have neither hyperventilation activation during EEG examinations nor intravenous contrast with CT unless specially indicated, as these procedures may exacerbate neurological deficits.

The congenital or acquired thrombophilias (e.g. due to protein C or antithrombin III deficiency or lupus anticoagulant) should be considered in unexplained stroke and appropriate studies performed in consultation with the haematologist.

Haemorrhagic shock and encephalopathy syndrome (HSES)

In this disorder with hypotension, hypoglycaemia, increased transaminases, and coagulation disorder, the EEG accompaniment of the epileptic seizures is characteristic of severe hypoxic-ischaemic damage, but needs more than a single-channel CFAM to demonstrate it adequately. The EEG can be described as multivariable: for much of the time, repetitive spike or sharp and slow complexes vary in their location over the cerebral hemispheres, in their rate, and in their form.

Haemolytic uraemic syndrome (HUS)

The diagnosis is made by the biochemical and haematological findings, but additional tests do not usually help in understanding the neurological complications. CT may show late brain-stem or basal ganglia low densities in children with sequelae.

Hypoxic–ischaemic conditions

Most acute encephalopathies of hypoxic–ischaemic origin will have an obvious explanation, for example, cardiac arrest after bleeding or inhaling a foreign body. One situation, in which the history confuses, needs emphasis.

Suffocation (Meadow's syndrome)

A child who is suffocated for more than 2 minutes or so, but not long enough to cause death, may present as an acute encephalopathy with epileptic seizures and an EEG showing stereotyped high-voltage triphasic waves, together with transient hyperglycaemia and prolonged blood neutrophil leucocytosis. In contrast to herpes encephalitis, the CSF is likely to be entirely normal, and of course herpes titres will not increase. Serial CT scans may show hypodensities in watershed zones.

Tumours

Occasionally brain tumours, especially when there is coincident fever, may be confused with meningitis. However, the history tends to be of more than 2 weeks, and neck stiffness from tonsillar herniation tends to be more of a feature than the depression of consciousness. CT scan must be performed as an urgent matter, and lumbar puncture avoided, if tumour seems a realistic possibility.

Toxic disorders

Of the various chemicals which may be ingested or inhaled and lead to a clinical picture resembling an encephalopathy, some can be measured, such as carbamazepine and toluene, others such as tricyclics may have to be inferred from clinical signs.

Benzodiazepines

Benzodiazepine ingestion is common, whether by accident or as deliberate poisoning. A single-channel EEG with facilities for frequency analysis as in CFAM will give immediate support for (or exclude) this diagnosis. Benzodiazepine ingestion is always accompanied by a high proportion of fast (beta) activity in the EEG. Similar but less regular fast activity excess occurs in the EEG after barbiturate ingestion.

Children who are on sodium valproate may present with an acute encephalopathy resembling Reye's syndrome. Liver biopsy may be necessary to distinguish this from the situation found in progressive neuronal degeneration of childhood (Alper's disease, *see* below).

Carbon monoxide

Carbon-monoxide-induced encephalopathy sometimes presents without the tell-tale history. Early estimation of carboxyhaemoglobin confirms the diagnosis. Follow-up CT scan may show atrophy of the caudate.

Lead

Papilloedema is usually present even when lead encephalopathy appears to be acute. Reduced haemoglobin and increased density at the end of long bones are usually present. An increased CSF protein is a constant finding, but lumbar puncture is not advised. Blood lead estimation confirms the diagnosis.

Metabolic conditions

Diabetic coma and hepatic encephalopathy should not present diagnostic difficulties.

Hypoglycaemia will be recognized at the onset and corrected, but this may give a clue to the explanation of the encephalopathy. Low glucose levels occur in Reye's syndrome, organic acidaemia, fatty acid oxidation defects, and in the rare situation of adrenal unresponsiveness to ACTH (suggested by excessive pigmentation of a taller-than-expected child). Hypoglycaemia is also a feature of fulminant hepatitis, in which increased bilirubin is the rule.

Severe resistant metabolic acidosis suggests an inborn error of metabolism and in these circumstances serum pyruvate and lactate, plasma and urine amino acids and urine organic acids must be measured.

Hyperammonaemia will suggest Reye's syndrome or a disorder of the urea cycle, or of fatty acid or organic acid metabolism.

Low plasma carnitine suggests idiopathic Reye's syndrome or a fatty acid oxidation defect. In most cases urine organic acid analysis is abnormal, showing dicarboxylic aciduria in particular. In primary carnitine deficiency (carnitine transport defect) plasma carnitine is severely reduced, but urine organic acids are normal, with no dicarboxylic aciduria.

Reye's syndrome

Reye's syndrome is recognized from the history and increased ammonia and transaminase levels. Urine will be frozen for gas chromotography mass spectroscopy or other sensitive method of organic acid analysis. Intracranial pressure monitoring will be indicated if the child does not localize to pain, once coagulation defects have been corrected. In idiopathic Reye's syndrome liver histochemistry and electronmicroscopy are characteristic (*see* Chapter 7).

Fatty acid oxidation defects

In particular medium-chain acyl coenzyme A dehydrogenase (MCAD) deficiency may resemble Reye's syndrome. The hypoglycaemia is said to be hypoketotic, but in practice, ward tests of ketones in urine may be strongly positive. The finding of octanoyl carnitine after L-carnitine loading (100 mg/kg) confirms the diagnosis. Urine and preferably plasma also, should be frozen for later sensitive organic acid analysis.

Urea cycle disorders

When they present as acute encephalopathy, urea cycle disorders often have markedly increased ammonia concentrations. A high ammonia without the full clinical and biochemical picture of Reye's syndrome (ammonia may be elevated, but not to high levels, in MCAD deficiency) is highly suggestive. Excess orotic acid in the urine confirms the diagnosis of OTC deficiency, the usual defect in these circumstances, but a protein load may be required to demonstrate this.

Leigh's disease

As a manifestation of a mitochondrial disorder, Leigh's disease may present as an acute encephalopathy. Peculiar eye movements and breathing patterns are suggestive. Increased lactate and pyruvate and subtle low-density areas particularly in the basal ganglia on high-resolution CT will support the diagnosis. Further investigation needs muscle biopsy and special mitochondrial studies (see Chapter 10).

Explosive onset of neurological disease

A number of neurological disorders may present in such an acute and dramatic manner that they masquerade completely as acute encephalopathy. These disorders may be truly progressive or completely static in the pathological sense.

Progressive neuronal degeneration of childhood with liver disease
(Alper's disease or Huttenlocher's disease)

Although there may be a long history of subtle neurological impairment or very mild developmental delay, this disorder commonly presents in an explosive manner with a true virus infection and fever. Repeated epileptic seizures and impaired consciousness are accompanied by a substantially increased CSF protein with no increase in cells. Repetitive slow proximal twitchings may be accompanied by very high-voltage sharp and slow activity on the EEG with notched wave crests which may suggest the diagnosis. CT scan may be normal or later show low densities, including the grey and white matter. VEPs may show asymmetrical conduction defect. The transaminases are not always increased in the acute phase, but gradually rise terminally when coagulation defect and high lactate and pyruvate in blood and CSF become apparent. Liver biopsy is possible, provided the diagnosis is considered before the coagulation defect makes the biopsy impracticable, showing cirrhosis and fatty change.

Prenatal brain lesions

Prenatal destructive brain lesions such as periventricular leucomalacia, or in particular certain asymmetrical disorders of neuronal migration, may have onsets which closely resemble acute encephalopathy. Hemimegalencephaly or hemipachygyria may present with repeated seizures and an apparently acquired hemisyndrome and decline in consciousness associated with a febrile illness. The EEG in these disorders may show repetitive high-voltage stereotyped lateralized complexes, very closely resembling those seen in herpes encephalitis. A clue to the diagnosis is very high-voltage activity in the alpha frequency (or later, beta frequency), predominantly over the hemisphere opposite the apparently acquired hemiparesis. A standard CT scan may not show these lesions clearly, but high-resolution CT should do so, and MR will give absolute confirmation.

Epilepsy onset

No great difficulties arise when a previously known patient with epilepsy relapses in status either spontaneously or after drug withdrawal. Epilepsy may present *de novo* masquerading as an acute encephalopathy. This is the mode of presentation of the epileptic syndrome called polymorphous epilepsy of infancy, or severe myoclonic epilepsy of infancy (sometimes called Dravet's syndrome). The hemiclonic febrile status epilepticus under the age of 6 months is not likely to have any distinguishing features, but follow-up EEG is likely to show photosensitivity at around the age of one year, and others seizure types will precede overt mental handicap in the second year of life.

Outcome prediction

Evidence on the predictive power of the various tests available is accumulating. If the ICP has been measured, a persistent CPP of less than 35 mmHg is usually but not always followed by handicap. The EEG appears to have a clear adverse predictive value when there is loss of rhythmic activity with an amplitude under $2 \mu V$. Provided the EEG is obtained while the child is neither severely poisoned by sedative drugs nor under deep hypothermia, then a flat EEG appearance suggests permanent loss of cerebral hemisphere function but not necessarily 'brain death'. The CFAM is the easiest way of testing the EEG continuously in the course of an acute encephalopathy, using one or sometimes two channels. A diffuse ground-glass appearance of the cerebral hemisphere on CT scan followed by progressive shrinkage (atrophy) predicts profound handicap. However, it is most important to note that brain shrinkage resembling 'cerebral atrophy' may be the (temporary) result of corticosteroid therapy. Brain biopsy is not a satisfactory way of predicting outcome, because of the patchy distribution of many lesions. A biopsy may show extensive or even total necrosis of cortical neurons in the area sampled, yet the child may have only minor handicap in due course.

The diagnosis of 'brain death' is made on clinical criteria in children as in adults. It must always be borne in mind that the first criterion is the diagnosis of a lesion expected to lead to death of the brain. If this diagnosis is not clear, evidence of a flat EEG will have to be sought in addition to the clinical criteria.

Case illustrations

See 1.6, 5.1–5.3, 10.7–10.9.

Further reading

Barthez, M. A., Billard, C., Santini, J. J. *et al.* (1987) Relapse of herpes encephalitis. *Neuropediatrics*, **18**, 3–7

Carstensen, H. and Nilsson, K. O. (1987) Neurological complications associated with mycoplasma pneumoniae infection in children. *Neuropediatrics*, **18**, 57–58

Di Mauro, S., Bonilla, E., Zeviani, M. *et al.* (1987) Mitochondrial myopathies. *Journal of Inherited Metabolic Disease*, **10**, 113–128

Dravet, C., Roger, J. and Bureau, M. (1985) Severe myoclonic epilepsy of infants. In *Epileptic Syndromes in Infancy, Childhood and Adolescence* (ed. J. Roger, C. Dravet, M. Bureau, F. E. Dreifuss and P. Wolf) John Libbey, London, pp. 58–67

Editorial (1985) Haemorrhagic shock and encephalopathy. *Lancet*, **2**, 534–536

Goutières, F. and Aicardi, J. (1982) Acute neurological dysfunction associated with destructive lesions of the basal ganglia in children. *Annals of Neurology*, **12**, 328–332

Hallam, N. F., Eglin, R. P., Holland, P. *et al.* (1986) Fatal Coxsackie B meningoencephalitis diagnosed by serology and in situ nucleic acid hybridisation. *Lancet*, **2**, 1213–1214

Harding, B., Egger, J., Portmann, B. and Erdohazi, M. (1986) Progressive neuronal degeneration of childhood with liver disease. *Brain*, **109**, 181–206

Kelley, R. E. and Berger, J. R. (1987) Ischemic stroke in a girl with lupus anticoagulant. *Pediatric Neurology*, **3**, 58–61

Kennedy, C. R., Chrzanowska, K., Robinson, R. O. *et al.* (1986) A major role for viruses in acute childhood encephalopathy. *Lancet*, **1**, 989–991

Kurokawa, T., Chen, Y. J., Tomita, S. *et al.* (1985) Cerebrovascular occlusive disease with and without the moyamoya vascular network in children. *Neuropediatrics*, **16**, 29–32

Lacey, D. J., Duffner, P. K., Cohen, M. E. and Mosovich, L. (1986) Unusual biochemical and clinical features in a girl with ornithine transcarbamylase deficiency. *Pediatric Neurology*, **2**, 51–53

Launes, J., Nikkinen, P., Lindroth, L. *et al.* (1988) Diagnosis of acute herpes simplex encephalitis by brain perfusion single photon emission computed tomography. *Lancet*, **1**, 1188–1191

Mitchell, G., Ogier, H., Munnich, A. *et al.* (1986) Neurological deterioration and lactic acidemia in biotinidase deficiency. *Neuropediatrics*, **17**, 129–131

Neves, J. F., Lopes, D., Casal, M. I. *et al.* (1988) 'Botryoid nuclei' of leucocytes in the haemorrhagic shock and encephalopathy syndrome. *Lancet*, **1**, 112

Pasternak, J. F., De Vivo, D. C. and Prensky, A. L. (1980) Steroid-responsive encephalomyelitis in childhood. *Neurology*, **30**, 481–486

Perdue, Z., Bale, J. F., Dunn, V. D. and Bell, W. E. (1985) Magnetic resonance imaging in childhood disseminated encephalomyelitis. *Pediatric Neurology*, **1**, 370–374

Roe, C. R., Millington, D. S., Maltby, D. S. and Kinnebrew, P. (1986) Recognition of medium-chain acyl-CoA dehydrogenase deficiency in asymptomatic siblings of children dying of sudden infant death or Reye-like syndromes. *Journal of Pediatrics*, **108**, 13–18

Rowe, P. C., Newman, S. L. and Brusilow, S. W. (1986) Natural history of symptomatic partial ornithine transcarbamylase deficiency. *New England Journal of Medicine*, **314**, 541–547

Shih, V. E., Abroms, I. F., Johnson, J. *et al.* (1977) Sulfite oxidase deficiency. *New England Journal of Medicine*, **297**, 1022–1028

Tasker, R. C., Boyd, S., Harden, A. and Matthew, D. J. (1988) Monitoring in non-traumatic coma. Part II: electroencephalography. *Archives of Disease in Childhood*, **63**, 895–899

Tasker, R. C., Matthew, D. J., Helmas, P. *et al.* (1988) Monitoring in non-traumatic coma. Part I: invasive intracranial measurement. *Archives of Disease in Childhood*, **63**, 888–894

Tonsgard, J. H. (1986) Serum dicarboxylic acids in Reye syndrome. *Journal of Pediatrics*, **109**, 440–445

Vomberg, P. P., Breederveld, C., Fleury, P. and Arts, W. F. M. (1987) Cerebral thromboembolism due to antithrombin III deficiency in two children. *Neuropediatrics*, **18**, 42–44

Wintzen, A. R., Broekmans, A. W., Bertina, R. M. *et al.* (1985) Cerebral haemorrhagic infarction in young patients with hereditary protein C deficiency: evidence for "spontaneous" cerebral venous thrombosis. *British Medical Journal*, **290**, 350–352

Chapter 25

Regression

The process of development means that it is often difficult to distinguish disorders with true neurological regression from static non-progressive disorders in which a ceiling of development has been reached. Disorders with regression are important to recognize and differentiate because some of them are treatable and many more have specific genetic implications. In others, the provision of a diagnostic label is helpful to the family.

Some clinical clues are helpful in reducing the range of tests necessary for diagnosis, and at any given age some disorders are likely, others unlikely or impossible. Certain somatic features found on physical examination will narrow the diagnostic possibilities. Also the pattern of neurological involvement with or without epilepsy will distinguish others. Where absolute differentiation is not possible on the basis of these three aspects, the battery of screening tests may still be reduced to manageable proportions.

The more one knows about the subject, the more one might be able to discriminate between individual disorders and therefore reduce the number of tests needed. This is an argument for onward referral.

Deterioration in infancy

Deterioration with no obvious clinical clues

T_3, T_4, *TSH*. Neonatal hypothyroid screening tests may not be in operation, or hypothyroidism may arise later.

Plasma and urine amino acids. The various types of hyperphenylalaninaemia should have been detected by a neonatal screen. Screening for homocystinuria is not universal.

Organic acids. Organic acid disorders may present with regression even in the absence of metabolic acidosis. If additional features suggest biotinidase deficiency (sparse hair, skin rash) plasma biotinidase should be estimated and a trial of biotin given.

Urine free sialic acid. Salla disease and variants may have very slow regression without obvious additional clinical features.

Blood film for macrocytosis and measurement of serum B_{12}. B_{12} deficiency is a treatable cause of regression even with severe CT scan 'atrophy'.

Regression with seizures

Electroencephalography. EEG detects hypsarrhythmia which may be present in the absence of overt spasms or other seizure type, and may be reversible.

Diagnostically suggestive EEG features are found in Angelman's syndrome (posterior high-voltage sharp waves and posterior spike and wave on eye closure), confirmed in some cases by prometaphase banding of chromosome 15 or flow karyotype, and also in pachygyria (very high-voltage activity in the alpha or beta frequency).

Computerized tomography. CT scan will often confirm tuberous sclerosis before hypopigmented patches are visible by Wood's light.

Uric acid. Low plasma uric acid (confirmed by a low urine uric acid) suggests molybdenum cofactor deficiency. (Dysmorphism and lens dislocation may be absent.)

Copper and copper oxidase. Low plasma copper and copper oxidase confirm Menke's kinky hair disease, even when the clinical clue of pili torti is not obvious.

Cerebrospinal fluid glycine. Markedly increased CSF glycine indicates glycine encephalopathy, even when plasma glycine is not increased. The usual more severe case will have been diagnosed in the neonatal period.

Irritable and often-extending infants

Krabbe's disease. Tendon reflex loss is the clinical clue. Markedly increased CSF protein suggests the demyelinating neuropathy which is confirmed by very slow motor nerve conduction velocity. Confirmation of diagnosis must be galactocerebroside-beta-galactosidase estimation, using a natural substrate.

Glutaric aciduria type I. Dystonic presentation after a febrile illness with regression is usual. The diagnosis may be missed by organic acid analysis. Specific assay of glutaryl CoA dehydrogenase in fibroblasts will be confirmatory.

Canavan's disease. Visual loss often with megalencephaly prompt CT scan, which shows extensive and highly characterized hypodensities in cerebral white matter and thalami. Histological diagnosis has previously required frontal brain biopsy, but recently n-acetylaspartic aciduria with aspartoacylase deficiency in fibroblasts has been reported in this disorder.

Infantile Gaucher's disease. Loss of the saccadic eye movements and splenomegaly prompts confirmation by blood glucocerebrosidase. Bone marrow examination is probably not necessary if the clinical clues are present and the enzyme assay available.

GM 2 gangliosidosis (Tay–Sachs etc.) An excessive startle to noise and a cherry-red spot at the macula should be enough to prompt hexosaminidase estimation.

Aicardi-Goutières syndrome. Spasticity, dystonia, nystagmus and evolving microcephaly accompany global regression in early months. CSF shows lymphocytosis without evidence of infection and in due course CT reveals symmetrical basal ganglia calcification.

Molybdenum cofactor deficiency. Seizures plus ectopia lentis prompt discovery of low uric acid in blood and urine.

Lesch–Nyhan disease. Regression commonly begins in the first year of life, although the extensions and other extrapyramidal signs do not usually occur until the second year of life. Elevated plasma uric acid and urine uric acid : creatinine ratio suggest the diagnosis, confirmed by low red cell hypoxanthine–guanine–phosphoribosyltransferase.

Pelizaeus–Merzbacher disease. Clinical clues are nystagmus and dystonia. Progression may be so difficult to detect that cerebral palsy is suggested. These findings should prompt MR imaging, which shows striking abnormality on T2 weighted images of white matter.

Classical Niemann–Pick disease. The phenotype is striking, with large abdomen, splenomegaly, cherry-red spot, and hypotonia with areflexia. Very slow motor conduction velocity indicates a demyelinating neuropathy. Bone marrow shows foamy lymphocytes, and leucocyte sphingomyelinase is grossly deficient.

Foramen magnum tumour. The clinical picture with extension and irritability may mimic genetic degenerative brain disorder. Lateral skull X-ray and high-resolution CT scan will be supplemented by high-resolution CT scan and/or MR imaging.

Sandifer's syndrome. Infants with static disorders may appear to regress with dystonic extension of the neck in the presence of reflux through a hiatus hernia.

Deterioration in the second and third years

'Autistic' presentation

Rett's syndrome. No tests are available at the present time for this common disorder of girls. The EEG appears normal to start with but later shows slowing and decreased organization of the background activity, and spikes and sharp waves at first only in sleep. Earlier suggestions of an abnormality of CSF biogenic amines have not been confirmed.

Disintegrative psychosis. In psychological evolution, disintegrative psychosis has certain similarities to Rett's syndrome, but is predominantly a disorder of boys. Once again there are no tests which give positive results.

Angelman's (happy puppet) syndrome. In the early stages this disorder may superficially resemble Rett's syndrome, but the distinguishing feature is the EEG finding of high-voltage posterior sharp waves.

Neuronal ceroid lipofuscinosis. The infantile type of lipofuscin storage disease presents with hand-knitting behaviour and autistic appearance at the end of the first year. Progressive lowering of the ERG, which becomes extinguished, suggests the diagnosis. Confirmation is by rectal biopsy using ultraviolet autofluorescence, and fat stains and electronmicroscopy for the 'snow-storm' inclusions ('Finnish snow-balls'). Electronmicroscopy of white cells (buffy coat) and skin biopsy can be attempted in advance.

Missed phenylketonuria. Phenylketonuria would by this stage show autistic features. It is advisable to have plasma amino acids and indeed urine organic acids in this situation when regression is otherwise unexplained. Another rare disorder has been described in which succinylpurines are increased and may be detected in CSF and urine (*see* Chapter 18).

Regression with seizures

Progressive neuronal degeneration of childhood. Otherwise called Alper's disease or Huttenlocher's disease, this disorder is suggested by increased CSF protein and high-voltage lateralized runs of spike and wave (the slow waves having a notched apex), together with gradually increasing AST and ALT concentrations in plasma. High CSF (and blood) lactate and pyruvate, and hepatic failure with coagulation defect are late features.

Late infantile neuronal ceroid lipofuscinosis. Ataxia and dementia may be so rapidly followed by a difficult epilepsy that the decline in mental competence and the cerebellar signs are attributed to the epilepsy. *Diagnostic tests:* Flat ERG, giant VEP, and curvilinear bodies on electronmicroscopy of white cells in buffy coat or in biopsy of conjunctiva skin or rectum.

Polymorphous epilepsy. This epileptic syndrome, otherwise called severe myoclonic epilepsy of infancy, is associated with developmental arrest and regression in the second year. Stroboscopic activation during EEG commonly induces a photoconvulsive response.

Disorders with neurological signs

Metachromatic leucodystrophy. Clinical evidence of peripheral neuropathy accompanying the ataxia, dementia and bulbar signs suggest the diagnosis. *Diagnostic tests*: Increased CSF protein, prolonged motor conduction velocity, metachromatic material in renal tubular epithelial cells stained with toluidine blue, and deficient arylsulphatase A in leucocytes and fibroblasts.

Juvenile Sandhoff disease. This disorder may present as progressive cerebellar ataxia and mild dementia. *Diagnostic tests*: Very low hexosaminidase A and B in leucocytes and in plasma.

Ataxia telangiectasia. Ataxia, choreoathetosis, and 'oculomotor apraxia'
  with tiddleywink tonsils suggest the diagnosis. *Diagnostic tests*: Raised
  alphafetoprotein in plasma, DNA repair defect in fibroblasts.

Infantile neuroaxonal dystrophy. A combination of both peripheral
  motor and possibly sensory defect and mental regression and ocular
  wobble suggest the diagnosis. Normal CSF protein and motor nerve
  conduction velocity, but denervation evidence on EMG, indicate
  axonal neuropathy. Prominent diffuse fast activity (beta activity) is
  present on EEG from the age of 2 years. Axonal spheroids in skin or
  conjunctival biopsy are diagnostic, but one may need brain biopsy
  with esterase staining.

Leigh's disease. Deteriorating disorders, including impairment of eye
  movement control and respiration and ataxia and possible peripheral
  neuropathy may be caused by various mitochondrial defects.
  Diagnostic tests: Urinary organic acids and if in doubt plasma
  biotinidase to exclude biotinidase deficiency; CSF protein, nerve
  conduction studies; urine amino acids for evidence of renal tubular
  leak; blood and CSF lactate and pyruvate; high-resolution CT scan
  looking for low densities in putamena, cerebellum and brain-stem.
  Special biochemical studies on the mitochondria isolated from muscle
  are needed to identify the various mitochondrial defects. Techniques
  exist for similar studies on fibroblasts

*Neurovisceral storage disease with vertical supranuclear ophthalmo-
  plegia.* Impaired saccadic eye movements in the vertical plane suggest
  this disorder, in which splenomegaly may be only borderline. Cataplexy in humorous situations may be striking, *Diagnostic tests*: Even if
  the bone marrow does not show sea-blue histiocytes and Niemann–
  Pick cells, rectal biopsy shows diagnostic morphology. Despite the
  disorder being classified as Niemann–Pick disease type C, sphingomyelinase activity is not decreased in leucocytes.

Regression without specific features

The three conditions which we include here commonly have specific
features but these may be very subtle.

Sanfilippo disease. Even if there are no obvious dysmorphic features,
  the spleen is not palpable and the rib ends are not expanded, there is
  usually impairment of complete extension of the fingers. Clues are
  not obtained from neurophysiological or imaging studies. Urinary
  excretion of GAGs may be missed by screening tests. Twenty-four-
  hour urine for heparan sulphate, repeated if necessary, should be
  undertaken if this disorder is thought possible. Once this abnormality
  has been shown, then the four enzymes of Sanfilippo A, B, C, and D
  are assayed to see which one is defective.

Moya-moya disease. Though arterial narrowing around the circle of
  Willis, of whatever cause, commonly presents as (alternating) hemi-

plegia, this pathology may manifest as dementia with regression and no other clue. This is an argument for SPECT and/or MRI imaging, which will show the vascular abnormalities when dementia is otherwise unexplained.

HIV dementia. There may be an obvious clue in that the child has known congenital HIV infection (dementia from HIV infection complicating haemophilia treatment appears at a later age). CT atrophy is not specific. Tests for HIV are essential for diagnosis.

Regression in the schoolchild

The problem of a child whose progress slows or stops or who seems to regress at school is a common one. In a normal school, the solution may be that the child has an unrecognized non-progressive mental handicap of mild degree or a previously unrecognized specific learning disorder leading to secondary behavioural difficulties. Sometimes specific sensory deficits of vision or hearing may have been unrecognized, particularly when these are progressive. There may be family disturbances or there may be true depression. Within the totality of epilepsy it is unusual for the presentation to be a school failure without the seizures having been recognized, but compared with the neurodegenerative disorders to be discussed, epilepsy is common. Most often, the epilepsy will be characterized by absences, and a standard EEG with hyperventilation activation will demonstrate the regular approximately 3-Hz spike and wave. Complex partial seizures do not usually present in this way, but if an epilepsy with 'blanks' is suspected and standard EEG does not reveal anything, then cassette EEG monitoring can be undertaken.

Similar considerations apply to children attending special schools for the visually handicapped, for the deaf, and for the mentally and physically handicapped. In these circumstances the incidence of epilepsy is increased, and absence epilepsy is not uncommon in children with simple mental handicap. In these schools children thought to have isolated sensory deficits or static mental and physical handicap may have unrecognized progressive disorders. In particular, the child who becomes blind in early schooldays may have juvenile neuronal ceroid lipofuscinosis (*juvenile Batten's disease*) presenting as school failure with later extrapyramidal features. A low ERG, with an EEG containing too much slow activity and some spikes should be followed by blood film for vacuolated lymphocytes and, irrespective of whether or not these are found, microscopy and electronmicroscopy of white cells, and rectal biopsy. In children with mental and physical handicap, reversible regression may have been induced by so-called psychotropic drugs and by antiepileptic therapy. True regression may occur due to malfunction of shunts in hydrocephalus.

The rare disorders which may have previously masqueraded as static disorders in the schools for the mentally and physically handicapped include amino acid disorders (previously undetected phenylketonuria), biotinidase deficiency, Sanfilippo disease, sialic acid storage disease, and Alexander's disease. Juvenile paretic neurosyphillis may have been previously manifest as non-progressive mental handicap and then deteriorate dramatically. Hypothyroidism may appear insidiously without coarsening of the features. In contrast, some disorders such as tuberous sclerosis, cerebral malformations, and prenatal cerebral destructive lesions and Rett syndrome, may appear to decline without any definite evidence of progressive cerebral pathology.

Regressive disorders which most often present during school years are discussed in convenient groupings.

Disorders in which epilepsy is not usually a presenting feature

Juvenile metachromatic leucodystrophy, juvenile Krabbe's and juvenile GM1 gangliosidosis may have similar presentations, with dementia or behaviour disorder or ataxia with or without pyramidal signs. EEGs and other neurophysiological tests are not helpful. CT scan may show some asymmetrical white matter hypodensity which is not specific. Juvenile Sandhoff disease has been mentioned in the section on the 1–4-year presentation. These four disorders may be detected by leucocyte enzyme assays of arylsulphatase A, galactocerebroside-beta-galactosidase, beta-galactosidase, and hexosaminadase A and B. It is important to employ a reliable laboratory using special substrates for galactocerebroside-beta-galactosidase and hexosaminidase A and B estimation.

Hypothyroidism, HIV infection, Sanfilippo disease and moya-moya have been discussed in the 1–4-year section.

Adrenoleucodystrophy (ALD) and subacute sclerosing panencephalitis (SSPE) have a similar presentation with vague dementia and subtle neurological deficits which include difficulties in processing visual or auditory information.

SSPE. Electroencephalography usually though not always shows periodic polyphasic complexes with several seconds of reasonable EEG background between, but often frontal slowing. A CT scan may show asymmetrical posterior white matter hypodensities indistinguishable from those seen in ALD. CSF protein is often but not always increased. Increased globulin is present in the CSF so that the Lange colloidal gold test gives a paretic curve and an increase of specific measles IgG immunoglobulin may be detected. In the blood, measles-specific IgM is positive. Epilepsy sometimes brings SSPE to the doctor's attention but schoolwork will have declined before this.

ALD. The CSF protein is increased and oligoclonal bands are commonly present. CT scan shows symmetrical white matter hypodensities predominantly around the occipital horns of the lateral ventricles. Very long-chain fatty acid levels and ratio of C26 to C22 fatty acids are increased. Although this type of very long-chain fatty acid increase occurs in many different peroxisomal disorders, in this particular clinical situation it is specifically diagnostic.

Striatal signs may be prominent in Wilson's disease, juvenile Huntington's disease and in Hallervorden–Spatz disease.

Wilson's disease ought to be considered in any unexplained regressive neurological disorder from age 5 years upwards. Before that, hepatic involvement is evident and the diagnosis is not so difficult. Special neurological investigations are not necessarily helpful aside from non-specific hypodensity within the basal ganglia; slit lamp examination of the cornea, plasma copper and copper oxidase, and urinary copper and amino acids indicate the diagnosis in most cases.

Juvenile Huntington's is suggested by a history of the disorder in the father and often by a disorder of horizontal saccadic eye movements. Caudate atrophy on CT scan may not be obvious.

Hallervorden–Spatz disease. CT shows low-density areas in the putamena and globus pallidus, but a specific diagnosis is not to be expected in life.

Of the various disorders which are difficult to diagnose in life, Alexander's disease presents considerable difficulties because of variability of age of onset and insidious symptoms. It may masquerade as simple hydrocephalus or epilepsy, and dementia may be very slowly progressive so that it resembles mental handicap. CT scan shows low density of white matter, predominantly anteriorly. Brain biopsy (Rosenthal fibres, etc.) is diagnostic.

Four other rare chronic infective disorders should be borne in mind.

Juvenile paresis. This manifestation of congenital syphilis may present with regression on a background of apparently static mental handicap. Retinitis may be present so that a 'cerebral retinal degeneration' is suggested. The CSF normally contains a few lymphocytes, some increase in protein and a paretic Lange colloidal gold curve. Serological tests for syphilis are positive in the CSF.

Borrelia burgdorferi infection. The late dementia which has been reported following treated infection is confirmed by an increased Borrelia burgdorferi specific IgG antibodies in serum and CSF.

Rubella panencephalitis. Rarely, after ordinary rubella infection or in a child already handicapped by congenital rubella infection, a panencephalitis occurs years later. The EEG is not specific and shows only slow activity and not periodic complexes as in measles SSPE. CSF contains lymphocytes and increased protein IgG and oligoclonal bands, and there is specific rubella immunoglobulin present. Rubella IgM is present in the blood.

Chronic encephalitis in the immunocompromised patient. The suggestion of this diagnosis is indicated by the clinical setting.

Regressive conditions in which epilepsy is prominent

As indicated above, many epilepsies may appear to be associated with regression even though there is no underlying progressive neurological disease. Regression is often associated with a disruption of the EEG which shows much spike and wave, but this association is not constant. An epileptic syndrome characterized by prominent myoclonus, known as Unverricht's disease or Balkan myoclonus epilepsy, may be manifest as dementia if seizures are treated with phenytoin, whereas no dementia occurs if sodium valproate is employed. The use of valproate and its beneficial effect is sufficient to distinguish this disorder and avoid the other special tests discussed below. On this particular point it should be mentioned that phenytoin or carbamazepine may exacerbate other more common myoclonoic epilepsies (such as the juvenile myoclonic epilepsy of Janz), whereas sodium valproate will be markedly effective.

Early juvenile neuronal ceroid lipofuscinosis. In early school years the child may begin with a difficult epilepsy with ataxia and dementia. Before visual failure develops the ERG is found to be low, with exaggerated VEP. Skin biopsy will show fingerprint profiles on electronmicroscopy, but if the skin biopsy is inconclusive a rectal biopsy will be necessary.

While it must once again be emphasized that most cases of myoclonic epilepsy with ataxia and apparent regression are not true progressive diseases but simply 'epilepsy', a number of rather specific disorders can be recognized on rare occasions.

Lafora body disease. Presentation is in later childhood with grand mal tonic–clonic seizures. The initial EEG has a normal background and may have spike and wave or polyspike and wave and a photoconvulsive response (spike and wave on stroboscopic activation without myoclonus). Later, myoclonic jerks and then dementia and neurological deterioration occur. Diagnosis is by skin biopsy, which shows PAS-positive polyglucosan bodies in sweat glands.

Cherry-red spot myoclonus syndrome (sialidosis type I). Neuraminidase is deficient in leucocytes, with additional beta-galactosidase deficiency in some cases.

MERRF (myoclonic epilepsy with ragged red fibres). Muscle biopsy may indicate this disorder of mitochondrial function, which may be further investigated by biochemical studies on muscle samples. Although increased lactate may be a clue to mitochondrial disorder, lactic acidosis is not always present.

Juvenile Gaucher's disease. Enlargement of the spleen and a defect of horizontal saccadic eye movement will suggest this disorder. Diagnosis is by defective glucocerebrosidase activity in leucocytes.

Juvenile neuroaxonal dystrophy. Skin or conjunctival biopsy may show spheroids, but brain biopsy may be required.

Late infantile or juvenile GM_2 gangliosdosis may present with myoclonic epilepsy before dementia and other signs develop. *Initial test*: Hexosaminidase A and B in serum; if abnormal, special substrate assay on cultured fibroblasts.

Summary

The tests that may be indicated in school-age regression are listed below, but the diagnostic pointers discussed above should limit considerably the range needed.

Urine
    Renal epithelial metachromatic granules
    Heparan sulphate (24-h GAGs)
    Amino acids.
Plasma
    T_3, T_4, TSH
    Copper, caeruloplasmin (copper oxidase)
    Lactate and pyruvate
    Cholesterol
    Uric acid
    Amino acids
    Very long-chain fatty acids
    Immunoglobulins
    Measles IgM
    Rubella IgM
    Syphilis titres
    Borrelia titres.
Leucocytes
    Arylsulphatase A
    Beta galactosidase
    Galactocerebroside-beta-galactosidase
    Hexosaminidase A and B
    Neuraminidase
    Glucocerebrosidase.
CSF
    Immunoglobulin (Lange, IgG, oligoclonal bands)
    Cells (Cytospin)
    Measles IgG
    Rubella IgG
    HIV testing
    Syphilis titres
    Borrelia burgdorferi titre.
EEG
Cassette EEG
ERG and VEP
Nerve conduction studies
CT brain scan
MR brain imaging

Blood film microscopy
Electronmicroscopy of buffy coat
Skin biopsy
Muscle biopsy
Bone marrow biopsy
Rectal or appendix biopsy

This daunting list may serve to emphasize the importance of the initial decision as to whether true organic regression has occurred. If a single investigation is to be done, this should be the EEG.

Behaviour disorder with possible regression

Most behaviour disorders in childhood do not have a neurological basis, at any rate in the sense that tests might be helpful. Sometimes it is difficult to know whether deterioration in the child's intellect or personality has occurred. If clinical and psychological studies suggest that there is a dementia, then investigations as previously discussed in this chapter are indicated.

Some questions that are commonly asked:

Is this epilepsy?

Conduct disorders and outbursts or rage (*see below*) are not usually epileptic manifestations. If episodes of altered behaviour have a description suggesting a high probability that they are complex partial epileptic seizures, then some means of obtaining an EEG during the episode may clarify the diagnosis.

Episodes of minor epileptic status are easy to diagnose by standard EEG, provided arrangements can be made for the child to be brought to the EEG department as soon as a change in behaviour has started.

Is there a brain tumour?

Unlike the situation in adults, brain tumours causing a prominent psychiatric disorder as the sole manifestation are rare. In craniopharyngioma hallucinations may complicate regression. If the clinical features do not specifically suggest craniopharyngioma, then a lateral skull X-ray is an adequate investigation. If there is growth failure and endocrine disturbances, then CT scan is indicated. Cerebral hemisphere tumours may occasionally present with episodic behaviour disturbances and hallucinations. The absence of headache or visual field defect or other defect on standard neurological examination would allow conservative management, but a combination of headache and declining school performance should prompt CT scan to exclude a frontal glioma in particular.

Is it a rare, treatable disorder?

Wilson's disease may show behavioural disturbances without dementia or neurological signs. Investigations are as above.

Homocystinuria. A folic-acid responsive form may present with rage reactions or even a schizophrenia-like picture. Urinary amino acids specifically seeking this disorder will confirm or exclude.

Urea cycle disorders (initial test blood ammonia) have very rarely presented in this way, but usually vomiting is the clinical clue.

Endocrine disorders should have clinical clues, e.g. alterations in growth rate in hypo- and/or hyperthyroidism.

This group of children, who may present to school Medical Officers or Child Psychiatrists, are not likely to give a high yield on investigation. In the absence of dementia, EEG, lateral skull X-ray, and urine amino acids are reasonable when investigation seems justified but the doctor thinks that the likelihood of any particular disorder is low.

Delay or regression with 'coarse' facies

In some of the storage disorders with neurological involvement the diagnosis is apparent on clinical grounds and one can go directly to enzyme confirmation. In many cases the differential diagnosis within the group of children with 'coarse' facial appearances is not obvious. The battery of tests which will be done for a positive diagnosis in most cases is:

Skeletal survey
    dysostosis multiplex
        mucopolysaccharidosis
        mucolipidosis
        gangliosidosis.
T_3, T_4, *TSH*
    hypothyroidism
Blood film microscopy
    metachromatic + other granules in leucocytes
        mucopolysaccharidosis
    vacuolated lymphocytes
        mucolipidosis, gangliosidosis, etc (*see* Chapter 7).
Urine protein
    glutamyl ribose-5-phosphate storage disease.
24-h urine GAGs
    mucopolysaccharidosis
24-h urine oligosaccharides
    mucolipidosis, fucosidosis, mannosidosis

24-h urine amino acids
  N-aspartylglycosamine
    aspartylglycosaminuria
24-h urine sialic acid
  sialic acid storage disease (infants)
  Salla disease (coarse later)
Plasma arylsulphatase A
  increase in I-cell disease
Leucocyte enzymes
  beta-galactosidase
    GM_1 gangliosidosis and some sialidoses
  arylsulphatase A, B, C
    multiple sulphatase deficiency
  neuraminidase
    sialidosis
  fucosidase
    fucosidosis
  mannosidase
    mannosidosis

Additional specific lysosomal enzyme assays will be undertaken when urine GAG excretion suggests a mucopolysaccharidosis.

Failure to find any abnormalities in such tests where storage disease is suspected, particularly if additional features such as corneal clouding are present, will lead to biopsy of accessible sites (such as conjunctiva or skin) to look for storage material.

Case illustrations

See 1.3, 1.4, 2.4, 3.1, 3.2, 4.3, 4.5, 5.3, 7.1–7.3, 8.1, 9.2, 10.2, 10.3, 10.5 and 10.6.

Further reading

Adams, C. and Green, S. (1986) Late onset hexosaminidase A and hexosaminidase A and B deficiency: family study and review. *Developmental Medicine and Child Neurology*, **28**, 236–243

Aicardi, J. and Goutières, F. (1984) A progressive familial encephalopathy in infancy, with calcifications of the basal ganglia, and chronic cerebrospinal fluid lymphocytosis. *Annals of Neurology*, **15**, 49–54.

Aukett, A., Bennett, M. J. and Hosking, G. P. (1988) Molybdenum cofactor deficiency: an easily missed inborn error of metabolism. *Developmental Medicine and Child Neurology*, **30**, 531–535

Berkovic, S. F., Andermann, F., Carpenter, S. and Wolfe, L. S. (1986) Progessive myoclonus epilepsies: specific causes and diagnosis. *New England Journal of Medicine*, **315**, 296–305

Biggemann, B., Voit, Th., Neuen, E. *et al*. (1987) Neurological manifestations in three German children with AIDS. *Neuropediatrics*, **18**, 99–106

Boulloche, J. and Aicardi, J. (1986) Pelizaeus–Merzbacher disease: clinical and nosological study. *Journal of Child Neurology*, **1**, 233–239

Burk, R. D., Valle, D., Thomas, G. H. *et al*. (1984) Early manifestations of multiple sulfatase deficiency. *Journal of Pediatrics*, **104**, 574–578

Clayton, P. T. and Thompson, E. (1988) Dysmorphic syndromes with demonstrable biochemical abnormalities. *Journal of Medical Genetics*, **25**, 463–472

Dravet, C., Roger, J. and Bureau, M. (1985) Severe myoclonic epilepsy of infants. In *Epileptic Syndromes in Infancy, Childhood and Adolescence* (ed J. Roger, C. Dravet, M. Bureau *et al*.) John Libbey, London, pp. 58–67

Eldridge, R., Iivanainen, M., Stern, R. *et al*. (1983) "Baltic" myoclonus epilepsy: hereditary disorder of childhood made worse by phenytoin. *Lancet*, **2**, 838–842

Feder, H. M., Zalneratis, E. L. and Reik, L. Jr. (1988) Lyme disease: acute focal meningoencephalitis in a child. *Pediatrics*, **82**, 931–934

Garcia Silva, M. T., Aicardi, J., Goutières, F. and Chevrie, J. J. (1987) The syndrome of myoclonic epilepsy with ragged-red fibres. Report of a case and review of the literature. *Neuropediatrics*, **18**, 200–204

Hagenfeldt, L., Bollgren, I. and Venizelos, N. (1987) N-Acetlyaspartic aciduria due to aspartoacylase deficiency – a new aetiology of childhood leucodystrophy. *Journal of Inherited Metabolic Disease*, **10**, 135–141

Harding, B., Egger, J., Portmann, B and Erdohazi, M. (1986) Progressive neuronal degeneration of childhood with liver disease. *Brain*, **109**, 181–206

Jaeken, J. and Van der Berge, G. (1984) An infantile autistic syndrome characterised by the presence of succinylpurines in body fluids. *Lancet*, **2**, 1058–1061

Levin, S. D., Hoare, R. D. and Robinson, R. O. (1983) Childhood moyamoya presenting as dementia. *Developmental Medicine and Child Neurology*, **25**, 794–797

Lipkin, P. H., Roe, C. R., Goodman, S. I. and Batshaw, M. L. (1988) A case of glutaric acidemia type 1: effect of riboflavin and carnitine. *Journal of Pediatrics*, **112**, 62–65

Matalon, R., Michals, K., Sebesta, D. *et al*. (1988) Aspartoacylase deficiency and n-acetylaspartic aciduria in patients with Canavan disease. *American Journal of Medical Genetics*, **29**, 463–471

Mitchell, G., Ogier, H., Munnich, A. *et al*. (1986) Neurological deterioration and lactic acidemia in biotinidase deficiency. *Neuropediatrics*, **17**, 129–131

Murphy, J. V., Thome, L. M. Michals. K. and Matalon, R. (1985) Folic acid responsive rages, seizures and homocystinuria. *Journal of Inherited Metabolic Disease*, **8** (Suppl. 2), 109–110

Neville, B. G. R., Lake, B. D., Stephens, R. and Sanders, M. D. (1973) A neurovisceral storage disease with vertical supra-nuclear ophthalmoplegia and its relationship to Niemann–Pick disease. A report of nine patients. *Brain*, **96**, 97–120

Pachner, A. R. (1986) Spirochetal diseases of the CNS. In *Infectious Diseases of the Central Nervous System* (ed J. Booss and G. F. Thornton) *Neurologic Clinics*, **4**, 207–222, W. B. Saunders Co, Philadelphia

Petty, R. K. H., Harding, A. E and Morgan-Hughes, J. A. (1986) The clinical features of mitochondrial myopathy. *Brain*, **109**, 915–938

Van de Kamp, J. J. P., Niermeijer, M. F., von Figura, K. and Giesberts, M. A. H. (1981) Genetic heterogeneity and clinical variability in the Sanfilippo syndrome (types A, B and C). *Clinical Genetics*, **20**, 152–160

Ylitalo, V., Hagberg, B., Rapola, J. *et al*. (1986) Salla disease variants. Sialoylaciduric encephalopathy with increased sialidase activity in two non-Finnish children. *Neuropediatrics*, **17**, 44–47

Chapter 26

Movement disorders

Many neurological diseases have movement disorders as their presenting feature or as a dominating aspect of the illness. Most of these individual diseases may lead to more than one type of movement disorder. In an attempt to steer between oversimplification and excessive complexity we have grouped the neurological diseases under the headings of the movement disorder most likely to be dominant, but it must be emphasized strongly that these groupings are in no way exclusive.

Certain conditions may lead to virtually any type of movement disorder and will be considered first. One such example is *tumour* and this is one of the reasons why all children with acquired movement disorders should have high-resolution CT brain imaging in the first instance. If the CT scan is normal and a focal lesion is suspected, e.g. in hemidystonia, then MRI scan is indicated.

Wilson's disease

From the age of 5 years tremors, psychiatric disturbance and the various movement disorders outlined below may be a manifestation of Wilson's disease. Investigations have to be rigorous. Many additional extra neurological tests may give clues, particularly blood count, liver function, renal tubular function and bony appearances. CT scan may not show low densities in the striatum. All clinically compatible cases must have serum copper and copper oxidase estimated and in all cases 24-h urine copper excretion. If these three copper studies are negative and the disorder still seems compatible with Wilson's disease, then liver biopsy for copper content is necessary. If doubt remains ^{64}Cu uptake studies may have to be undertaken.

Akinesis–Rigidity

As in all the categories except that of myoclonus, Wilson's disease will be the most important condition to diagnose.

Juvenile Huntington's disease does not have specific neurological test findings in childhood, and diagnosis depends on a positive family history.

Juvenile Parkinsonism with diurnal fluctuation in severity of the disorder has no specific tests except the response to L-dopa.

Hallervorden–Spatz disease may, like several of the disorders to be discussed, show low density areas on high-resolution CT scan in the putamen and globus pallidus. The ERG may show decline in amplitude.

Subacute sclerosing panencephalitis. Periodic EEG and measles studies in CSF and serum confirm this condition.

Akinesia in babies may be due to tetrahydrobiopterin deficiency, described in the following section.

Dystonia

Acute hemidystonia from a putamenal infarct may be clarified by immediate SPECT or MRI after several hours, or after several days by CT scan. Angiography is indicated in all cases.

The most common form of acquired dystonia, *'dystonia musculorum deformans'*, remains a clinical diagnosis, and neurological investigations do not contribute.

An important member of this group is *Dopa-sensitive dystonia*. In this disorder the disability, which begins in the lower limbs, is not always fluctuating. Low homovanillic acid levels in the CSF are to be expected, but this test may not be available. Trial of low-dose L-dopa is necessary in all compatible cases.

Tetrahydrobiopterin (BH_4) deficiency. With rare exceptions the plasma phenylalanine level is high and will have been detected by neonatal screening, when the finding of hyperphenylalaninaemia is followed by measurement of pterins (biopterin and neopterin) in blood and/or urine, or, in some centres, assay of dihydropteridine reductase activity on dried blood spots. However, if screening was not performed or if the result was a false negative, then the presentation may be later in infancy, with progressive dystonia and rigidity. In the severe form there is also truncal hypotonia, seizures, microcephaly, general and facial immobility, drooling, and temperature instability. Milder clinical forms of BH_4 deficiency with isolated movement disorder have been described. If the plasma phenylalanine level is normal in such patients, then a defect in biopterin metabolism is most unlikely.

Glutaric aciduria type I disorder, a potentially treatable disorder, is discussed under 'Athetosis' (*see below*).

Leigh's disease may rarely present with prominent dystonia. Tests of mitochondrial function are indicated (*see* Chapter 10).

Findings in certain other identifiable neurometabolic disorders are listed below.

Neurovisceral storage disease with vertical supranuclear ophthalmoplegia. Bone marrow reveals sea-blue histiocytes and foamy cells, and rectal or appendix biopsy inclusions are seen.

Metachromatic leucodystrophy. The diagnosis is often doubted in the late form of metachromatic leucodystrophy in which dystonia is prominent, because of the very slow progress of the disease. As always, investigations for this disorder should be sound (*see* Chapter 25).

Juvenile Sandhoff. Leucocyte hexosaminidase A and B.

Chronic GM$_1$ gangliosidosis. Beta galactosidase in leucocytes.

Neuronal ceroid lipofuscinosis. The various juvenile types may present with generalized or hemidystonia. Diagnosis is established following identification of a sufficient number of characteristic profiles on electronmicroscopy, bearing in mind that with different genetic variants, fingerprint bodies, curvilinear bodies, and granular 'Finnish snowball' inclusions may be seen irrespective of the age of the child.

Lesch–Nyhan syndrome. Dystonia, chorea and spasticity dominate the picture before self-mutilation appears towards the end of the second year. Elevated blood uric acid and 24-h urinary urate excretion are suggestive; the findings of absent hypoxanthine-guanine phosphoribosyltransferase in red blood cells and fibroblasts confirm the diagnosis.

Dystonia is also a feature of a rare X-linked recessive disorder due to phosphoglycerokinase deficiency. Haemolytic anaemia will prompt enzyme assay in red blood cells.

Athetosis

Glutaric aciduria type I presents with acquired athetoid/dystonic deficit during or after acute febrile illnesses. CT or more likely MRI will show alterations in the signals from the caudate nucleus. Glutaric acid may be difficult to detect in the urine except as an acyl-carnitine after L-carnitine loading (100 mg/kg), and diagnosis depends on assaying this specific enzyme in fibroblasts, as a precursor to therapy with riboflavin, etc. Demonstrating a reduced CSF GABA concentration gives some rational basis for baclofen treatment in addition.

Athetosis may also be found in Salla disease variant. Skin biopsy showing typical inclusions and increased urinary free sialic acid will confirm this.

Chorea

Sydenham's chorea. The diagnosis of Sydenham's chorea is based on the history and physical findings, as anti-streptolysin titres are usually negative.

Hypoparathyroidism usually has other clues such as corneal inflammation with photophobia. Calcium, phosphorus and alkaline phosphatase indicate the diagnosis. CT scan may show basal ganglia calcification, a non-specific finding.

Systemic lupus erythematosus may present with sudden-onset chorea or focal or generalized dystonia without asymmetrical EEG slowing. Immunological studies will usually show elevated antinuclear antibody titres and/or anti-double-stranded DNA and other autoantibodies, and characteristic changes on immunohistology of skin biopsy.

Myoclonus

The dancing eyes syndrome often has myoclonus dominating over ataxia. The only helpful investigations are directed towards the discovery of occult neuroblastoma by urine HVA and HMMA and general imaging studies (chest X-ray etc.) to look for the tumour.

The other disorders with myoclonus and also epileptic seizures are discussed in more detail in Chapter 25 on Regression. More or less well-defined conditions with the key investigations are as follows.

Progressive neuronal degeneration of childhood with liver disease. Characteristic EEG with trains of semi-rhythmic large, slow waves, topped or notched by polyspikes; elevated CSF protein from the beginning; a progressive rise in hepatic transaminases and a later rise in blood and CSF lactate.

Neuronal ceroid lipofuscinosis. Low ERG; decline in EEG in infantile type and huge voltage responses to slow stroboscopic activaton in late infantile type; one or other category of profile on electronmicroscopy of white cells, skin or rectum.

Neuraminidase deficiency ('Cherry-red spot myoclonus syndrome' and mucolipidosis I). Estimation of this enzyme in leucocytes.

Lafora disease. Skin biopsy for characteristic inclusions (*see* chapter 25).

Myoclonic epilepsy with ragged red fibres, (MERRF). Muscle biopsy with trichrome stain confirms. Further studies are indicated of mitochondrial electron transport chain function (Chapter 10).

Paroxysmal dyskinesias

Of the various types described, one is associated with pyruvate decarboxylase deficiency in which there is paroxysmal choreoathetosis. Determination of pyruvate and alanine in the blood during attacks supports this diagnosis.

Rapid onset movement disorders

A number of disorders referred to above may have an acute onset. The most important are tumours, putamenal infarcts, Wilson's disease, Leigh's disease, progressive neuronal degeneration of childhood with liver disease, dancing eyes syndrome, Sydenham's chorea, systemic lupus erythematosus and glutaric aciduria type I.

Summary

It will be seen that the number of tests applicable in this group of disorders is large, but in practice the clinical features, both general and neurological, will reduce this number considerably. It is important that rare, treatable metabolic disorders be recognized. Those detectable by appropriate investigations include at the present time Wilson's disease, dopamine-sensitive dystonia and Parkinsonism, glutaric aciduria type I, dihydropteridine reductase deficiency and vitamin B_{12} deficiency. Various other treatable disorders of amino acid and organic acid metabolism, for example maple-syrup urine disease or methylmalonic acidaemia, may be associated with movement disorders but other aspects of the illness tend to dominate the clinical picture.

Case illustrations

See 4.7 and 10.8.

Further reading

Costeff, H., Gadoth, N., Mendelson, L. *et al.* (1987) Fluctuating dystonia responsive to levodopa. *Archives of Disease in Childhood*, **62**, 801–804

Deonna, T. (1986) Dopa-sensitive progressive dystonia of childhood with fluctuations of symptoms – Segawa's syndrome and possible variants. *Neuropediatrics*, **17**, 81–85

Garcia Silva, M. T., Aicardi, J., Goutières, F. and Chevrie, J. J. (1987) The syndrome of myoclonic epilepsy with ragged-red fibres. Report of a case and review of the literature. *Neuropediatrics*, **18**, 200–204

Hagberg, B., Kyllerman, M. and Steen, G. (1979) Dyskinesia and dystonia in neuro-metabolic disorders. *Neuropediatrics*, **10**, 305–320

Harding, B., Egger, J., Portmann, B. and Erdohazi, M. (1986) Progressive neuronal disease of childhood. *Brain*, **109**, 181–206

Lipkin, P. H., Roe, C. R. Goodman, S. I. and Batshaw, M. L. (1988) A case of glutaric acidemia type I: effect of riboflavin and carnitine. *Journal of Pediatrics*, **112**, 62–65

Marsden, C. D., Obeso, J. A., Zarranz, J. J. and Lang, A. E. (1985) The anatomical basis of symptomatic hemidystonia. *Brain*, **108**, 463–483

Neal Rutledge, J., Hilal, S. K., Silver, A. J. *et al.* (1987) Study of movement disorders and brain iron by MR. *American Journal of Neuroradiology*, **8**, 397–411

Neville, B. G. R., Lake, B. D., Stephens, R. and Sanders, M. D. (1973) A neurovisceral storage disease with vertical supra-nuclear ophthalmoplegia and its relationship to Niemann–Pick disease. A report of nine patients. *Brain*, **96**, 97–120

Quinn, N., Bydder, G., Leenders, N. and Marsden, C. D. (1985) Magnetic resonance imaging to detect deep basal ganglia lesions in hemidystonia that are missed by computerised tomography. *Lancet*, **2**, 1007–1008

Smith, I., Leeming, R. J. Cavanagh, N. P. C. and Hyland, K. (1986) Neurological aspects of biopterin metabolism. *Archives of Disease in Childhood*, **61**, 130–137

Stuchfield, P., Edwards, M. A., Gray, R. G. F. *et al.* (1985) Glutaric aciduria type I misdiagnosed as Leigh's encephalopathy and cerebral palsy. *Developmental Medicine and Child Neurology*, **27**, 514–518

Ylitalo, V., Hagberg, B., Rapola, J. *et al.* (1986) Salla disease variants. Sialoylaciduric encephalopathy with increased sialidase activity in two non-Finnish children. *Neuropediatrics*, **17**, 44–47

Appendix I Predictive value of investigation results

In the introduction and in the body of the book stress has been put on making the significance of a test result depend on the likelihood of the disease or disorder being present. In this section some simple calculations of likelihood or probability are preceded by definitions of the terms employed. A binary table helps to clarify the simple algebra used in this section:

Table A1

Disease		Present	Absent	
	Positive	true positive	false positive	
		a	b	a + b
Investigation				
		c	d	c + d
	Negative	false negative	true negative	
		a + c	b + d	a + b + c + d

Definitions

Sensitivity. The probability that the investigation result will be positive when the disease is present, i.e. the true positive rate (a/a + c).
Specificity. The probability that the investigation result will be negative when the disease is not present, i.e. the true negative rate (d/b + d).
*False positive rate. The probability that the investigation will be positive when the disease is not present (= 1 minus specificity, i.e. 1 − [d/b + d]

*In the definitions listed here an asterisk indicates that *prediction depends on the prevalence* of the disease or disorder, that is, how probable the clinician expects that to be the diagnosis. The major exception is the ROC (receiver operating characteristic) curve (*see* p. 230), which is ideal for comparing the diagnostic power of two investigations such as CT and ultrasound or CT and MRI. Unfortunately, at the time of writing the literature on neurological investigations in children contains very few studies backed by ROC evidence. The remainder of this section will thus be confined to some calculated examples of the effect of estimates of prevalence on the interpretation of neurological investigations. Many further calculations are available to the interested reader.

False negative rate. The probability that the investigation will be negative when the disease is present (= 1 minus sensitivity, i.e. $1 - [a/a + c]$).

Likelihood ratio for a positive investigation (LR+). The sensitivity divided by $[1 - \text{specificity}$, i.e. $[a/a + c]/[1 - (d/b + d)]$

Likelihood ratio for a negative investigation (LR−). [1 minus sensitivity] divided by specificity, i.e. $[1 - (a/a + c)]/[d/b + d]$.

Prevalence. The proportion of patients in the population investigated who have the disease in question, i.e. $[a + c]/[a + b + c + d]$. Commonly this has to be interpreted as the proportion who are expected to have the disease or disorder in question, thus becoming the *prior probability*.

Prior odds. The odds that a disease or disorder is present as estimated before obtaining the result of the investigation in question. It is the probability of the disease being present divided by the probability of the disease not being present.

Posterior odds. The odds that the disorder is present as estimated after the result of the investigation in question, on the basis of the assumed sensitivity and specificity of the investigation. The posterior odds equals the prior odds multiplied by the likelihood ratio. If the investigation is *positive*, posterior odds = [prior odds × LR+]. If the test is *negative*, posterior odds = [prior odds × LR−].

Probability. This is another way, besides odds, of describing the frequency or expected frequency of a disorder. Mathematically, probability = odds/ [1 + odds].

Positive predictive value (PV+). The probability that the disease is present if the investigation result is positive, i.e. $a/[a + b]$.

Negative predictive value (PV−). The probability that the disease is not present if the investigation result is negative, i.e. $d/[c + d]$.

True positive proportion (pTP). The proportion of true positive results at any particular degree of diagnostic confidence. This is also called the true positive fraction. It is the same as the true positive rate, i.e. sensitivity.

False positive proportion (pFP). The proportion of false positive results at any particular degree of diagnostic confidence. This is also called the false negative fraction. It is *not* the same as the false positive rate, the latter being dependent on the prevalence of the disorder.

True negative proportion (pTN). The proportion of true negative results at any degree of diagnostic confidence (also called the true negative fraction). It is the same as the true negative rate, i.e. specificity.

False negative proportion (pFN). The proportion of false negative results at any degree of diagnostic confidence (also called the false positive fraction). It is *not* the same as the false negative rate, the latter being dependent on the prevalence of the disorder.

Cut-off point. An arbitrary value separating positive and negative results in any given investigation.

Receiver operating characteristic (ROC) curve. A graphic plot of the true positive proportion (pTP) against the false positive proportion (pFP) at each of a number of cut-off points. This is the same as a plot of the false negative proportion (pFN) against the true negative proportion (pTN). Put another way, the ROC curve is a graph of sensitivity $(a/[a + c])$ plotted against one minus specificity $(1 - [d/(b + d)])$ at different levels of diagnostic confidence in one's ability to discriminate a and d.

Example 1. Does the 'fit' at age 3 signify epilepsy?

Let us assume that (i) EEG spikes are seen in 80% of those with epilepsy, (ii) that 2% of normal children at this age have EEG spikes, and (iii) that there is no positive evidence in the history to support epilepsy of any kind. None the less, the physician obtains an EEG 'for reassurance', only to discover that clear-cut spikes are recorded.

From the first two assumptions, the sensitivity of the EEG is 80% or 0.8, and the specificity is 98% or 0.98. The likelihood ratio for epilepsy given the presence of spikes (LR+) is thus $0.8/[1 - 0.98] = 0.8/0.02 = 40$. However, from the third assumption the expected prevalence has to be regarded as no different from that in the general population, say 5/1000 or 0.005. The prior odds are thus $0.005/0.995 = 0.005$ to 1, and the posterior odds $0.005 \times 40 = 0.2$ to 1. The posterior probability, being odds/[1 + odds], is thus $0.2/1.2 = 0.17$, or 17% in favour of epilepsy and 83% against.

In this example the probability of epilepsy remains low despite the presence of EEG spikes, so that the EEG is not of value as a positive diagnostic tool. Had spikes been absent, the likelihood ratio of epilepsy (LR−) would have been $[1 - 0.8]/0.98 = 0.2/0.98 = 0.2$, and the posterior odds $0.005 \times 0.2 = 0.001$ to 1, or 0.001 probability. This is the result the physician wants, but in the example the prior odds were so low that the EEG result was a luxury.

Example 2. Does a very premature neonate have brain damage?

For this example we make use of the data of Hope et al. (1988). These authors compared blind the results of ultrasound brain scanning and the 'gold standard' of neuropathology in an unselected series of babies with a gestational age of less than 33 weeks. For the diagnosis of any intraparenchymal brain lesion (haem-orrhagic or hypoxic–ischaemic) sensitivity was 0.44 (44%), specificity 0.82 (82%), LR+ 2.4 and LR− 0.68. For intraparenchymal haemorrhage separately, sensitivity was 0.82 (82%) specificity 0.97 (97%), LR+ 27.3 and LR− 0.19, whereas for hypoxic–ischaemic damage sensitivity was 0.28 (28%), specificity 0.86 (86%), LR+ 2.0, and LR− 0.83. The low likelihood ratios for hypo-xic–ischaemic lesions mean that when the prior odds are low the posterior odds will not change in a useful manner. If such a lesion seems more than probable, a positive scan may be helpful, as follows: prior probability 0.55 (55%) equals odds 1.22 to 1; posterior odds $= 1.22 \times 2.0 = 2.44$ to 1, giving a posterior probability of 0.71 (71%). However, a negative scan would leave the probability at around 0.5 (50%).

Some normal values

A selected number of 'normal' value are included in this section. In many instances the available data are based on statistical assumptions of normality, such as coming within two standard deviations (SD) of the mean ($\bar{x}$) or between the 2nd and 98th percentile. In practice, the concepts of likelihood ratio related to prior odds or the positive and negative predictive value as defined in the previous section, are more helpful in deciding whether a particular test result influences a clinical diagnosis.

Motor nerve conduction velocity (metres per second)

Velocities are fastest in the ulnar, slowest in the posterior tibial and intermediate in the median and common peroneal nerves. The lower limit is based on
2 SD below the mean ($\bar{x}$), but pathological slowing may require a velocity of
60% of the mean ($\bar{x}$), or less. Values for the ulnar (U) and posterior tibial (T)
are listed as -2 SD[$\bar{x}$]. Places of decimals are not used since the basis of the
measurements does not allow of such accuracy.

Neonate	U	20–22[28]	1 year	U	40[46]
	T	17[22]		T	31[38]
3 months	U	31[35]	3 years	U	45[55]
	T	22[26]		T	40[44]
6 months	U	35–37[42]	Adult	U	49[60]
	T	26[32]		T	40[45]

Sensory nerve conduction velocity

Velocities in sural and median nerves approximate to those in the faster motor
nerves.

Flash VEP (latency in ms)

Neonate	190
3 months onward	100

BAEP: I–V latency (ms) (mean and [upper limit])

Neonate	5.1 (6.0)	1 year	4.2 (4.9)
3 months	4.8 (5.6)	Adult	4.1 (4.8)
6 months	4.6 (5.3)		

BAEP: V/I ratio (mean and [lower limit])

Neonate	1.2 (0.4)	6 months	2.3 (0.5)
3 months	1.7 (0.5)	1 year	2.8 (0.5)

Cortical grey matter maximum depth

5 mm

CSF protein (g/l)

(The upper limit is based on 2 SD above the mean.)

Neonate	1.2	5 months onwards	0.25
2–4 months	0.6	late childhood	0.3

CSF special biochemistry

IgG/albumin ratio ≤ 0.27
Lactate 0.8–2.4 mmol/1
Pyruvate 40–80 μmol/l

Glycine up to 15 μmol/l
CSF : plasma glycine ratio 0.025 or
   less, i.e. plasma : CSF glycine
   ratio 40 or over.

Case illustration diagnoses

1.1 Vasovagal (convulsive) syncope
1.2 Specific learning disability
1.3 Autism (mild) with Valsalva-mediated anoxic seizures
1.4 Landau–Kleffner syndrome
1.5 Lissencephaly type I
1.6 Hemipachygyria

2.1 Vaccine polio(encephalo)myelitis
2.2 Chronic relapsing polyneuropathy
2.3 Hereditary motor and sensory neuropathy type I
2.4 Infantile neuroaxonal dystrophy
2.5 Emery-Dreyfuss muscular dystrophy

3.1 Infantile neuronal ceroid lipofuscinosis
3.2 Brain-stem glioma

4.1 Hemimegalencephaly (pachygyria)
4.2 Septal agenesis with hemispheric cleft
4.3 Canavan's disease
4.4 Tuberous sclerosis
4.5 Moya-moya disease
4.6 Severe mental handicap: spinal osteoblastoma
4.7 Atlanto-axial rotatory subluxation
4.8 Syringomyelia
4.9 Dancing eyes syndrome: thoracic neuroblastoma
4.10 Osteopetrosis

5.1 Herpes simplex encephalitis
5.2 (Sub-)acute disseminated encephalomyelitis
5.3 Progressive neuronal degeneration of childhood with liver disease

6.1 Pompe's disease (acid maltase deficiency)

7.1 Ophthalmoplegic neurolipidosis
7.2 Juvenile metachromatic leucodystrophy
7.3 Adrenoleucodystrophy

8.1 Subacute sclerosing panencephalitis
8.2 Prenatal alloimmune thrombocytopenia

9.1 Hereditary motor and sensory neuropathy type I
9.2 Angelman's (happy puppet) syndrome
9.3 Ataxia telangiectasia

10.1 Glycine encephalopathy
10.2 Tay–Sachs disease (infantile GM_2 gangliosidosis)
10.3 Krabbe's disease (galactocerebrosidase deficiency)
10.4 Duchenne progressive muscular dystrophy
10.5 Leigh's disease (cytochrome c oxidase deficiency)
10.6 MELAS
10.7 Reye-like encephalopathy (MCAD deficiency)
10.8 Glutaric aciduria type I
10.9 Ornithine transcarbamylase deficiency

Further reading

Cooper, L. S., Chalmers, T. C., McCally, M. *et al.* (1988) The poor quality of early evaluations of magnetic resonance imaging. *Journal of the American Medical Association*, **259**, 3277–3280

Department of Clinical Epidemiology and Biostatistics, McMaster University Health Sciences Centre (1981) How to read clinical journals: II. To learn about a diagnostic test. *Canadian Medical Association Journal*, **124**, 703–710

Griner, P. F., Mayewski, R. J., Mushlin, A. I. and Greenland, P. (1981) Selection and interpretation of diagnostic tests and procedures: Principles and applications. *Annals of Internal Medicine*, **94**, 553–600

Hope, P. L., Gould, S. J., Howard, S. *et al.* (1988) Precision of ultrasound diagnosis of pathologically verified lesions in the brains of very preterm infants. *Developmental Medicine and Child Neurology*, **30**, 457–471

Miller, R. G. and Kuntz, N. L. (1986) Nerve conduction studies in infants and children. *Journal of Child Neurology*, **1**, 19–26

Mizrahi, E. M. and Dorfman, L. J. (1980) Sensory evoked potentials: clinical applications in pediatrics. *Journal of Pediatrics*, **97**, 1–10

Moosa, A. and Dubowitz, V. (1976) Motor nerve conduction velocity in spinal muscular atrophy of childhood. *Archives of Disease in Childhood*, **51**, 974–977

Phillips, W. C., Scott, J. A. and Blaśczcynski, G. (1983) How sensitive is 'sensitivity'; how specific is 'specificity'? *American Journal of Roentgenology*, **140**, 1265–1270

Sheps, S. B. and Schechter, M. T. (1984) The assessment of diagnostic tests. *Journal of the American Medical Association*, **252**, 2418–2422

Simel, D. L. Playing the odds. *Lancet*, **1**, 329–330

Stephenson, J. B. P. and King, M. D. (1987) Clinical justification for cerebrospinal fluid investigation. *Lancet*, **1**, 222

Appendix II Recent advances

This short Appendix highlights some recent advances in neurological investigations in children.

Philosophy of the use of tests

The philosophy of the use of tests as outlined in the Introduction has not changed. Rather, the principles have been sharpened by a combination of rising costs and an increase both in the range of possible investigations and in the number of diagnosable disorders[1, 2]. It is even more necessary to emphasize the clinical approach to which diagnosis is most probable so that the physician may be selective in the choice of tests.

Since this book was first written some novel investigations have come into use, but of more importance has been the better and more discriminating use of established investigations. Some 'new' disorders have appeared and once again we have drawn attention to those with either a genetic or prognostic implication, and particularly to situations however rare in which effective treatment has become available. Updating of individual references has not been possible within the constraints of a revised reprint, but computerised data bases should provide a stop-gap.

For the reader's convenience we will discuss recent developments under the same chapter headings as used in part two of this book.

The neonate

Attempts have been made to predict the neurodevelopmental outcome of premature and apparently damaged term babies by various neurophysiological investigations such as SEP. High magnetic field strength (1.5 tesla) MRI seems likely to improve the capacity for prediction of neurodevelopmental outcome, but this is not yet established at the time of writing. It is already evident that high field MRI is better than ultrasound and much better than CT in detecting most brain lesions in high-risk neonates. High field MRI may also date haemorrhages in so far as the different signals of breakdown products of haemoglobin signify prior bleeding.

When cerebral malformations are detected by whatever method of imaging, a search may have to be made for the cause of the malformation which may in some cases be a genetic metabolic error. For example, the finding of agenesis of the corpus callosum should lead to lactic acid estimates to detect congenital lactic acidosis.

Another cause of a baby with a 'peroxisomal' appearance is glutaric aciduria type 2 (severe multiple acyl co-enzyme A dehydrogenase deficiency) easily detectable if urinary organic acids are estimated. Plasma pipecolic acid may be markedly increased in this disorder, giving a false confirmation of the suggestion of a primary peroxisomal disorder. The finding of apparent cerebellar 'hypoplasia' in a floppy neonate may indicate the 'new' carbohydrate deficient glycoprotein syndrome detailed in the next section.

Floppy baby

There is still a dearth of laboratories able to provide useful analyses of CSF neurotransmitters. A rare treatable cause of hypotonia and seizures is aromatic acid decarboxylase deficiency in which the CSF contains increased L-dopa and 5-hydroxytryptophan and reduced dopamine and serotonin. Recognition allows therapy with a monoamine oxidase inhibitor. Another such disorder which does not require CSF evaluation for diagnosis is 4-hydroxybutyric aciduria, detectable on urine organic acid analysis by GC-MS. It must be re-emphasised that urine organic acids must be measured in any undiagnosed hypotonic infant. The carbohydrate deficient glycoprotein (CDG) syndrome, previously called disialotransferrin developmental deficiency syndrome, has been briefly mentioned in the text but deserves further description. Presentation is commonly with hypotonia and failure to thrive and slow development. There may be joint restriction, fat pads on the buttocks, pericardial effusions and mild non-progressive liver disease. Convergent strabismus is common. Brain imaging shows cerebellar hypoplasia which reflects the underlying pathology of olivopon to cerebellar atrophy. Blood thyroid binding globulin is low. At older ages there is retinopathy and evidence of denervation suggesting anterior horn cell disease (SMA).

Now that the gene for severe infantile SMA has been localised (5q) it is important to take blood for DNA extraction and storage in all suspected cases. Another and quite likely genetically distinct variety of SMA has been described in which neck muscles are predominently involved with poor head control: EMG studies must include affected muscles.

Abnormal head size

Metabolic microcephaly

Blood glucose and CSF glucose estimations are now essential in undiagnosed acquired microcephaly in infancy with developmental delay with or without seizures. Acquired microcephaly has been described as the sole feature of chronic hypoglycaemia from nesidioblastosis, and has reversed (as did the developmental delay) when the hypoglycaemia was permanently corrected. Another rare treatable disorder is glucose transporter defect, presenting as acquired microcephaly, delay and seizures. The CSF glucose has to be measured specifically since this is low while the blood glucose is normal. Medium chain triglyceride oil is curative.

Metabolic megalencephaly

Unexplained accelerated head growth in infancy demands urine organic acid estimation since organic acidurias may present solely in this fashion. Head imaging in such cases may show both a large brain and excess CSF.

Wobbly-eyed baby

Major advances have occurred in the diagnosis of Pelizaeus-Merzbacher disease. Temporary laryngeal stridor in early infancy, rotatory nystagmus, and postural hypotonia prompt BAEP (absence of waves beyond wave I) and brain MRI (lack of myelin). The more common X-linked variety may rarely be diagnosed with certainty by DNA studies, since point mutations have been identified in the proteolipid protein gene which is on Xq22. However, from a practical point of view, in accurate clinical diagnosis is of paramount importance and in most families this forms the basis for genetic prediction using informative poly-morphisms.

The child who is not speaking

Oromotor dysfunction with drooling, swallowing difficulty and dysarthria or anarthria is a feature of the anterior opercular syndrome (the opercula are the lips of the frontal, temporal and parietal lobes which overhang the insula). In the congenital opercular syndrome accompanied by refractory epilepsy, high resolu-tion brain imaging (preferably high field MRI) shows central macrogyria. This diagnosis is an indication for consideration of section of the corpus calluosum. When the opercular syndrome is acquired without a well-known brain damaging cause such as herpes simplex encephalitis, EEG studies are mandatory. Very frequent lower Rolandic spike discharges suggest a type of localised status epilepticus which may be reversable by anti-epileptic drugs or corticosteroids.

Mental handicap and autism

The diagnostic use of blood and CSF glucose estimations has been alluded to above. Accelerated linear growth in a profoundly retarded and unresponsive infant suggests GABA transaminase deficiency. Diagnosis is by CSF GABA and homocarnosine estimation.

In two newly described related genetic syndromes, alpha-thalassaemia (*not* inherited from either parent) is linked to mental handicap. In the deletional type, mild to moderate retardation is associated with variable dysmorphism and DNA analysis shows 16p deletion. In the non-deletional variety, which is usually inherited in an X-linked fashion, severe to profound mental handicap is asso-ciated with microcephaly and unusual facies and genital anomalies. These children have no more than mild anaemia and it is necessary to think of the possibility of the condition and if the mean cell haemoglobin (MCH) is low to ask the laboratory to look for haemoglobin H inclusions by brilliant cresyl blue preparations of blood smears. Molecular genetics is becoming of major import-ance in the diagnosis of the cause of mental handicap, since at the time of writing a probe has become available for the fragile X gene. Other chromosome micro deletions are invisible by cytogenetic methods and it is thus important to pursue molecular genetic studies if there is a strong clinical suspicion of a particular chromosomal syndrome, for example Wolf syndrome (4p–).

Cerebral palsy

Unexplained and particularly ataxic types of cerebral palsy require investigation by urinary organic acids to detect for example 4-hydroxybutyric acid (succinic semi-aldehyde dehydrogenase deficiency – in which oculomotor apraxia may be a clue) or glutaric acid (glutaric aciduria type 1). The clinical picture of the cerebral palsy in purine nucleoside phosphorylase (PNP) deficiency has become clearer being a disequilibrium syndrome with pyramidal signs. The importance of diagnosis by finding very low plasma uric acid followed by absent red cell PNP has been increased by the eventual potential of gene therapy to cure the immune deficiency.

In unexplained cerebral palsy, high field MRI may not only show evidence of the underlying brain lesion, but in some instances will allow an estimate of the gestational age at which a hypoxic-ischemic insult occurred.

Peculiar gait

Plasma Vitamin E must now be added to the investigations necessary in spino-cerebellar ataxia resembling Friedreich's ataxia when there is no septal thickening on echocardiography. Low plasma vitamin E will lead to special vitamin E absorption studies, before curative therapy.

Febrile seizures

In a suspect child with fever and hemiconvulsions, there is now the possibility of improving the early diagnosis of herpes simplex encephalitis by detection of HSV in CSF by polymerase chain reaction.

Epilepsy and non-febrile seizures

Advances have occurred in the diagnostic investigation of absences. When absences are the presenting feature in a child who will later have early morning myoclonus and possibly the generalised tonic/clonic seizures of juvenile myoclo-nic epilepsy (JME) it appears that these absences have EEG features subtly different from those of childhood absence epilepsy. In JME polyspikes may separate some of the waves in the spike and wave train, and also a spike may not accompany each wave. Since JME now has a chromosomal localisation (6p22) further advances in molecular investigations are expected. Another type of absence has been described which requires EEG or better video-EEG for diagnosis. Loss of awareness of the child occurs during the slow waves of induced hyperventilation *without* spike discharges.

Progress in MRI investigation in epilepsy illustrates the need for the investi-gator to be clear about the precise problem presented. Thus, when the clinical history suggests mesial temporal sclerosis (previous febrile hemiconvulsions) then appropriate angled and sequenced high field MRI will show this lesion in a high proportion of cases.

It is now known that the major cause of MERRF syndrome is a point mutation (bp8344) in mitochondrial DNA and analysis of blood for this mutation is a good screening test, but not wholly reliable, since this phenotype and MELAS syndrome also (see below) are most probably genetically heterogeneous.

Headache

MELAS may present with a combination of migraine and with partial epileptic seizures. A point mutation in the mitochondrial DNA (at a different site from that in MERRF, bp3243) allows diagnosis from a blood sample in a proportion of cases.

Acute encephalopathy

The use of the polymerase chain reaction (PCR) in the early diagnosis of HSV encephalitis has been alluded to earlier. Likewise, tuberculous meningitis and enteroviral encephalitis may be diagnosed by PCR studies of lumbar CSF.

When the explanation of an acute encephalopathy is thought to be non-accidental injury, high field MRI may provide information not available from brain CT by giving some idea of the age of previous haemorrhages.

Stroke is now an indication for urine organic acid analysis (propionic acidaemia has presented as such).

When a child has died from an acute encephalopathy without obvious explanation, it should be remembered that techniques are now available for molecular analysis of DNA in fixed post-mortem tissue, using PCR. MCAD may be diagnosed retrospectively in this manner.

Regression

One of the most exciting and potentially useful investigative methods, not yet widely available, is magnetic resonance spectroscopy using a high field magnet. This non invasive technique allows, for example, the demonstration of neuronal loss by inference from *reduced* concentration of N-acetylaspartic acid and also the recognition of metabolic disorders such as Canavan's disease in which there is an *increased* concentration of N-acetylaspartic acid. Step-wise regression with a neurological picture suggesting Leigh's disease may be a manifestation of a mitochondrial respiratory chain disorder (for example cytochrome c oxidase deficiency) confined to the central nervous system. Magnetic resonance proton spectroscopy shows clearly the increased brain lactate in such patients, even when the CSF lactate is not unequivocally raised. In suspected multiple sclerosis in children brain MRI (as in adults) is the most useful investigation. The mild form of multiple acyl co-enzyme A dehydrogenase deficiency may simulate a demyelinating disorder and is diagnosed by finding ethylmalonic and adipic acids in urine on GC–MS: it responds to riboflavin.

The apparent success of bone marrow transplant in reversing the neurological features of early treated adrenoleukodystrophy and metachromatic leukodystrophy have highlighted the need for precise diagnosis. It has now been shown that the plasma VLCFA concentration may be normal in ALD. If the family history or the clinical features suggests that ALD ought to be the diagnosis then, if plasma VLCFA are normal, the VLCFA oxidation rate should be estimated in cultured fibroblasts. A strong caution is in order in relation to the diagnosis of metachromatic leukodystrophy in a child who does not have the expected neurological deficits. In ayrlsulphatase A *pseudodeficiency*, the measured enzyme is very low but no disease develops. The finding of this pseudodeficiency is one hazard of investigating lysosomal enzymes without the right clinical indication.

At the time of writing the clinical suspicion of juvenile Batten's disease (retinal blindness in a school child with later subtle regression) is one of the remaining indications for rectal biopsy (whether or not lymphocyte inclusions are present). A new indication for rectal (or appendix) biopsy is neuronal inclusion disease, in which characteristic profiles are seen on electron microscopy of neurones. The suggestive clinical picture includes behaviour disorder, blepharospasm, oculogyric crises and, later, lower motor neurone signs.

Movement disorders

It has become apparent that the most usual relapse of HSV encephalitis with ballismus or similar movement disorder is not associated with positive tests for HSV in CSF nor with increases in CSF alpha-interferon: it is considered to be an immunological disorder.

McKusick numbers

From the ninth edition (1990) of *Mendelian Inheritance in Man*, McKusick numbers have six figures instead of five. For major entries this only means that an additional zero is added so that for example Friedreich's ataxia which was 22930 becomes 229300.

References

1 Anonymous (1989) Routine diagnostic testing. *Lancet*, **2**, 1190–1191
2 Kassirer, J. P. (1989) Our stubborn quest for diagnostic certainty. A cause of excessive testing. *New England Journal of Medicine*, **320**, 1489–1491

Index

McKusick numbers are given in brackets. Page numbers in italics refer to tables.